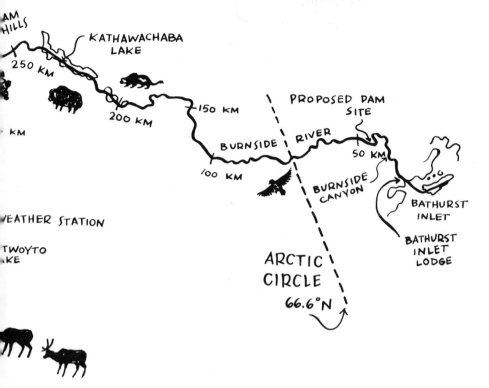

KATHAWACHABA LAKE

250 KM

200 KM

150 KM

100 KM

BURNSIDE RIVER

PROPOSED DAM SITE

50 KM

BURNSIDE CANYON

BATHURST INLET

BATHURST INLET LODGE

ARCTIC CIRCLE

66.6°N

WEATHER STATION

TWOYTO LAKE

AM HILLS

KM

SUMMER

NORTH

OF SIXTY

SUMMER NORTH OF SIXTY

BY PADDLE AND PORTAGE ACROSS THE BARREN LANDS

James Raffan

KEY PORTER BOOKS

To my Celtic parents,
Hamish and Elizabeth Raffan,
who chose Canada

Canadian Cataloguing in Publication Data

Raffan, James
    Summer north of sixty

ISBN 1-55013-224-5

1. Northwest Territories – Description and travel – 1981- .*2. Canoes and canoeing – Northwest Territories. 3. Raffan, James – Journeys – Northwest Territories. I. Title.

FC4167.3.R33 1990   917.19′2043   C89-095264-7
F1095.5.R33 1990

Key Porter Books Limited
70 The Esplanade
Toronto, Ontario
M5E 1R2

Design: Scott Richardson
Map: Kathryn Adams
Typesetting: Southam Business Information and Communications Group Inc.

Printed and bound in Canada

90 91 92 93 94 95 6 5 4 3 2 1

CONTENTS

PREFACE

SOMEWHERE ABOUT THE MIDDLE OF A LONG WILDERNESS JOURNEY, I awake and revel in a sleeping-bag that smells of outside and old socks. It's early. I gaze left and see my partner, a heap of blue nylon; no sign of life except the rhythmic rise and fall of her shadow on the opposite wall. Delaying the torment of putting dry feet in wet boots, I sit up, untangle the sweater that has been my pillow, draw it on, and unzip the door just enough to savour one of the best-kept secrets of wilderness–morning.

Outside, warm familiar air in the sweater is replaced by an infusion of the coolness and possibilities of a new day. I am alone with uncluttered thoughts. Yesterday, we hauled canoes over a frozen July river-bed; today, we will leave the boats and maybe hike among tundra wolves and caribou. Tomorrow, if the weather allows, we'll pack up and parallel the shore of this grand lake, at a rate of thirty-two strokes per minute–transcendental monotony that bonds us to this place and lifts into imagination the essence of these experiences. An arctic tern wafts by. As it disappears in the brightness of the northeastern sky, I kneel to a small pile of willow twigs, anticipating coffee and camp bacon. Dry flames take hold and

I look up across the lake to the edge of arctic infinity. A shiver feels like feathers ruffling.

Mornings such as this are spawned by adventure quest, but to say that adventure alone motivates wilderness journeys is to deny the fact that trail living affords a luxurious inner peace and an open invitation to ponder the origins of such contentment. Journeying itself has been the most significant teacher in my life. And after adventuring on wild rivers and northern coastlines, in mountain passes and the deep snows of boreal winter, I know that the wisdom of the journey is elusive and perhaps best explained by Harold Horwood's hero in *White Eskimo*. Esau Gillingham is asked why he travels, to which he replies: "How can I tell you why I'm going? I could never tell you why. I suppose this new journey that I want to make is what the Eskimos call a journey in pursuit of itself–one that has no purpose other than its own accomplishment. My whole life, in some degree, has been such a journey."

All venturers since Odysseus share the urge to journey; social historians say the North American fascination with wilderness is rooted in frontier history. Covered wagons in America and canoes in Canada may indeed be icons, but their effect on our lives has blurred with time. Somehow, maybe because adventurers are more interested in doing than reflecting, maybe because our English culture does not have the language or mythology to understand spiritual matters related to the land, the greater significance of journeying has been lost in sensation and in the powerful gloss of wilderness photographs.

More and more, as the world is brought into our lives in pre-packaged, sanitized chunks, we have lulled ourselves into thinking that Walt Disney was a documentary film-maker. We pour chemicals into the earth and talk about agribusiness. We clearcut old-growth forests to make paper cups. We think the solution to pollution is dilution. In the short term, technology sustains, but largely by illusion; in the long term, we are rapidly losing any real sense of belonging with the natural world. We are adrift in our luxury liner and haven't looked shoreward long enough or hard enough to realize that there will soon be no place to land. Enough is enough. We've got to start figuring out ways to get back in tune with the earth.

My principal purpose in this book is to explore, using the myth of perhaps the most significant journey in my experience, the attachment, or reattachment, to the land engendered by wilderness travel. By myth, I mean *mythos*, or story, in the Shakespearean sense. Canadian critic Northrop Frye said that "if Shakespeare is writing a historical play, you'll find that he alters some details. He makes Hotspur and Prince Henry the same age, where historically they were 20 years apart. Well then, we say that the story, the play, follows history except for some poetic licences, but that's got the whole thing backwards. The myth of Shakespeare's play incorporates historical material, but it twists the events around so that they confront the audience. You cannot listen to a myth without moving into a higher dimension of time than the purely sequential one." Myths are stories that explain who we are, or who we might wish to be.

Physical journeys like this arctic odyssey on the Burnside River are fun and adventuresome, but fleeting: one prepares, separates, encounters dragons in unexpected places and returns. The details fade, leaving a journey of the imagination, a mythical encapsulation of places and people on one's internal landscape. As much as memory, journal notes, photographs and recollections allow, this story celebrates a 438-mile (700-kilometre) journey, over three heights of land, from treeline to arctic tidewater, as etched on a traveller's imagination.

I have always been drawn to native voices, as they have turned up in transcripts of land-claim hearings or in literature or as spoken at public and private meetings, not so much for what they say but because they have confirmed what I have felt about the land on extended wilderness journeys. Seattle, Chief of the Squamish, responding to a treaty proposal, said: "How can you buy or sell the sky, the warmth of the land? The idea is strange to us. If we do not own the freshness of the air and the sparkle of the water, how can you buy them? Every part of this earth is sacred to my people. Every shining pine needle, every sandy shore, every mist in the dark woods, every clearing and humming insect is holy in the memory and experience of my people. The sap which courses through the trees carries the memories of the red man." These words impart a message of what it means to be native, what it means to belong to a place, instead of the other way around. Canadian writer M.T. Kelly, in accepting the 1988 Governor-General's Award for fiction, said: "Listen to these Indian voices, harken: they seem to me to be the very breath of the Americas."

Like many Canadians, I have not been exposed to much native teaching. Going to the land in a canoe may be the next-best thing. The boon of these journeys is a sense of belonging, a meshing of human spirit and the land that, for lack of a better term, I'm calling *nativity*. The concept tries to catch the best of what it means to be native to a place. Wilderness travel certainly holds within it the possibility of a renaissance in thinking, a rebirthing of awareness, which gives this term meaning, but the principal meaning is belonging derived of the land. There is a chance, I dare say, that one need not be an aboriginal to be native to a place, to have a sense of belonging, a sense of nativity related to a particular place.

How one comes to belong to the land in a special way on a canoe trip, I hope is woven through the experiences described in this book. At this point, I will say simply that I think music had a great deal to do with the transmutation of the physical journey into a journey of the imagination. Whether or not this would be true for someone else, or whether, in fact, it is true at all, is of little consequence. That I believe music to be significant in this regard has been important in the playing out of my own understanding. That is the key. The myth of this journey is set to music in my imagination.

The possibility of music as a metaphor for understanding a wilderness journey dawned on a job-related canoe trip in Northern Quebec on which I was upset by the photographer who insisted on wearing a Walkman. We had to co-operate to "get the coverage" for the book we were working on, but I asked him, finally, what on earth he was listening to. He handed me the unit and I put on the earphones. I soon handed the thing back. It was wrong, I told him, in the whispers of a northern sunset, *not* to pay attention to the music of the land. But . . . there was *something* about that music that seemed to enhance his journey.

After returning home, I was editing a slide presentation about the experience and chose a stirring Canadian Brass arrangement of the Pachelbel Canon to accompany images of the journey. Pachelbel was a teacher and mentor to J.S. Bach; the river had been a teacher and mentor to me–the selection made sense. But, in listening to the Canon repeatedly as the dissolve sequences came together, I was deeply moved by the similarities between the simple melody and how, as new harmonies and nuances of meaning emerged with each new voice repeating the same tune, this was the perfect analogue for my trail experiences. Wilderness journeying is superficially and fundamentally a repetitive process: you get up, you travel, you go to sleep; you get up, you travel, you go to sleep; and so on. But what elevates this circular and rather mundane process to the imagination is the fact that every time the journey melody is reiterated by the voice of another day, you hear new harmonies and become cognizant of new meaning and new understandings. The longer the journey, the more you listen, the richer the music, the richer the potential reward. My hope is that this book will let readers in on the music of this journey, and perhaps teach them a new way of paying attention to their own life travels.

This is a story about a journey by canoe across the barren lands of the Canadian Arctic, a story about ordinary people being moved by circumstances to extraordinary things on occasion; a story of grit, hard work, adventure, wild animals, suspense, tough questions and clear sailing in one of the last remaining wilderness areas on the globe. This is also an account of the gradual, and maybe even musical, transition of a physical journey to a mythical journey of the imagination. It is the story of the most remarkable and memorable canoe trip of my life. It is a story of hope and possibility derived of the natural world.

THIS BOOK BEGAN, REALLY, ON THE DOCK AT LIVERPOOL, SOON after the Second World War, when my Scottish mother and English father decided to emigrate from Great Britain. They had friends in both South Africa and Canada and thus reason to go to either. Whatever life might have been like in Africa, I am grateful they decided on west instead of south. And grateful too, although neither of them has been on a canoe trip, that they taught four kids to look north.

The journey on which the story is based would not have been possible without the adventurous spirit, companionship and good humour of the Burnside River crew: Catherine Laing, Norm Frost, John Fallis, Lorraine McDonald and especially Gail Simmons, my partner now in all ventures.

Special appreciation to R.H. Horwood, my colleague, friend, and mentor at Queen's University Faculty of Education, who always listened and always replied.

For quiet places to write, thank you to: Rob and Karen Filipkowski, Baker Lake, Northwest Territories; Joan and Len Whiteford, The Farm, Seeley's Bay, Ontario; Florence and Creighton Marney, Amherst Shore, Nova Scotia; Erma Simmons, Kingston, Ontario; Richard and Bronwyn Cooke, Eugene, Oregon. Hugs to daughters Molly Claire and Laurel Cole who knew when to break the quiet and how to put writing in pre-school perspective.

I am also indebted to colleague Mac Freeman who got excited about nativity; to musicologist Michael Kerwin who brought shape and form to ideas about six/eight time; to David Stafford, Bill Brookes, and M.T. Swanson with the Geodetic Survey of Canada who helped sort out astronomical observation points; to Jocelyne Revie at the Canadian Permanent Committee for Geographic Names who tracked down verification of place name origins; to librarian John Barton at the National Aviation Museum who helped unearth the significance of Bellanca Rapids; to paddler George Luste whose encouragement came at crucial times; to Glenn and Trish Warner who made us welcome at Bathurst Inlet Lodge and who were helpful in providing research information; to my camp pal Bob Wolfe who read the manuscript with care and knew when to challenge; and to Jan Carrick, the Dragon Lady-critic reader, loose-end-chaser, phone answerer, and friend-to whom, as to all of the others, I am most grateful.

Seeley's Bay, Ontario
November 1989

1.
PREPARATION

IT WAS ON A COPPERMINE RIVER CANOE TRIP IN THE MID-1970s THAT Jake Fallis and I decided gaps between canoe trips should be filled by playing in a country-and-western band rather than by teaching. We had it all figured out. We would buy a van, load it up with cowboy paraphernalia and musical instruments and play in every sleazy bar from St. John's to Vancouver. Travelling from place to place would make every day an adventure, and there would be lots of time during the day to plan canoe trips. There was only one problem: Jake didn't play a musical instrument. "I'll sign up for lessons the minute we get back," he promised when we parted company in Yellowknife at the end of the trip.

That he did.

He would leave his job at the natural-science school north of Toronto a couple of times a week and travel to Orangeville for guitar lessons. On the phone out in eastern Ontario, where I was teaching high school, I would hear all about how sore his fingers were from practising. We would talk about the Coppermine, and when we should be getting together to look at the slides and relive whitewater thrills, night-paddling chills and the excitement of walking amid caribou by the thousands.

But I got suspicious. Group lessons turned into private lessons. He began to speak more about the teacher than the music. "She is a wonderful singer," he said, "and quite the fisherman. Since I told her about fifteen-pound arctic char, she's keen to see slides of the Coppermine."

She saw the slides. Lorraine was a convert. They agreed that the next trip, wherever it was (and it would be tough to top the Coppermine), would be together. That was the end of Jake as my paddling partner.

They made an excellent pair. Lorraine, the professional musician and music teacher, was a hundred-pound dynamo whose voice was as accomplished as her guitar-playing. She'd matched wits with hecklers and lounge lizards of every stripe. With scrawny Jake, would-be musician and outdoor educator, as straight man, they were happier together than not.

Jake and I had met at Kandalore, a wilderness canoe-tripping summer camp, where we had both been campers and staff members. There, we worked with Norm Frost, another Coppermine paddler. Probably more by accident than design, unless there is such a thing as synchronicity and the unconscious bonding of like-minded spirits, Jake and Norm ended up working at the same outdoor-education centre.

I met Norm in a bar in Guelph just before going back to university one fall in the early 1970s. He said they were looking for teaching assistants to fill in for a few weeks at the outdoor centre. Was I doing anything? "No." The biology studies could wait. It would be like old times.

There at the outdoor school, with the three of us together, reliving past trips and going over maps, looking for new routes, the idea of doing another arctic trip had its genesis.

Norm, since leaving camp, had met and married Catherine Laing, a math teacher and outdoor enthusiast. Free-spirited Norm–the one called "the human crane" after he single-handedly lifted a hundred-pound pack out of a sinking canoe at the edge of Obstruction Rapids on the Coppermine–and quiet, well-organized Catherine made a perfect canoe-tripping pair.

The Coppermine was the first arctic canoe trip for all of us: 28

days and 418 miles (669 kilometres) of remote tundra and 24-hour light; real risks, rough living; caribou, wolves, eagles; white water, walks, and swims in the Arctic Ocean. We touched the lives of Sir John Franklin, Samuel Hearne and the Inuit of Coppermine – it was our introduction to northern people and arctic lore. The flat, treeless green landscape; the wild, shallow, twisting river; the close encounters with wildlife combined to form an experience that smouldered well into the autumn, long after the fire of actually being there was out.

I showed slides to anybody I could trap near a projector and screen. After family and friends were sick of hearing about the Coppermine, I devised ways of retreading the tales for students and unsuspecting colleagues from school. Of those people there was but one person, a long-haired, winsome English teacher named Gail Simmons, who never tired of the photos and stories. She had never canoed in her life. One day she asked about going on such a trip. Eureka! A new paddling partner.

In late autumn 1979, we ordered 1:250,000-scale topographic maps for the entire mainland Northwest Territories. After school one day, in my geography classroom, we folded back the margins of forty-five or fifty maps, pushed all of the student tables together and pieced together a mosaic that was 20 feet × 30 feet (6 metres × 9 metres). Using a yellow highlighter pen, we marked all of the possible routes: from east to west, the Mackenzie, the Snare, Lockhart, Yellowknife, Coppermine, Hood, Burnside, Back, Hanbury, Thelon, Dubawnt, Kazan and others besides. And then, taking off our shoes, we got up on the tables and scouted the possibilities.

It was like viewing the North from outer space. The forest was coloured pale green. Against the white tundra on the maps, the limit of tree growth was clearly evident on a line that ran from northwest to southeast. It looked like the whole region was covered more by water than land. All the lakes, like the treeline, had a northwesterly flow to them, their longer dimension always on the diagonal, presumably a result of the last ice sheet's retreat. It was easy to see lakes and small unnamed rivers that could lead into various river trips and thereby shorten the flight from Yellowknife. The few tiny communities on the perimeter of the map along the coasts had evocative names–Eskimo Point, Whale Cove, Baker Lake, Repulse Bay, Gjoa Haven, Bathurst Inlet, Coppermine, Paulatuk, Tuktoyaktuk–but they were so overpowered by the expanse of the intervening land as to give us a disturbing sense of the remoteness of these rivers.

"What happens if somebody breaks a leg or something?" Gail asked.

"We carry a flare gun and a mirror for signalling airplanes," I replied, trying to sound encouraging.

"How often do planes fly over these routes?"

"It depends on the route, but some of them, not too often."

"Oh. So, I guess you try to make sure that nothing happens."

"That's the idea. . . ."

I bend down and draw three big arrows across Point Lake to show her where on the Coppermine trip we encountered stream upon stream of barren-ground caribou swimming south across the lake. There is a place where the light brown contour lines crowd together at a difficult rapid called Rocky Defile.

"That's where we found the granite monument I showed you in the pictures, the memorial to two canoeists who drowned. Jake and I almost dumped going through that canyon. I'll never forget how good it felt to have us all below that place in the river. It was nerve-wracking. There is an international scale of river difficulty. Rocky Defile might be a class three or four, made one notch higher because of the remoteness of the 45°F (7°C) water, but I have a different gauge. I had to pee at least six times while we were scouting; that, to me, is a *scary* rapid! That's also where we saw gyrfalcons for the first time and where we met those Swedes I was telling you about."

"I'm game for anything. Any one of these routes would be a new experience. If you could go anywhere on this whole map," asked Gail, "where would you go and why?"

There is no doubt in my mind that it would be good to cross at least one divide to get into the headwaters of a river. On the Coppermine, I had the sense that we just dropped into Lac de Gras and paddled downstream all the way. We didn't really work to get into the river. It was a physically demanding trip but I think the experience of paddling to the ocean would have been somehow more meaningful if we had crossed at least one height of land under our own steam to access the river.

Paddling over the treeline would be desirable; more happens at edges. Seeing caribou would be a plus; a couple of hundred thousand would answer a prayer. So would seeing musk-oxen and at least as many birds, especially birds of prey, as we saw on the Coppermine.

Seeing more of John Franklin's route across the tundra would be a plus too; touching history is the only way to really learn it. Ending at an Inuit community is a must; it could not help but open our eyes farther, to let us gaze, through the filter of their culture, at the landscape.

A little-travelled route would add to the adventure; so much the better if we could pioneer a route for which there are no trip reports. Something about six weeks long would give us time to adjust to the subtler rhythms of the landscape. A route with inexpensive access and egress was worth considering too.

For a couple of hours, Gail and I mulled over the possibilities and decided that a canoe trip ending on the Burnside River at Bathurst Inlet in the middle of the Territories' north coast could be the trip we were looking for.

Jake and Lorraine and Norm and Cathy had been thinking along similar lines. We opted to go in somewhere south of Aylmer Lake in the Lockhart River system, portage into the Back River, cross over another divide into Contwoyto Lake and then another into Nose Lake, from where we would, we hoped, be the first people ever to canoe down the Mara River, a tributary of the Burnside. It would be about a 500-mile (800-kilometre) route. We would pack for fifty days.

As it turned out, for almost unbelievable reasons we never did get to the Mara River. But we did get to Bathurst Inlet, just barely. Nothing before or since has rivalled this journey for physical intensity, emotional highs and lows, friendship, showing we all have much to learn, and inexorable growth of a sense that there is latent spirituality in every animal, every rock and every plant.

THIS TRIP IN THE SUMMER OF 1980 WAS THE REALIZATION OF A weathered yearning for blue lake and rocky shore. As a kid I used to long, as I did for nothing else, to get in a canoe and go somewhere. There was nothing at school that came close to the feeling of summer days in a canoe on the Canadian Shield. Boy Scouts came close from time to time, but not often enough.

A steady supply of British adventure tales such as *Camp Six, Gypsy Moth Circles the World, Scott of the Antarctic, The Worst Journey in the World,* and special exploration issues of the *London Illustrated News* kept me going with the adventures of Mallory, Chichester, Scott, Cherry-Garrod, Hillary and the rest. In the absence of television in our house I used to listen clandestinely in my room to adventures on the CBC's "Theatre Ten-Thirty." But one night, in December 1967, I happened to tune in to a program called "Ideas."

"This is Glenn Gould," a voice said, "and this program is called 'The Idea of North.'" Now you're talking!

"I've long been intrigued," he continued, "by that incredible tapestry of tundra and taiga which constitutes the arctic and subarctic of our country. I've read about it, written about it and even pulled up my parka once and gone there." I was hooked.

What followed was a series of people talking about their ideas of North, woven together by editing to give the impression that they are all riding north to Churchill on a train called *The Muskeg Express.*

The reason I remember this in such detail is that this groundbreaking radio documentary by Canadian virtuoso musician Glenn Gould was made into a phonograph record, which has been played countless times on my home stereo.

The narrator of the story was W.V. Maclean or, as he was known along the Winnipeg-to-Fort Churchill railway line and at all the hamlet sidings where his bunk car would be parked, simply "Wally." Wally Maclean was a retired surveyor. Gould explained that "Wally has parlayed surveying into a literary tool even as Jorge Luis Borges manipulates mirrors, and Franz Kafka badgers beetles. His relation to a craft which has as its subject the land enabled him to read the signs of that land to find in the most minute measurement a suggestion of the infinite to encompass the universal within the particular."

Wally Maclean said, "Most of us have got a built-in sense of direction. This need have nothing to do with north or with any direction that is physical. We all have a gyro-compass that gives us inner direction or a sense of possible purpose. This gyro-compass gives direction in this way: it points us to that point in our journey where we can say 'Ah, we've been there, we know this place.' We go from the known securely to the unknown. The only way I see getting this idea of north is to take an extended ride north–I mean a long, terrible, trying trip."

These guys knew what canoeing was about. Never before or since have I heard anyone come closer to the kind of experience with the land that I have had in the North. Whether my own ideas have been shaped by "The Idea of North" program, or whether we have all been influenced by the same northern landscape is problematic. I think Glenn Gould and Wally Maclean would both agree that, in the North, the journey is the most powerful teacher of all.

The journey in a northern landscape often teaches harsh lessons–sometimes fatal ones–but is always instructive. The essence of the northern landscape is stillness. The human experience in the North, whether it be that of an Inuk, a surveyor, a sailor, a paddler or a musician, is one of movement, of motion. The journey is central to the idea of north. So much the better, as Wally Maclean says, if it is "long, terrible, trying."

TROUBLES ON OUR JOURNEY BEGAN IN THE DARKEST DAYS OF THE WINTER, long before we got anywhere near the North. Norm was admitted into hospital just after Christmas for major knee surgery that put his whole leg in a cast for nearly two months. He was angry. Cath was worried. But neither of them ever doubted that somehow they would be on the trip. Cath went ahead with planning the menus and Norm spent more time with the maps than ever, checking out the details of our multiwatershed route, especially the places where we would surely have to portage seven weeks' worth of gear. It was easier not to think about what would happen if Norm had to drop out of the group, or, worse, what would happen if his knee failed in the middle of this ambitious trip.

Planning and purchasing went ahead. We agreed to plan meals on the basis of an eight-day rotation. There were eight different breakfasts: pancakes, granola, oatmeal, dried eggs for French toast and omelettes, double-smoked bacon, various multigrain cereals and muesli. Lunches were to be always the same: some combination of crackers, dark bread, bannock, peanut butter, honey and/or jam and a second source of protein, such as cheese, salami, canned meat or fish. Four out of eight suppers were to require fresh fish, with which we planned to combine dried potatoes, stuffing mix, rice and spices. The other four suppers were macaroni and cheese, dried steak and hash-brown potatoes, spaghetti and vegetable stew. Cath, the organizer, did most of the buying and packing.

Individual preparations also continued. As an avid horsewoman Gail was quite fit. In the early months of the new year, however, she worked into a pretty rigorous training schedule, complete with running, sit-ups and a variety of other exercises on her kitchen floor. I had no idea how strenuous this training program was until she phoned one day in early April to say she had spronged something in her back and couldn't move.

The local doctor said that there was nothing he could do beyond prescribing pain-killers. She would just have to lie on her back for six weeks until it got better.

"Will I be able to go on a canoe trip in the Arctic this summer?" she asked.

"Out of the question."

As soon as she could, Gail got on the phone to find out if this was really to be her lot. She found her way to the Carleton University Sports Medicine Clinic in Ottawa. A doctor there diagnosed the problem as an inflamed, or "slipped," disk in her lower back and prescribed special exercises, not rest. He explained that the disk was weakened, and that it would probably never be as good as new, but that with careful attention to how she walked, sat, lifted and worked, it was possible to live a full and active life.

"Will I be able to go on a canoe trip in the Arctic this summer?"

"Where are you going?"

"To Bathurst Inlet on the Mara River."

"It's your back and your decision," he said. "I don't think a trip like that will make your back any better."

"Will it make it worse?"

"I don't imagine it will."

In the middle of all this, as new teachers in the board, Gail and I were both declared surplus. There was the possibility of being hired back, or finding work elsewhere, but the stress didn't help her back any.

No work, Norm's knee, Gail's back – what next? Nothing. Plans for the trip continued in fine style. Slowly Gail and Norm healed. Their attitudes were good. They wanted the trip more than anything. Each canoe crew began to assemble the mass of necessary clothing and gear. By the end of May, all was going exceptionally well. Norm's recovery since the removal of the cast was quicker and more complete than expected, thanks to physiotherapy, and Gail was back at work with almost full strength and range of movement.

Jake and Lorraine had agreed to drive to Yellowknife with a large portion of the gear and our three canoes. The other four of us had purchased our plane tickets. We met, and in an all-night session, double-bagged and packed all of our food, except the fresh vegetables, which we would buy in Yellowknife. For the first time since about November, it looked like the trip was really going to happen. But then, in the second week of June, Lorraine was rushed to the hospital doubled over with abdominal pain. Kidney stone!

The likelihood that our long-awaited Arctic expedition would happen at all was never more uncertain than it was at that moment, only days away from our scheduled departure date. Although we were prepared in some way for all the trail risks, including cold, rough water, high winds, bears, isolation and rocky portages, it looked for a while as if we had been blind-sided by our own mortality. The doctors in Orangeville determined that Lorraine's passing of the stone was an isolated incident that was not likely to recur. Gail's dad, an ex-military pilot, insisted we carry a battery-powered emergency locater transmitter – the kind designed to go in small airplanes–so that we could be sure we would get attention, even in the middle of the barren lands. Finally, finally, it looked like we were set.

Gail and I had closed out our apartments and had put what furniture we had into storage, in anticipation of our both moving to new jobs for the autumn. We finished marking final exams in a flurry, handed in our marks, said our goodbyes and met in the parking lot after the last day of school. The little car was so loaded with packs and gear that I accidentally backed into the front bumper of the vice-principal's car while trying to exit. No damage. Somehow, nothing, at that point, seemed more important than getting onto the river. Nothing *was* more important. Driving to my family's home in Guelph, from where we would jump off to Toronto airport the following morning, the sense of freedom and possibility was intoxicating.

2.
YELLOWKNIFE

IT'S 5:30 A.M. AFTER A NIGHT WITH FAMILY IN GUELPH, ONTARIO, 50 miles (80 kilometres) west of Toronto, Gail and I head east on Highway 401 to meet Norm and Cathy for the early-morning flight to Edmonton. The car is cold. The sky is a velvet study of fading indigo. Beside an imposing promontory to the south, the spire of a small church is silhouetted. The car becomes a flying canoe in my imagination, like *la chasse-galerie*, skirting the steeples of Milton, Ontario, whirling, with the excitement of a magical journey, toward the rising sun.

On the outskirts of the city, a satellite streaks behind the bright lights of Carling O'Keefe Breweries and disappears into the glow of Toronto. We drive on and catch a glimpse of Lester B. Pearson International Airport. There is a picture of Toronto Airport zipping out of the solar system at 101,000 k.p.h. on the Voyager space probes. These ambassadors celebrate more than 20th century temples. They carry music as well.

Voyagers 1 and 2 were launched on August 20 and September 5, 1977, to explore the outer solar system from Jupiter to Uranus. When their scientific purpose is done, these spacecraft will leave our solar system, each carrying a gold-coated copper phonograph record describing who we earthlings are.

The Toronto airport image is one of 118 digitized pictures on the record. It also contains greetings from the president of the United States, a list of U.S. senators responsible for NASA activities, audio greetings in fifty-five languages and nineteen sounds of earth, including wild dogs and heartbeats, volcanoes and crickets, laughter and a kiss. The Voyagers also carry music–ninety minutes of the world's greatest compositions. This intrigues me.

Scientist and author Carl Sagan, the principal organizer of the Voyager record, did not include music as another measure of our knowledge and technical prowess. In *Murmurs from Earth*, Sagan writes, "Our previous messages [on the Pioneer spacecraft] contained information about what we perceive and how we think. But there is much more to human beings than perceiving and thinking. We are feeling creatures. . . . Music, it seemed to me, was at least a creditable attempt to convey human emotions." So, on the expedition that represents the ultimate extension of humanity's journey, it is music that is used to convey the essence of who we are. Music is part of Voyagers' myth.

Emotion–knowledge of the heart grounded in experience– that's what journeying, adventuring and exploration are about. The human experience is not well represented by facts and figures. If the six of us on this canoe expedition wanted to find out plain knowledge about the North, we would watch a film or read about it in a book. What we are seeking on our trip to the Mara River is the feeling of the river and of the land through which it flows, to find in the most minute measurement, as Glenn Gould said of Wally Maclean, a suggestion of the infinite, to encompass the universal within the particular.

It's no accident–it is sheer synchronicity, I dare say–that Gould, the man who had the vision to produce a radio program and record called "The Idea of North," is also one of the musicians represented on Voyager. Of the hundreds of pianists whose Bach recordings might have been chosen, it is Canadian Glenn Gould whom the extraterrestrials, in some other time and space, will hear playing Prelude and Fugue in C, No. 1, from Book 2 of *The Well-Tempered Clavier.*

To journey is to be linked to the Voyagers of this and every other age, and the spirit of exploration they represent. One step on the surface of the earth, if it is to have any meaning at all, must necessarily be linked in imagination to the universe. We will take with us what we know and hold to be true into another part of our world, travel and return with the perspective and teachings of our journey. But, with luck, what we derive from this experience will be guided and informed as much by our hearts as by our senses and our minds. The *possibility* that this kind of whole-mind, whole-body, emotion-laden learning will occur is what comprises most of my anticipation on our day of departure.

CATHY AND NORM HAVE MADE IT TO THE AIRPORT ON TIME AND the four of us have checked in our mountain of gear. After months of planning and preparation, the four of us are seated at last in early-morning sunshine on a Canadian Pacific Airlines jet destined for Edmonton and Yellowknife. Fully charged with expectancy and anticipation, we glance at each other and wonder out loud where on the road to Yellowknife Jake and Lorraine might be with their gear and our three canoes.

The music of Pachelbel's Canon drifts through the cabin as last-minute arrivals stuff their coats in the overhead bins and get seated. For me, music is a great integrator. Music, real or imagined, somehow blends thoughts, feelings and ideas like no other life force. Pachelbel's simple eight-note melody—*soh, reh, me, ti, doh, fah, doh, re*—dances around and upon itself over and over again, and weaves in among the images of morning and this canoe adventure that is beginning to unfold. Eight notes laid down on each other time after time after time create a richness of sound and cadence that blends beautifully with this occasion. Today the Canon is the music of the rising sun, the music of motion and possibility.

Mid-chord, the music stops, a chime pongs, the lights flash, a low whine builds without and vibrations shake the plane. Gail is stiff. She rotates her shoulders, peeks past the man in the window seat, then tips her head back onto the headrest and stares at the ceiling. Nothing green out that window–asphalt, concrete, steel, glass and aluminum. A day-pack that won't fit under the seat in front crowds her feet. She adjusts her seatbelt. I am conscious of her short, shallow breaths. The plane begins to move. Gail embeds her fingers in my wrist.

"We're finally on our way," I say. "Mara River, here we come."

She nods, nervously, without looking at me.

Take-off pushes us deeper into the seats. The bottom drops from our hold on the ground. We're airborne and falling toward the sky.

Several minutes into the flight, I'm conscious of a presence beside me in the aisle. A red-haired flight attendant with flashing green eyes asks, "Would you like something to drink?"

I turn to Gail, who, in contrast, looks wrung out.

"Yes, please, a double rye."

"Would you like anything to go with that?"

"Yes, please, a beer."

"And you, sir?" The flight attendant didn't miss a beat.

"A glass of orange juice would hit the spot."

"It's being shut into this airplane that I hate," Gail concedes. "I feel totally helpless and out of control. Here we are, trusting our lives to the pilot, and we don't know who he is. We don't even know what he looks like. In little planes, you can feel the air, and you can see who's flying. In little planes you can at least maintain the illusion that you still have some control over your destiny. Jetliners make me feel trapped. The only reason I'm on this plane at all is because I want this trip so badly."

Eventually she dozes off. The sooner we get to Yellowknife the better. Watching fear is a fearful experience. Gail had mentioned once or twice how afraid she was of flying, but I never really listened, never took it seriously.

Out the window and down through fives miles of summer air is the city of Winnipeg; four roads from north, south, east and west knotted into a city left alone on the prairie. Gail's still asleep. It's a good thing, but I want to show her how, from this altitude, southern Manitoba looks so much like it does on school maps.

Pressure change awakens Gail as we begin our descent to Edmonton. She's groggy, and not as fearful as before. We land, change planes and take off again. This time a military pilot sits beside her and explains the thumps and whirrs that shake our seats. Knowing the details of flaps, gears and hydraulics, she seems more relaxed.

The feeling of north envelops us quickly out of Edmonton. This provincial capital is at nearly fifty-four degrees north latitude. That's about 600 nautical miles (1140 kilometres) north of home. Maps have taught us to forget that the prairies are so much farther north than central Canada. Having driven in the deep south of Ontario, I know the sign announcing that that part of Canada is at the same latitude as sunny California, but it takes an airplane experience and a map in the in-flight magazine to show that Edmonton is on the same parallel as Kamchatka and the Aleutian Islands and not too far south of Copenhagen or Moscow.

We fly north over Canada's great Interior Plains. It's not long before regular fields of wheat and canola vanish, and scrub spruce and sand, ordered by well-spaced seismic survey lines, appear. We forget that the prairies stretch north to the Beaufort Sea. John Macoun, the first naturalist with the Geological Survey of Canada, knew this. He argued, in the late nineteenth century, on the basis of the rich plant life he found in northern Alberta, that the railway should be routed here and settlers encouraged to farm this region.

By now we're "north of sixty," north of the sixtieth parallel, the place where arctic magic begins. Strangely there's no line on the ground. My staring at the map too long has etched it in my brain, but not on the landscape. I've been over this route three or four times—on other canoe trips, on my way to Inuvik as a labourer—but still I'm glad of the opportunity to witness the borderland again. Down there somewhere, slicing across millions of continuous acres, is an invisible political line dividing Alberta and the Northwest Territories. All we have from the air is a gradually changing landscape. The only borders that make any sense here are the edges of rivers and lakes.

Before long we're over Great Slave Lake. To the west is Hay

River and the mouth of the mighty Mackenzie. To the east, the Canadian Shield. And to the north, 100 miles (160 kilometres) of water, over which we descend to Yellowknife. The nose of the plane tips down. Gail finds the old dents in my wrist and latches on for one final bout of panic, but this time she manages a smile.

WRITER CLAIRE DEANE CALLED YELLOWKNIFE THE CAPITAL OF THE national psyche. It is the capital of the Northwest Territories, she says, and the NWT comprise the largest part of the Canadian North. Since the Canadian North is embedded in the national psyche, Yellowknife is the key to the Canadian identity, capital of the national psyche.

"Welcome to Yellowknife, ladies and gentlemen. For your own comfort and safety please. . . ." Gail turns and flashes a smile that says "I made it. I made it!" It gets broader with the sound of the cabin doors being opened.

As we step onto the landing of the companionway, it takes a moment for our eyes to adjust to the intensity of the afternoon sun. Time to breathe. The air is dry and clear and sweet. From the companionway we see the van with three canoes lashed on top parked on the gravel beside the terminal. It's dirtier than when we last saw it, but it's here. And then we see at the window, looking out from inside the terminal, Lorraine waving madly to get our attention.

There's something delightfully simple about northern airports, like Yellowknife's. They're small and low, and every piece of building material is derived from the universally portable four-by-eight building unit.

Whether you're the prime minister, the pilot or the Pope, you get off your plane on this same bit of tarmac in Yellowknife and, if you want immediate shelter, washroom or a drink of water, you step into the building and mix with the folks inside–drillers, Sikhs, South Africans, roughnecks, midwives, mechanics and just about every combination of Indian, Inuit and European stock a Canadian might imagine. Kids, dogs and politicians–all mixed together at one time or another on the same worn, tiled floor under the same smoke-stained ceiling, sitting on the same chipped chairs under the same sign for Aero Arctic–Canada's first territorial helicopter company. "We deliver safely," the sign says.

We walk past a guy in dirty orange overalls holding the ramp door, through another door and into those arms. Hugs and handshakes all around.

Lorraine and John have had a great drive. Five thousand miles (8000 kilometres) and six days of highway bliss were punctured momentarily by a flat tire in Saskatchewan. Leave it to Jake and Lorraine to turn frustration into a funny tale.

The spare, as it turned out, was flat too, but they managed to limp to a garage. The mechanic, for their amusement, hauled out a wild assortment of springs, combs, nails and bits of glass, every sharp object he had taken out of thirty-five years of flat tires.

"Ninety percent of flats is in the back tires," he told them. "The front tires stand 'em up and the back tires drive 'em in."

Conversation within the group splits off in twos. Everyone is charged up by our reunion and is full of stories about the first leg of our journey. I tell Jake the story of Gail's drink order on the plane. He laughs and suggests to her that we get a few extra bottles to feed her habit while we're on the trail.

At the airport window we watch a fork-lift remove the luggage from the hold. A green Duluth pack pitches off the load and hits the pavement. No bounce. A thickish lad in a sleeveless black T-shirt and jeans grabs it by one strap. The strap breaks. Using two hands he dumps the load contemptuously onto the train of baggage carts. We watch the handlers load the items onto the conveyor just outside the window. An airline employee presses a button that activates the conveyor. Our gear rides through the wall with tool boxes, cardboard cartons, gym bags, wooden crates and various soft suitcases. Closer inspection of the broken pack reveals that somewhere along the way a bright red tag has been attached that says simply, "Caution: HEAVY! Bend your knees."

There's a greasy stain on another pack that needs immediate attention. A plastic bag-lined bottle of vegetable oil has exploded in transit and soaked through everything in the pack. Fortunately most items are wrapped in plastic bag-lined nylon stuff sacks, so it is the stuff sacks that are soaked, but the bags will all have to be changed. Two new paperbacks are swelled with oil. A loose sweatshirt is dumped in a greasy heap on the floor. There's a puddle of oil in the bottom of the pack. Ribbons of paper towel from the washroom soak up and wipe away most of the oil. No serious harm done.

On the way into town we pass an immortalized, guppy-like, Bristol front-loading cargo plane dressed in the characteristic blue and red of Wardair Canada. It's a monument to Max Ward's contribution to flying and happens to be the first wheeled aircraft to land at the North Pole. It's mounted on a cement pedestal, but against the stunted spruce outside the airport it looks like it's flying. Actually, with nose down, the plane looks like it's crashing.

YELLOWKNIFE IS AN ESTABLISHED SETTLEMENT THAT SEEMS TO ignore its northern disposition. The famous NWT white three-legged polar bear on blue background is everywhere, fostering the illusion of northness, but really it has most of the comforts of home. Claire Deane says of this aspect of Yellowknife that, while you can't get shoes fixed or treat your boss to a doughnut, you can hop into a cab whose driver, likely as not, is the treasurer of the Daughters of the Midnight Sun. He might turn out to be Fred, a black East African who works in the gold-mine, drives a cab and speaks fluent Danish, Swedish, Czech, German, Italian, Swahili, Russian and English, as well as his own language. Yellowknife has a local chapter of the Robbie Burns Society. It even has its own gang of bikers that roars up every summer from Saskatoon. This summer, the long-awaited Prince of Wales Northern Heritage Centre is nearing completion.

As we drive into town, all crammed into the loaded van, the previous connections to this place scroll through my imagination. Gail tells me about a transfer student from Yellowknife who wrote an English essay about a trip her family had taken by car all the way from Yellowknife to Edmonton–600 hot and dirty miles (960 kilometres) packed into the non-airconditioned family sedan–to go to McDonald's.

Yellowknife has been the capital of the Northwest Territories since 1967, and as such is the seat of power and government organization for most of Canada north of sixty. Yellowknife Dene, the city's namesake people, have been in the area since the early 1800s. Samuel Hearne, the first European to visit the shores of Great Slave Lake, passed through in 1771. Fort Providence, a trading post established as a result of Alexander Mackenzie's exploration of the area, lasted on the shores of Yellowknife Bay for thirty years, just long enough to be of service to Sir John Franklin on his journey in 1820. But it was the discovery of gold and the subsequent development of gold-mines in the 1930s that gave rise to modern-day Yellowknife.

The frontier feel to Yellowknife remains. We reach a T-junction on the way into town. To the left is the Giant Gold Mine. Straight ahead is the raw rock of the Canadian Shield.

In town, we scatter with last-minute lists of groceries and little errands. We meet back in the Miners Mess, a downtown cafeteria-style restaurant in the Yellowknife Inn that stretches the frontier motif. Beneath ornamental artefacts and photos of the men who worked the "Con," "Negus," and "Giant" claims in the early days, Jake tells us that he has found six charter companies with Twin Otters on floats, but all their machines are working elsewhere. One company has two machines ferrying helicopter fuel up at Great Bear Lake, one of which is due back the next afternoon at three o'clock. Jake has booked us in for that time: $3.10 per mile plus fuel surcharge. The charter works out to about $1100, or $183 per head. He has also managed a free flight to cache a third of our food on Contwoyto Lake at a weather station near our route.

That evening we step out of bright sunshine into a gaudy red-and-black tiled landing and tread down a darkened set of stairs to a steakhouse called the Hoist Room. There's an old mine elevator–a hoist–at the head of the stairs, but the name can also be construed as a verb. A quick scan of the place confirms the appropriateness of this interpretation. Six beers for the table! Hoist a toast. "To the trip!"

3.
NIGHT FLIGHT

By early afternoon the next day, we have bought all of our last-minute fresh groceries and supplies, checked route and schedule with the RCMP, written last-minute postcards and carted everything from canoes to canola oil to the wharf, ready to be loaded into our charter. Lines of planning and preparation have converged at one bright spot in old-town Yellowknife. But, no plane.

"He's weathered-in somewhere near Great Bear Lake," says the dispatcher, not understanding that we expect him to be substantially more specific about the whereabouts of his pilot and the company's million-dollar aircraft. "Come back at six o'clock."

At six: "Nothing new. Come back in two hours."

At eight: "He just took off. Should be here by ten-thirty. Why don't you guys go up to a movie to kill time until then? We should still have time to load, gas up and get out before legal darkness. Come back around eleven."

Jake has been stewing all this time about whether their eighteen-and-a-half-foot (5.6-metre) canoe will fit into the Twin Otter.

"How long is the cabin in the Twin?" he asks.

"You got me. All I know is it holds a lot of stuff. If I'm right, you can put five fuel drums deep from front to back." With the nervous energy of anticipation building by the minute, we take him up on his suggestion and head uptown in the empty van.

The movie at the Capital I Theatre that night is *The Goodbye Girl*. We watch. At the end, from a corner phone booth, the main character resolves conflict by making eye contact with his female counterpart who is standing at a window, looking down into the rain-filled pool of light containing the man who has come back. A human connection in urban chaos makes the difference. It's raining hard in Boston as the credits roll. We leave the theatre and step back into the long yellow light of 10:30 P.M. in Yellowknife. It takes a moment to separate fact from fiction. Norm flips the lights on as we drive back to the float base. Still no sign of the plane.

As we all pile out of the van, there is without warning an airy whistle overhead and we are left standing in turbine exhaust, watching the prodigal Twin Otter alight silently on the metallic mirror of Back Bay. It skims in a wide arc, leaving seersucker ripples of light and shadow as its wake. Just a few hundred yards off the dock, the pilot finally throttles the engines back, the tail drops, the craft ploughs then drifts to a near-perfect side landing. The front door opens and out jumps a wily-looking character in a blue flight suit. "You the canoeists? With you in a minute."

After five minutes we go inside and find the pilot studying a dog-eared handbook with the dispatcher. He turns to us and explains that it is light enough for take-off from here, but the legal-darkness charts tell them that it will be too dark to ensure a safe landing at the other end.

"It only takes one rock on a pontoon landing to ruin your whole day," he says.

The boss continues: "We'll get 'er loaded now, but you won't be taking off until three."

"Three A.M.? Three in the morning?"

"That's right. You want to get out there as soon as possible, right? There are cots in the back room if you want to lie down."

The pilot stretches both arms above his head, revealing mismatched sweat socks and scruffy white tennis shoes. "I've been at this now for thirty hours. I'm going home for a shower and a snooze," he says to the dispatcher. Turning our way he adds, "Hauling fuel is a dirty job. Those goddam drums would give you a triple hernia if you let 'em. Back in an hour."

Outside, the disproportionately large tail of the Twin Otter is silhouetted against swirling reds on the northern horizon. The plane sits quietly on still water at the wharf, its high-speed pontoons angled up toward the characteristic de Havilland nose cone. The port propeller is perfectly aligned with its starboard twin, their turbines reaching farther forward from the overhead wings than it appears they should, somehow compensating for the large tail. A bare bulb on the flight shack illuminates air-whipped exhaust stains on the near-side engine cowling. The monster is sleeping.

A silent youth breaks the stillness by dragging a stout orange fuel hose to nourish the beast. A cigarette hangs precariously from his lower lip. He steps onto the pontoon; the plane rocks gently in acknowledgement. He loosens the cap, flicks his cigarette into the lake, plunks in the right-angled brass nozzle and jams the fuel trigger on full flow with an old piece of wood. He walks back on the pontoon, staring blankly at the sky to his right; he reaches up over the three-step metal ladder and opens both rear doors and latches them open with rubber bungee cords.

Without speaking he comes over and eyes our load. Jake points at the white Woodstream. "Let's load that one first. I'm a little worried that it might not fit in," he says. The two of them pick up the long white boat and head for the plane. First try, there's still a 4-foot (1.2-metre) chunk hanging outside the door. With the canoe other-side up and a second person inside the cabin, we slide and wrestle it to within 6 inches (15 centimetres) of success. Out it comes for a fresh start.

Twice more we try, using variations of the previous strategies, and come up 6 inches short of cabin space. It's a lever problem: to angle forward into the cabin through the narrow double doors we must find a way to bring the ends of the boat toward the centre of the airplane, but the doorframe gets in the way. There's no way Jake is going to give up, but we take a break and lean over the boat for a rest. After this shared struggle, the hired hand speaks: "There's a skill saw in the office."

Suddenly we hear liquid pouring. The belly tanks are full and the nozzle is still jammed on full, and it's now overflowing fuel into the lake. The canoe blocks the rear doors. The hired hand jumps into the cockpit, out the pilot's tiny door, flips out the wood, and replaces the cap. Without a second look at the spilled fuel spreading muted rainbow colours in the water around the pontoons, he lugs the hose back to the reel and returns to the loading problem.

By this time, Jake is in the cabin and has found the pins that secure the aluminum tubing of the double canvas-backed folding seats against which the prow is pushing. With those temporarily removed, the boat is persuaded to inch forward enough to get the back end inside. By putting the prow past the bulkhead and up between the pilots' seats we are able to jostle the boat around and get it placed on the floor under the seven starboard windows. "Phew!" says Jake, with a broad smile.

Packs go into the big white canoe. The heavy ones have to be hugged to get them off the ground, and from that proximity the rich smell of damp canvas, oiled leather straps and dried food cuts through the fuel vapours surrounding us. The aroma reminds me of trips to the basement in the wintertime, just to smell that summer smell, the musty essence of freedom and adventure. The next canoe goes in without a fuss – this time it's Norm and Cathy's Miller, a foot and a half (45 centimetres) shorter than the Woodstream. It's loaded with packs, and in goes the third boat, our green ABS-plastic Old Town Tripper. More pliable than the other two boats, it bends around the corner and makes a triple-decker canoe pile. Remaining packs and gear go in the back cargo compartment, leaving six fold-down single seats for us on the port side of the plane. In the low light we don't notice the nasty bulge in the side wall of the white canoe made by the weight of two other canoes full of heavy packs. We leave the hired hand strapping down the load. A muffled crunch emanates from inside the plane as we cross the wharf. "Nothing we can do about it now," says Jake. "It's probably just the gel coat on the big white beauty. Get out the duct tape."

While we work, the bright spot on the horizon moves eastward. At this time of year, in this place, the sun really doesn't set and rise; it circles the sky and soaks a while in twilight over the midnight hour. I'm caught by the blue that stretches upward to infinity just above the beer-coloured band of gold.

With the packing all done, the others head for the cots, while I sit down on the flight-shack step and enjoy the privacy and stillness of night. These last few days have been a whirl.

It seems like months ago that Gail and I backed into the vice-principal's car on the way out of the school parking lot. It's been only two days. Since then we've been on remote control, driven along pre-ordained paths, all leading to this moment. But we're stalled by circumstances and left in a weird, placeless limbo. The frenzy has spun us to the very edge of our workaday lives. But the union of people and circumstances has yet to be consummated with a flight across the threshold of the unknown.

Headlights break the spell. The company pick-up rattles up to the side of the building and out hops our pilot. It takes two slams to get the door to shut. I hope they maintain their planes better than they do their trucks. "Wanna coffee?" he asks blithely, as he steps by me on his way in the door.

His name is Ted Allen. He's thirty-four and has been hanging around airplanes his whole life, cleaning them, gassing them up and now flying them. At fifteen he was a Ramp Rat, making minimum wage with a fixed-base operator at a strip in southern Saskatchewan. The boss carried his wages on a stick and gave it back in dual flight time–some of it, at least; the rest he forgot. At sixteen Allen had enough time for his private licence and, by eighteen, he'd gone commercial, flying sightseeing tours over prairie wheat fields. At twenty-two, he had his instrument rating and float rating and was in Yellowknife, hauling fishermen around in a Cessna 185 Skywagon, taking what time they'd give him in the right seat of the Twin. Four years later, he was captaining the Twin Otter. He's got four gold stripes on the shoulder of his flight suit to prove it. "Long hauls when I can get 'em," says Allen. "Mostly it's short runs and a lot of heavy lifting.

"Yeah, the Twin is a beautiful machine. For short take-off and landing and for space and cargo weight, there's nothing in the 12,000-pound (5400-kilogram) class that can touch it. Top speed, 175 knots (87.5 metres per second) and a range of over 900 nautical

miles (1710 kilometres). And those high-speed floats on the 300 out
there have their own lift-they fly themselves. Twins are at the
North Pole and the South Pole, and just about everywhere in
between. My buddy Al Philby just went to Kuwait to fly Twins.
Those turbine engines are pricey, but they can burn anything-JP4,
JP5, kerosene, diesel, AV-gas in a pinch. A guy down the street said
he ran one on whiskey one time. They'll do anything and they're
fun to fly. Way less bumpy than single-engine jobs. And the second
engine comes in handy sometimes.

"One time I took a bunch of bigwigs up to look at some mine
site over by the Thelon River. And I hear one of these guys talking
before we start about how these planes can fly on one engine. A real
big talker. Just for a laugh, when I got up to cruising altitude I shut
down the engine outside his window and let the prop stop dead. It
took him a while to see it, but you should have seen that bugger's
face go white when he figured out that the plane really was flying on
one engine. He looked out the window again, at that eight-
and-a-half-foot (2.5-metre) three-bladed Hartzell prop totally still,
and then across at the other one-just to make sure it was
running-and then back out his window. Yup, it really was stopped.
Man, was he scared!

"I was doing a medivac out of Coppermine one time and there
was this weird coastal fog hanging over the airport. You could see
the radio mast sticking through, so I knew roughly where I was. It
was the damndest thing. Clear skies overhead and out over the
pack-ice in the water. But right over the land at the edge of the water
was this fog. I knew I had to get in or somebody was going to die. So
I flew around and around with what fuel I had, waiting to see if
things would change. All of a sudden I saw a runway in a hole and
punched her down. Well, wouldn't you know it, I was almost at the
terminal. I got on the ground safe and just about piled off the end of
the runway. You might say it was almost a terminal landing. Get it?
That's the beauty of these planes. You put 'em on full reverse thrust
and they'll just about stand on their nose, but you can stop 'em in
500 feet (150 metres), less if you've got a good wind. Anyway the
nurse told me I was crazy and just about refused to fly with me, but
the old lady was so sick that we had to get her out, quick.

"And when things were frozen up last year I went down to the east end of the lake and took a bunch of native hunters out for caribou. Man, they don't fool around. We fly around until we see a herd. We go over the next hill and land. They get out and shoot sixty, seventy, maybe eighty caribou, quarter 'em with chain-saws and throw 'em in the back. Three or four trips it took, and the plane just reeked of blood. It was running all over the place. Toward the end they started getting tired and only threw in the hinds. What a mess! And you wouldn't believe how corrosive that stuff is. You've gotta clean the floor good or it'll eat right through the bottom. More coffee?

"It's pretty slow sometimes up here in the winter. Not much going on. So, in summer, we try to get in as much time as possible. Some guys even keep dual logbooks. You're only supposed to fly a certain number of hours at a time with a monthly maximum. The second logbook allows you to split up your time to keep everything legal, on paper at least. It's tough enough to make a living without federal rules getting in the way."

Sharp little eyes, recessed into darkened depressions in his sallow face, Allen talked the way you might expect a person to talk who'd had minutes of sleep and gallons of coffee in the last two days. He loves flying and the planes, but for him, with the exception of knowing the intricate details of a variety of landing spots around the NWT, the land is just a two-dimensional surface, a map, on which he draws flight lines. Much of the time, it seems, he flies using radio navigation beacons that require no attention at all to the land. He's buzzed a few caribou herds, checked in on a few unfortunate musk-oxen and caught the odd fish, but mostly it's just flying.

"It's two-thirty, time to go. Go rouse the others."

While we gather our things, Allen explains that technically it is against the rules to take off at this time of night because of the noise. Aside from Yellowknife residents living near Back Bay who will certainly be roused by the take-off noise, the only ones who care are the flight-service officers in the airport control tower west of town. He will forgo checking in with them this run and stay well below the hills between Back Bay and the airport to avoid detection until we are sufficiently far out of town. In short, we will sneak out of town in a Twin Otter. I begin to feel unsure about the whole affair. Allen scribbles a note and tosses it onto the dispatcher's desk. "Always file a flight plan," he says, with a maniacal grin. And we head out into the darkness.

The cabin is dark and quiet and smells of kerosene. We sit beside the cinched load in single file along the port side: Gail in front behind the bulkhead, me next, then Cath, Jake and Lorraine. Norm is tucked away in the seat right beside the second cargo door with a pack just about on his lap. Mixed with the fuel smell and metallic staleness is the familiar essence of dried food, oiled straps and musty packs.

Allen slams the back door from the outside. This was the point of most fear for Gail on the bigger plane. I touch her shoulder. It's rigid.

"No problem. I don't mind small planes," she says bravely, focusing her attention out the window. The excitement and expectation of the moment are written in her face, lit softly by light from the bare bulb on the flight shack.

Allen unties the lines and swings up into the cockpit. His door clicks shut. The steering column in front of the empty co-pilot's seat moves forward and back in testing fashion. A switch snaps, and instrument lights send a glow through the arched bulkhead door linking the cockpit with the cabin. More switches and the spiralling whine of the starting gyro-compass break the silence.

Another snap and the port propeller begins to turn, gently and smoothly at first, and then it begins to vibrate the plane. The starboard prop is turning. Allen's hand reaches up and behind to a bank of switches on the ceiling just inside the cockpit door. He flicks them all on and we see reflections of red and white lights on belly and tail bouncing off the dusky surroundings.

Gail turns and yells something. I lean closer, but fastened seatbelts make it impossible for us to connect. Can't hear. We share smiles instead.

Allen's hand moves to three sets of levers centred in the cockpit ceiling. With cocked arm–like a standing commuter in the subway–he holds the leftmost lever by its machine-aluminum roller handle and pushes it forward. The engine outside our window revs, and the plane rotates away from the wharf. He brings the other lever up to match it and we taxi out into the dim light, hanging onto the black waters of Back Bay. There is something sinister, clandestine and deliciously spooky about this exit from Yellowknife. Water begins to splash away from the pontoons. I'm awash with anticipation for the flight into morning, with the finality of leaving and with the uncertainty that moving in darkness breeds. Handwritten flight plans are decidedly wicked. We are in the hands of a genuine Canadian free-wheeling, hard-driving, bad-boy bush pilot–the kind you read about in Hammond Innes novels.

Low light, cold air and lack of sleep serve only to heighten the drama and intensify the fear in my gut. What lies ahead is unknown–the common denominator underlying all adventure. Living the uncertainty is much different from thinking about it, to be sure. Outside, the twilight world looks surreal. Dark shapes of houses and occasional lights stand against the weakening indigo sky. If we could see out the opposite windows we'd be able to savour pre-dawn colour, but for now we're locked into a dark and uncertain world that makes me tingle with fear and anticipation. If there was a time to bolt back to safety, this is it.

Allen shoves forward both throttles as far as they'll go. The turbines roar, the props accelerate the plane in a great slurry of noise and worried water. We push the water like an overloaded catamaran until the craft begins to plane and finally skims across it. On the darkened calm water we have only the heaviness of our bodies on the canvas seats to give us any indication of speed. But the escape from the water is unmistakable. Allen lifts one pontoon, and then the other. We're up. We're off and on our way. He reaches up and eases off on the pitch of the propeller blades. He turns a wheel beside his seat and lowers the nose away from a climbing angle. As promised, he stays close to the ground to keep hidden from the airport tower. We really are sneaking out of town.

The rock is black in the twilight. But as the plane swings round to our course–thirty-one degrees magnetic–light from the north-eastern horizon washes over the landscape and I become conscious of patterns on the land that falls away below us. It's rough and pitted, grey and vaguely green, and now stretches without human mark as far as we can see out the windows. Trees-the few that there are-stick to the edges of streams and lakes and to longitudinal cracks in the bedrock.

Higher now, we see sparkles of sun dance over the horizon and spin off the countless water surfaces below before recoiling to infinity. There is not a straight line below: the rock and the shadows and the trees and the edges are an infinite study of randomness. But wait. The bodies of water, the streams, the sloughs, the ponds and lakes are all narrower than long. They begin in the northwest and flow to the southeast, roughly perpendicular to our flight line. Let your eyes go out of focus and they seem united by currents of energy flashing across the land as we race toward morning.

"Run toward the dawn" is an Indian teaching. The glaciers, it seems, ran beside the dawn, leaving these megalithic scratches-footprints in time-on their way. Maybe if we run toward the dawn, only then will we get to see the tracks of the power that shaped this wild land. But how, I wonder, can you scratch granite? These ice sheets must have come with great power.

The sun pokes over the horizon and turns every water surface to the brilliant patina of precious metals-gold, silver and old-fashioned General Motors chrome. The lakes are twisting shapes on a black background: a horse, a canoe, a face. Natural artwork in twos: two colours, two dimensions. There is nothing for scale: are the lakes oceans, are the streams rivers, are the trees giants? Where is the third dimension when you are lost in space?

I think of another pilot acquaintance, so different from Ted Allen. For years he has flown a Single Otter from Baker Lake in the Keewatin to Chantry Inlet Lodge up on the Back River. The plane for him was just a tool. You knew how to fly it. You knew how to fix it. But it was a tool that took you out onto the landscape. The route from Baker to Chantry Inlet for him was a series of shaped lakes. He'd given them all his own names: Cat's Paw Lake, Beaver Tail Lake. He could recite his route by heart, and he might tell you, if you asked, where he would stop when he was alone and walk out over the tundra. He knew the route. He had some kind of map of it etched on his brain. He belonged on his route. He'd made the land's shapes and messages his own. For him the barrens were home, summer home. If he had time he would camp and fish–spend time on the land–and then take off again to ferry another load of rich American anglers over the Arctic Circle and beyond the lure of Saturday-morning TV.

As we fly into the morning, the sun angles in and lights up the cabin. Below, wash after wash of colour spreads over the land as the day breaks. Shadows begin to define the third dimension of the Shield. By now the land is green, the water still a metallic blaze, but right below us the edges of water are blue and we can get some idea of the depth of water, more map-like than I remember.

Like a pair of tuning forks just out of pitch, the propellers set up beats in their sound as one slows or quickens relative to the other, but Ted Allen reflexively reaches up and fine-tunes the throttles, and we carry on our way. The excitement of the moment is visceral. The air is rich and full. The fear and uncertainty are there to be savoured. How sad it must be for the map-reader who is never able to connect his map with the land it represents.

The throb of the propellers is mesmerizing; it's a noise much like the train sounds in the background of the "Idea of North" program. Gould, the musician, thought of the train throb as what he called the "basso-continuo" onto which were superimposed the voices of people talking on the train. Gould called it "contrapuntal radio." A catchy idea. "It's perfectly true," writes Gould in the program notes on the record jacket, "that in the dining-car not every word is going to be audible, but then by no means every syllable in the final fugue from Verdi's *Falstaff* is either.... Few opera composers have been deterred from utilizing trios, quartets or quintets by the knowledge that only a portion of the words they set to music will be accessible to the listener–most composers being concerned primarily about the totality of the structure, the play of consonance and dissonance between the voices–and, quite apart from the fact that I do believe most of us are capable of much more substantial information-intake than we give ourselves credit for, I would like to think that these scenes can be listened to in very much the same way that you'd attend the *Falstaff* fugue." I begin to wonder if the whole journey, with its myriad impressions, emotions, sensations and physical imperatives, can be understood in a similar way. Should I stop paying attention to detail and listen instead to the harmonies created by the overlay of detail, people and impressions onto the journey itself?

Suddenly, I have to urinate. At this point on another bush-plane flight–that time on a de Havilland Single Otter, which was, with the exception of a band-saw in the CIP paper mill in Temiska-ming, Quebec, the noisiest machine known to humanity–I motioned my dilemma to the pilot. He handed me a green garbage bag and pointed to the rear of the cabin. The ceiling was too low to stand under, so I knelt. With perfect timing, he put the plane into a sudden steep dive followed by an impressive variety of other confounding manoeuvres. Pilot humour. This time I'll hold it.

By now it's quite light and we're settled into the rhythm of the flight. For all the beauty below us to the west and to the north, the land has a certain sameness about it. We're flying northeast from Yellowknife into a chain of lakes that feed the Lockhart River system. There is no navigation beacon on our chosen drop-off point, Munn Lake. Looking ahead, the corner of a 1:500,000-scale aero-nautical topographical map is visible just off the edge of Ted Allen's lap. Gail is up there with him now, in the co-pilot's seat. She has the other headset on and is chatting away. He holds the map over her way and points out our position. I have a map on my knee too, but I've lost my place. One lake looks like the next. Or the lake I think to be that lake on the map turns out to have an extra island or a whole set of finger bays that don't make sense. I'm lost, and hoping furiously that Allen knows where he is. Is this what Leif Eriksson felt in the year 1000, or Jacques Cartier in 1534 when they sailed over the edge of the charted world? Is this what William Beebe felt when he broke all previous underwater records and dived to 3028 feet (924 metres) in his bathysphere in 1934, or what Yuri Alekseye-vich Gagarin had going through his mind when he became the first human to leave the earth's atmosphere in 1961? Tame though this adventure may be, it is exploration nonetheless. I feel today a kinship with fellow explorers, even if it is nothing more than a shared belief in our ability to survive the challenges ahead. And we believe that there is value in going over the edge, even if now we are crossing only the borders of our own preconceptions about ourselves and about the world.

Ears pop. Wish I'd remembered to buy a package of gum. We're getting close. I get a sudden feeling of fear and alienation, wondering what would happen if Allen dropped us on the wrong lake. We must be sure of where we think we are before he leaves us stranded. Allen points over the dashboard and draws Gail's attention to the horizon. Munn Lake. She turns and points excitedly for us to see. We're getting close. A sandy beach next to a rocky point in the lake seems a fine landing spot. Allen drops the plane a little more and then makes several passes over the adjacent bay to check for shoals and rocks. Looks good. He banks the plane steeply over the landing beach and heads out over the main body of the lake. Wheeling again, I turn sideways and the lake is right there, straight down. I can see waves and streaks on the water. The plane drops steeply toward the water, but just before landing Allen pulls the nose up, pulls back the throttles, and we glide silently over the lake. A satisfying hiss and a slight pull on the seatbelt were all we heard and felt on landing. As he had done before, Allen then revs the plane up and keeps it planing across the water until we are very close to the beach. Then, using the ingenious reverse-thrust system unique to the Twin Otter, he turns the plane around and backs it into the beach.

Unloading is a matter of team work, with Ted in the plane and the rest of us spread out evenly to the shore, some on the pontoon, some in the water and one on the beach. There is no time to fathom the fact that we are here finally, and that when the plane takes off, that's us on the tundra for seven weeks, unless we set off our emergency locater transmitter and call down on us the entire resources of the Search and Rescue Squadron out of Nameo Canadian Forces Base in Edmonton.

Before we're conscious of place or time, Allen says goodbye and is starting up the plane again. We walk up the beach and gain a little elevation on the land to watch him leave. In the foreground is Gail, standing silhouetted against the 5:00 A.M. sky. She waves as Allen rises from the cloud of spray and again as he turns and descends on us with a tree-top fly-past before leaving for home. There is an emptiness in the scene: one woman in the wilderness. And there is emptiness in our ears: the place, filled until now with turbine noise, is unable to receive the subtlety of tundra sounds. Ted Allen and his machine become a dot and disappear on the horizon. Slowly, the rustle of wind on arctic willow enters our senses.

4.
FIRST STROKES

LIKE THE LAST CAR IN THE PARKING LOT OF SOME SUPER SUBURBAN mall, we are alone. The finality of our situation is unnerving. A lone wind gusts through my pile sweater, cooling the moisture in the T-shirt next to my skin. I shiver and pull on my yellow raincoat and blue nylon rainpants. It's not raining, but they will help break the wind. Besides, another layer might help me feel less vulnerable. Without trees, or mountains or buildings to block vision, we are alone in a world that stretches to the horizon to the east, to the west and to the south.

This is a world in which nature does for the colour green what dawn does for blue. The idea of greenness is feathered in somewhere in this enchanting monochromatic landscape. Higher regions of land are peppered with various dusty green and yellow lichens that give only a hint that there is life there at all. Dominating this landing place is a mixture of pastel green caribou moss, patched with polymorphous colonies of dark green arctic heather, tending to black in the shadows. Spruce patches run deep chrome green, with vertical brown and black bars for texture. Creases in the landscape, where summer creeks might run, are lined with the jade hues of alder and arctic willow bushes. And completing the spectrum in this arctic land are phosphorescent green perennials such as sedge and horsetail that thrive in marshy bowls atop the permafrost.

Twenty-four hours without sleep cause Jake, Lorraine and Cathy to set up tents. Jake and Lorraine's tan and brown Deer Creek Dome is consumed by the landscape, as is Norm and Cath's green Timberline, except that their homemade red nylon vestibule stands out like a tee on a freshly mown fairway. Gail is standing still, blending in at the place from which she watched the plane disappear, all bundled up in her new green rainsuit, long chestnut hair tucked up into her deep green felt "crusher" that still looks catalogue new. Mixed rays of red and yellow light push over the landscape from the southeastern horizon, highlighting the wonder in her face. She is not sleepy. Unlike me, perhaps because I have told her enough about what this moment would be like, she is not afraid.

"The air here is so clear. The sky is so big," she says with a broad smile. "It's better than I ever imagined. Look at this place! It goes on forever." She beckons to the sky with both hands outstretched.

To the north of us is a rising plain with map-patterned growths of lichens and low grasses intermixed with the sand and gravel. And yet, although we can see perhaps 20 miles (32 kilometres) or more through the southern panorama, the scene is strangely two-dimensional–the flat treeless land like a variegated green brush stroke across the bottom of a piece of paper of the purest cobalt blue. From this low angle distant lakes come to our eyes as parallel lines of silver in the band of green.

"Hey what's that on the water there?"

A pair of red-throated loons cavorts on the water a few dozen yards offshore, cutting the near lake's silver surface with wake lines as they run and turn, dive, rise and light again. Their characteristic shape is similar to the silhouettes of common, yellow-billed and arctic loons, who also make this a summer home, but with subtle differences. The necks of the red-throats are more snake-like than those of their dagger-billed cousins and their beaks are thinner and have a distinctive up-turn. But, in the sunshine, the dead giveaway is the silver-grey head and the male's rufous throat patch. The grey checkered blue-black backs intermixed with sprays of sun-sparkled water and flashes of white belly plumage is eye-catching. They're chasing each other like a couple of mad fools.

To the Cree Indians, whose James Bay watershed homelands I paddled through as a kid, the loon is Mookwa, spirit of the North. This morning, the spirit is alive and playful. This bird is synonymous with north, perhaps because it has been around longer than human beings. Loons get the first page of bird books because their family record is the longest of any living bird. Their family fossil record goes back to the Paleocene, about 65 million years ago. Not long ago, a 54,000-year-old fossil of this very bird, in exactly the same form as it is before us today, was found by scientists in the Old Crow Basin in the Yukon.

Play climaxes with a flurry of wings on water. Their little webbed feet pedal furiously for take-off; whacka, whacka, whacka. The feet are the last part of the bird to touch the water, leaving splash prints spaced farther and farther apart by acceleration. The birds are airborne. The rippled pools widen into a V on the still water. The birds, hunchbacked in flight, wheel by against the bright southern sky. They come close enough for me to hear the rhythmic squeak in their wings.

In the pause predicated by their disappearance over the nearby hill, I am chilled by a strange sensation that the pilot has dropped us off somewhere other than Munn Lake. Trusting a guy who's been flying for a day and a half non-stop is not a good idea. Maybe he thought we knew where we are.

I open the map case and pull out the full topographic sheet. Orienting it to what I can see, I look south to a large point of land: it's there but it's so flat, giving the impression of being much farther away than one might expect. And to the southwest, the lake goes on forever, nearly to the horizon. That makes sense, relative to the map. We're here, or at least it's possible to convince oneself that one is in the right place. Nothing can be done for now about the stray-dog idea that we're not, except maybe get some elevation and look at the land one more time from there.

"Would you like to go for a walk?" I ask.

"Thought you'd never ask. We can sleep later. I can't get over this place!"

"Maybe we'll see the loons nesting over the hill."

Two of us trudge up the hill, conscious, at least initially, of the "sweet-sweet-sweet" sound of the legs and arms of our nylon raingear rubbing together as we walk. There seems to be a worn path that is going roughly in our direction, so we follow that. Gail spots a moss-covered caribou antler and runs over to it. She picks it up.

"Look at this claw at the front. It's like a shovel with fingers," she says with a kid's zeal.

It's half a set of antlers really. Judging by the amount of green moss covering much of its creamy white surface, it was shed quite a number of years ago. Gail holds it up to her head to try to understand how it would be oriented on the animal.

The end that attaches to the animal's head is round, with a pitted convex surface, somewhat like the surface of a molar a kid might leave for the tooth fairy.

"I wonder if it hurts when they shed these?" she asks, handing it to me.

"Maybe you can ask when we see one of these in the flesh."

The antler hangs naturally upside down. I turn it in my hands and look at it as it would be on a buck's skull. It's heavier than it looks. It weighs as much as an ordinary brick, but for all its perfection in shape and form, it's an unwieldy object. We try to imagine what it might be like to run thousands of miles with this on one's head. The antler has one curving stalk that breaks into three smaller branches. The shovel bit faces forward, while the other three branches face upward, relative to the animal. The horn has a muscley feel to it, smooth, hard and strong. We can see patterns of the blood vessels that nourished its growth. It's like a delicate sculpted arm, in alabaster. At the ends of bifurcations in the antler are widenings that look like human hands with fingers outstretched and spread. The hand on the shovel branch has fingers that are crooked and more animated than any of the others. I hand it back. She turns it over, feels it, bends and scrapes the ground with the shovel tine and then gently sets the rack back where she found it.

We continue walking and catch sight of the two loons, now swimming on a shallow tundra pond. Somewhere near that pond is a nest. And because both adults were fishing on the pelagic waters of nearby Munn Lake, I can only guess that they are not incubating the eggs. Either this female has yet to lay eggs, or, more likely, somewhere in the dark grasses at the side of that slough are a few pairs of small loon eyes, staring out in wonder at what we are. "We'd better stay clear," I say.

Beyond the tundra pond is a copse of spruce trees. We walk toward them for fifteen minutes without apparently getting any closer. Distance is deceiving. We walk for more minutes and realize that there is what looks like a very wet valley between here and there. It would likely take at least another hour to get there. There is another grouping of trees off to the east. We make those and are surprised to find that what we'd imagined to be large trees, based on their spruce-like shape, are, in reality, only just slightly taller than we are.

In fact, there are two clumps of trees, one in front of the other. The front clump contains about a dozen individuals of roughly similar size and shape, but the rear clump looks more like a ground-hugging shrub, much like a juniper, and in its middle is a Dr. Suess-Lorax-style tree with a 6-foot (2-metre) spindly stalk and topknot of thick bushy branchlets. The form of this spruce tree is a wonderful example of what an organism will do to survive at the edge of its limits for growth.

Although I have seen shedding or bug-bothered musk-oxen rubbing the trunks of stunted spruce trees raw, which results in a similar-looking plant, it is more likely that this tree has grown in response to snow abrasion, which is one of the most serious threats to plant survival in the Arctic. Wind-driven ice crystals can savage plants. In this case, the lower branches, within a foot or so of the ground, are protected by early snowfalls. The buds above the level of the early soft snows are abraded by ice and sand particles in the wind, leaving this bare stalk that looks so much like the spindly stem of a golf-green flag. The terminal buds, by contrast, have the protection of needles and a whorl of tiny lateral branches that allow them to survive. Sometimes, especially in very exposed locations, even the terminal buds are destroyed too, leaving nothing more than a lowly shrub creeping along the ground.

Even though there is light around the clock during summer, the growing season in these parts is short. It is impossible for spruce to develop seeds every year. In response to this challenge, layering has developed as an alternative reproductive form. Lower branches take root in the layering process and send up secondary trunks that result in a grouping of trees of the same genetic origin. Each one of these trunks plays a part in protecting its mates by setting wind eddies that reduce wind effects on the plant as a whole. This layering is really the principal adaptation of spruce to snow abrasion.

This clonal grouping of spruce trees is a marvel of mutual support in a group, one stalk protecting the other. Poking in around the roots Gail finds some golden-flecked 38-calibre ptarmigan droppings, which reveal this spruce community as a provider of protection for the Arctic's only year-round bird. In a little dry hollow under a rich green branch, a hollow as might be formed by cupped hands, two wisps of white down and a tidy pile of recycled spruce pickings bring images of a willow ptarmigan with its feathered toes huddled in here for protection. Dried wing bones and a few desiccated fox scats complete the interdependent chain of sacrifice that is this spruce island on the tundra.

We count eighteen trees in the closer group, smaller ones growing in the protection of the larger ones. There is black earth around the roots of these plants, but right underneath that is sand–plain sand. Was it the tundra version of the chicken-and-egg problem that got this compact little community started? Was it a dead animal, or an old hunting camp that made the soil here right for growth? Or was it some hardy spruce seed that came here on the wind and somehow germinated, thereby setting up the protection necessary for further development?

"I thought the trees would just end at the treeline," said Gail, after pondering the complexity of this place. "I had no idea that trees actually *do* anything in response to anything. I thought they just grow where they can and don't grow where they can't.

'Treeline' is not really an accurate term, when you see something like this. If you imagine these little islands of trees all across the Arctic, the treeline is more like a zone where trees eventually disappear."

She is right. Only as a *zone* of change between the forest and the tundra does the treeline idea make sense. It's a wide line. These trees before us may be some of the more adventuresome individuals of the black spruce species, the ones that can withstand the impoverished growing conditions at the extreme northern edge of the forest.

I begin to appreciate the value of studying the edges of things. Watching living beings, such as these trees, at the outer limit of their tolerance for cold and impoverished soil and for shelter and water tells us a great deal about the organism itself, but also about the two environments that overlap here.

Closer to camp, we stop and watch several terns hovering over a gravelly ridge. With short pauses between strokes of their scimitar wings, they waft their way to and from the lake. Far off, we can see them hovering over the water before diving for minnows. Terns are delicate, agile in the air and strong. They're my favourite bird of the North. Just watching them go about their business brings back memories of the toughest terns of all.

The encounter happened on the Elk River, en route to Baker Lake. We were in a rush to set up camp in the moments before a storm. A pair of terns dive-bombed us. Just as the storm hit, too late to move the tent, I noticed one of the birds settle on a nest, not 20 yards (6 metres) away. A quick look revealed four aggie-sized green-mottled eggs set neatly, little ends together, into an indentation in the gravel.

The storm stormed with a vengeance. Gale-force winds flattened the wands of our "wind-proof" dome tents. For forty-five hours we lay in sodden sleeping bags, worrying about the tent being blown willy-nilly across the tundra and into the lake–with two people in it! When we came up for air after things had settled down somewhat, the terns rose to meet us with renewed vigour. A quick look to the nest revealed a miracle. The eggs had hatched in the storm. The young were dry, fluffy and hungry. So were we, more or less, but we had a tent to fix.

The whole idea of wilderness as a physical place seems silly when you see the animals, like the tern, and plants, like the spruce, that belong here, who have lived in this land for millenia, and even more so when you consider that this land has been hunted for centuries by a variety of native peoples.

But wilderness as an idea or a state of mind is really nothing more or less than an environment relatively free of technological distractions in which to travel to the edge of what we know and believe. There is nothing certain about our existence here, nothing except uncertainty that can be taken for granted. The fact that we speak of vulnerability and alienation in this vast land is a sure sign that already something is happening.

By the time we're back at the campsite, the sun has warmed the air, bringing out legions of mosquitoes and black flies. We dig out our bee-keeper's bug hats and hastily put up the tent. Gail ducks inside while I finish rocking down the parachute-cord guy-lines. Gail's first priority on entering the tent is to trash, squash and otherwise annihilate every living blood-sucking creature in the place.

Northern historian Alan Cooke once wrote: "All other discomforts of wilderness travel pale beside the continuous torment offered by hordes of biting insects–this scourge being beyond easy description." They are numerous enough at this point to compel me to do three laps of the tent at a dead run to try to exceed the speed of bugs. The manoeuvre seems to work, only as I leave the cloud behind on one pass around the tent, I pick it up again on pass two. Pass three, I take a new course and call to Gail to open the zipper on the count of three. One . . . two . . . three, and into the tent I go with hundreds of faithful companions. We spend the next ten minutes smearing blood-filled bugs against the delicate white nylon of our new tent.

When we finally lie back on the pile of gear, what sounds at first like light rain on the taut tent fly turns out to be just bugs, millions of them, seemingly chafing to get at two new hapless hosts for the all-important blood meal. But, this time at least, we're one step ahead; the very latest fine-mesh netting keeps them all out.

"Happy Canada Day, partner. Welcome to the buggy barrens."

"Shall we drink a toast?"

"Where's the Sigg bottle with the Drambuie in it?"

"Outside."

"Forget it! Let's *imagine* we're drinking a toast."

I remember another Canada Day on the trail. I was guiding a group of people–five Canadians and an American–on a hike through the Pangnirtung Pass on Baffin Island and we were having lunch on the north shore of Summit Lake. Ice candles jostled on the surface of the lake, producing the euphony of the most delicate wind chimes. Behind us, Turner Glacier rose to the Penny Ice Cap and famous flat-topped Mount Asgard. Before us were the raw, cold mountains of Baffin. In deference to a Canadian sense of fair play, we'd had a crack at the American national anthem and learned that we knew more of the words than our eagle. He had no idea about our national anthem, but showed he was a good sport on our national birthday by conducting the rest of us with a ski pole. Right at the part that goes "with glowing hearts, we see thee rise, the true north strong and free" I felt the strangest shiver. The only other place I had felt such a shiver was in church, usually at the end of the service, when the organist would wind out the pipe organ with a stirring recessional that would usually turn the building and everyone in it into one resonating, reverberating instrument.

This Canada Day on Munn Lake I feel somewhat the same, even though we are trapped in this little tent by bugs. At least they're Canadian bugs, and they're probably related to the bugs that have eaten every human who has ventured into this northern wilderness since the last ice age. There could be no better day on which to begin our journey, and no better way to mark our initiation to the North than with a symbolic donation of blood, feeding the land that feeds us.

I'm dead tired, but can't sleep. Among inflatable sleeping-pads, three-season sleeping-bags, books, raincoats, bug hats, cameras and stuff sacks full of clothing, film and toiletries, we spread out the maps–seven of them at 1:250,000 scale, all marked with the highlighter routes from the geography classroom. We cut out one of the bar scales and mark off the route in 6.25-mile (10-kilometre) sections from Bathurst Inlet, up the lower Burnside River to the

Mara, upstream to Nose Lake, over the divide to Contwoyto Lake, down through a lake system to the mighty Back River, over the divide into Aylmer Lake, upstream on the Lockhart River and then overland on streams and small lakes to where we are now. Our goal in simple terms is 437.5 miles (700 kilometres) in forty-two days. Aylmer Lake, one of two with water horizons, each more than 94 miles (150 kilometres) long, looks ominous, even on the map. It is almost a certainty that we will get hung up on both of these bodies of water by ice or wind, probably in combination. The 19-mile (30-kilometre) divide between Contwoyto Lake and the Mara River looks possible–at least there are blue lines, indicating water, for most of the way–but it has never been done before. The pencil snaps as I note the position of today's campsite.

We awake to sweat-soaked bodies and stifling heat. These dome tents may be wind- and weather-proof, but the cost is lousy ventilation. I sit up and unzip the nylon shells that cover the door and window screens. The sun has moved westward enough to give the impression that we have slept well into the afternoon. A breeze brings with it the welcome vapours of wood smoke and frying fish. We dig out our bug hats and bug jackets, slather a healthy dollop of McCurdy's citronella on all exposed flesh and head down toward the beach.

Lorraine, in hunter green wellies with the yellow lace tie-ups, jeans and a bright yellow turtleneck under her citronella-soaked netting bug jacket, is hunched over a paddle, filleting the first fish of the trip.

"Hey, you guys, check this out," she says, proudly holding up a half-filleted fish that's as long as her arm. "It's a laker! Check it out. Thirty inches, twelve pounds. Isn't that right, Frosty?"

Norm is standing beside her with a combination measuring tape and scale called the "De-liar." He's brought this along as a little surprise for the crew and to keep track of the ongoing fishing derby. "That's right," he says, with a big smile. "She beached it! Ran it right up on the rocks. Otherwise it would surely have broken the line. Nice work, but the best part is yet to come. Hurry up and fillet that fish so we can cook it and eat it, Lorraine."

After years of fishing with her dad, Lorraine's strong, compact

and bug-covered hands move a filleting knife with practised authority along the fish's ribs, separating deep orange flesh from the
whitish connective tissue that surrounds the body cavity, until all
that is left of the fish is thick pieces of succulent flesh sizzling on the
griddle and a skeleton whose head and gaping mouth seem right for
a fish twice the size.

"My dad would kill to catch a fish like that."

Jake has collected enough spruce driftwood on the shore of the
lake to make a bright, hot fire. This being our first meal on the trail,
the rest of us dig in the packs to see what else we'll have. We settle
on fresh broccoli, rice, powdered chocolate pudding and coffee. To
get out of the bugs, the meal is served up onto six tin plates in Norm
and Cath's A-style Timberline tent.

The fish flakes apart easily into steaming forkfuls of freshwater
sweetness. The morsels hardly need chewing, but you bite down
anyway to feel the squeak on your teeth. Six of us–like kids, sitting
cross-legged inside a tent meant for three–chew contentedly with
silly smiles. The rice is burned and the broccoli overcooked, but
nobody mentions it. The fish–the fish is what we came here
for–from water to pan in less than half an hour.

"Norman, old chappie, would you like some more of my
fish?"

"Certainly, Lorraine, you're so kind. I thought you'd never
ask."

"And you, Gail? Catherine? James? John?"

"So kind of you to catch it, Lorraine!"

"And it's beautifully cooked."

"Lorraine, you're a wonder in the kitchen."

"John?"

"Yes, Lorraine?"

"Shall we do a little paddling today?"

"Why not? I believe that's what we came here to do, is it
not?"

"Maybe you did, I came here to fish."

"I came here to eat."

"Yeah, let's do some paddling. It would be a shame to miss the
lake while it's as calm as it is right now."

When all is packed up again and divvied up into three piles, Norm sallies up to a food pack, plants his feet firmly at shoulder width, bends his knees, arcs over, takes a quick half-breath, holds it and prepares for major exertion in the way of a constipated grizzly bear. Lorraine, little Lorraine, stands in front of him, waiting for the inevitable crushing force. This one is heavier than most. She struggles into the straps and can hold the weight, but only just. There is no possibility of moving without turning one of her knees inside out.

"No way, Norman. Get this thing off me. What the *hell* is in this pack?"

"There's a 56-pound (25-kilogram) pail of peanut butter in there, a big bag of flour and other baking supplies, and who knows what else," says Norm.

Cath, the organized one with the excellent memory for detail, pipes up. "There's a fibreglass repair kit with two litres of resin, hardener, acetone, brushes and a big piece of 6-ounce (160-gram) cloth. There are also two great-big dried salamis in there. They must weigh at least 10 pounds (4.5 kilograms) each. By the time you add all that up, with two big rolls of duct tape and the regular repair kit with the wire, and screws, tools and all that stuff, you're getting into a pretty heavy pack. It probably weighs more than you do, Lorraine."

"Let's try a little lighter one," says Lorraine. "I'm only going to the canoe, but let's be realistic about this business of carrying things."

They find a slightly smaller and lighter pack – a "supper pack" loaded with a collection of vacuum-packed plastic bags. Norm strikes the "Caution: Heavy! Bend your knees" stance and hefts it up onto Lorraine's back. She totters slowly downhill toward Jake, who is waiting to unload her and place the pack in the canoe.

"I can hardly stand up with this on," says Lorraine, "let alone walk with it. If I fall down with one of these brutes on, I'll be turtled for the rest of the day. And I sure hope I never have to move fast with one of these things on."

Jake places the pack in the canoe, looks at the other two partially loaded canoes, and then at the gear still left on the shore, and says: "There's no way we're going to get all of this stuff into these three boats and still have any freeboard left."

Somebody had to say it. The process of getting onto the water would be incomplete if there wasn't at least one person who had doubts about whether all of the stuff would fit in the available space. It happens on every trip. Even if you cut yourself back to cornmeal mush and pemmican, this problem would still arise, and it has something to do with three universal laws: (1) Packers always find out how much space will be available for storage and then purposely take a little bit more just to show that they can jam it in; (2) Stuff always looks bulkier when it's spread out on the ground; (3) Humans need with them, on journeys, reminders and comforts of home, technological "essentials" to allow them to survive. For Winnebago-ists, "essentials" may include colour televisions, microwave ovens and dozens of matching sets of pastel-coloured co-ordinated sportswear. Our "essentials" stopped short of electrical appliances (if you discount battery-powered cameras and tape recorders). Nevertheless, emergency locater transmitter, ultra-light gas stoves and various other necessary consumer products added up to a substantial volume of goods. But fundamentally, whether you're in a canoe or a motor-home, the problems are the same. The difference on a wilderness canoe trip is that you cannot simply put the lawn furniture back in the garage if there is no room left. Either you leave it on the tundra, thereby creating a puzzle for future archaeologists, or you take it with you.

Finally, we're all in with nothing left ashore, taking a couple of tentative stokes to make sure the boats are actually floating and not still beached. We're concerned about freeboard, and reach down from the outside gunwale to see how far it is to the waterline.

Norm calls over, "How's our trim?"

"You're a little stern heavy, but what else is new," replies Lorraine, with a sadistic cackle.

In a few hundred strokes we begin to move with the rhythm of the boat, a few hundred more to synchronize with our partners. But the lake is calm and forgiving this afternoon. Voices carry across still water. We laugh. Everything has fitted in and we're still afloat.

It's a miracle. I just hope we don't have waves over 6 inches (18 centimetres) until we eat some of this food.

The boat feels fat and unresponsive, but it is deeply satisfying to be back on the water and underway. An arctic tern approaches, quickly, with short, well-spaced wing-beats. It almost rests between beats. Economic motion. The bird's head-down concentration on the surface of the water seems broken by our presence. It swerves to miss us and continues down the shore on its original course. It dives, enters the water, comes up with a tiny fish and is back in full flight without missing a beat.

In a couple of hours, we're settled, more or less–thirty-two strokes a minute, 3 miles (5 kilometres) per hour. It's slow progress: 384 strokes per kilometre, around half a million strokes for the whole trip. We stop first to remove our bug hats. The breeze of our motion has left most bugs behind. We stop again to take off our outside layers of clothing. We switch paddling sides, and settle in once more. Stroke, stroke, stroke, stroke.

Home and work by now seem a long way off, over horizons that are clean and uncluttered. The only break in the blue arctic infinity in which we're immersed is the stripe of familiar green sandwiched between air and the water. We paddle amid the reflected filigree of scattered high clouds. I stare down into the still water slipping past below my thigh and watch as power from the paddle is transferred to pools of energy that whirl quietly past the stern of the boat and join with Gail's from the bow. Just beyond the paddle and the V'd wake of the canoe are deceptive reflections. Water becomes sky, sky becomes water, and we are left as *la chasse galerie*, floating above the steeples of another life.

Even on this first day of paddling, I'm becoming conscious of an essential contradiction in this journey that I've felt before on canoe trips. On the one hand, we have burned up a substantial quantity of fossil fuels in creating these circumstances–our boats are plastic, our clothes are plastic, our food is packed in plastic and the airplanes we have utilized to make this a one-way, a linear as opposed to circular journey, have drunk large quantities of fuel. We can't be too righteous about what we are doing here. On the other hand, the life of contrived simplicity and hardship – self-imposed hardship – we have cast for ourselves forces us to cope minute by minute, hour by hour, stroke by stroke, mile by mile, with problems that *are*, rather than the problems we *create* in that other life. Wilderness canoeing is hardship, pain and real problems, a pragmatist's paradise. But simultaneously this rugged journey breeds inner peace. Survival and spirituality, hell and heaven, enlightenment and profound contradiction, all together in the same wilderness package.

We make it 5 miles (8 kilometres) to the mouth of Margaret Lake and camp on a sloping hillside on a site that is protected by a soldiery of black spruce. Setting up camp that night we have our first accident of the trip. Jake has gathered a few large rocks from the shore, which he is arranging into a fireplace to cook the evening meal. He's set on baking with the Coleman oven tonight; hence, he takes time to make a semi-circular design that will minimize wind (while still allowing the fire to breathe) and provide a sturdy base for the oven. As he's placing the last boulder in the structure, he stops to speak to me, momentarily breaking concentration, and I watch in horror as he crushes the tip of his finger between two rocks. It's one of those delayed-pain, under-the-nail bleeders that take a moment to spiral to an agonizing peak. In a minute, he is prancing around in circles like a chicken on hot sand, issuing general pejoratives to anyone within earshot. It is only when he gets the finger immersed in the lake that I'm able to tell him how entertaining he has been. Fortunately, the wound is not as serious as it at first looked. He'll likely lose the nail, but the finger seems to work okay. It doesn't stop him from contributing loudly to a rousing sing-song, with Lorraine strumming "Stella," the official trip guitar.

5.
ARCTIC FEVER

WE AWAKEN TO THE WING FLUTTER AND THE SOUND OF LITTLE birds' feet scratching on the tent fly as they land and slide back into flight.

"How'd you sleep?" I ask.

"Bright skies twenty-four hours a day are going to take some getting used to," she says, with a smile. "I slept, but not a lot."

We're both a little stiff from paddling and from sleeping on the ground. Before we have time to open the screen to see what the weather is like outside, we again hear the sound of dots hitting the fly. This time it is rain, which increases in intensity as we get dressed.

"No sense in getting soaked today. I'm for staying put until this blows over."

"So soon we stop?"

"By the time we get the tents down and the stuff all packed up, it will all be pretty wet. We could do that, but at this point at least, we're not really in any hurry. We've factored in at least one day in five or six for this kind of thing. There's no sense in trying to push the weather."

"Sounds good to me," Gail replies, lying back on the mound of clothing that has served as her pillow through the night.

"Let's see what the others are up to."

Jake is fishing. Lorraine is still in the tent. Cathy is making breakfast, and Norm is nowhere to be found. Apparently they have all come to the same conclusion and are adjusting to our first "pit" day.

Walking the few dozen yards past the tents to gather dead branches from the spruce trees is a sensory experience. The dusty caribou moss (which is really a lichen–a plant that is an alga and a fungus growing in harmony) in this sheltered valley is nearly knee-deep. It seems to be supported by the gnarled and rusty twigs of a lower layer of Labrador tea shrubs. When disturbed by walking boots, the lichen emits a heady odour of mushroom and musk that is most pleasing, especially when intermingled with piquant spruce essence emanating from the wet grove beyond.

A small fire produces a pot of steaming coffee and scrambled eggs. Jake has caught a 2-pound (1-kilogram) arctic grayling, on a hairy Mepps lure, which we fry up as a complement to the breakfast we have brought with us. A couple of gulls squawk and bicker over the guts Jake has left on the shore. The rain intensifies and we retreat to our tents. There is no safer feeling than having a full stomach and stretching out in a dry tent on a rainy day. Time to revel and read and let the fullness of this place sink in.

I tell Gail about my buddy Bert's two-letter classification scheme for trail days. There are M-days and F-days. The F-days are fine ones, high pressure, sunshine, no wind. These are the days you forget. Then there are the M-days, with rain, bugs, wind, sleet and snow–the miserable ones. Those are the days that are memorable.

"So, what kind of a day is this?" Gail asks.

"So far, it's an F-day, but the moment our bags get wet, we'll be sliding into the M-day category in short order. Whatever the case, staying put today will give us a chance to settle into some campsite routines."

The whole business of who does what on trips with a bunch of friends is more complicated than it might at first seem. Commercial trips and organized clubs always tend to have set schedules and routines to which everyone must express allegiance. Friends are inclined to murder efficiency with niceness or with unwillingness to exert undue influence on the decision-making process. It's management by default, and as long as you're in no hurry for norms to become established, the system works.

Breakfast, as Gail has seen, is the responsibility of whoever gets up first. If nobody gets up, no breakfast. We travel after breakfast. No breakfast, no travel, unless other arrangements are made.

Lunch is the responsibility of the crew with the wanigan. Of course, picking up, unloading and loading this hundred-pound plywood box is accomplished by the person with the most persistent hunger. Reloading the staple containers inside the wanigan is done by the first person who needs the likes of brown sugar or coffee, unless of course that particular menu is altered by the spectre of food-pack wrestling required to find the motherlode of the staple in question.

At supper time, one person from each pair joins a tent-set-up party, and one person joins a firewood and cooking crew. Supper fare is the choice of the person or persons doing the cooking. The rule is this: you complain about the food, you cook the next meal; otherwise, we continue on an ad hoc rotation system. Dishes are the responsibility of anybody who decides to do them; we agree, though, that hot-water washing in a plastic dishpan is important to keep some semblance of sanitation. The dishwasher also permits a sneaky hand-wash.

Elimination employs the cat-hole principle – dig a small hole in the surface of the tundra, do your business and cover for bacterial breakdown. Of course, canoeing in a land of little sticks where privacy is a southern myth, we make no agreements about looking or not looking at people in the tell-tale crouch – it's potential after-dinner sport.

None of this has been talked about, which leaves Gail full of questions and somewhat baffled by the whole process, even this early in the trip. She is not comfortable with the privacy problem, but has resigned herself to potential loss of dignity with the realization that, on most campsites, unless there happens to be a tree or large shrub nearby, you can walk for hours and still be in plain view.

She has watched Norm, who took a book last evening and hiked to the crest of the nearest windy (and therefore bug-free) ridge where he settled onto a rock to commune with life. From the campsite, he presented a contemplative silhouette against the evening sky—a casual observer would think he was reading, Gail observed.

We make our way over the next couple of days to a peninsula on the north end of Back Lake. The rhythm of daily travel and shared campsite responsibility falls nicely into line. Gail perseveres with learning the unspoken rules and finds a niche in the group that allows her to contribute fully to the collective effort. But that night, the strangest thing happens.

Sometime before midnight, just as the amber sun is settling into its hammock on the north horizon, she says—even after a full day of paddling—that she's going for a walk. I watch from the back window of the tent as she strolls with her camera, stopping every so often to savour the view or to examine a flower on the ground. It feels good to see her gaining the independence and confidence that she has in her teaching life. As she fades into the distant hillside, I get a glimmer of the strength it must be taking for a fiercely independent soul like Gail to adapt to a totally new context.

What seems like hours later, she is shaking me and saying with soft but urgent tones that I *must* join her to appreciate the magic of this moment on the tundra.

"Can't it wait?" I ask groggily, still wondering if I'm dreaming. The sleeping-bag is a perfect temperature. I hate to even move for fear the cell of warm air will escape.

"Come on, you've got to see this," she insists through the screen, her breath condensing in the cool twilight air.

I roll onto my back and sit up, trying to keep the top of the sleeping-bag closed, but it still manages to suck in a swallow of frigid night air.

"Are you sure?"

"Come on. Get dressed and come out to see this. It's absolutely breath-taking!"

Pants are cold and wet, boots even worse. I unfold the thickest pile sweater that has been serving double duty as a pillow and pull it on over the turtleneck. Even at that, as I unzip the tent, the damp chill of arctic night floods into the sweater and makes me shiver. At least the bugs are gone. This better be good.

"Come on," she says, taking my hand and dragging me up the hill behind our camp. Without looking back, I follow in the dim light, stepping stiffly at first, but, as the blood begins to move and the sleepiness fades, I'm almost keeping up. On a gravel plateau several hundred metres above our campsite, she stops and turns, waiting for me to catch up. "Look," she says, with an appreciative sigh.

From this vantage-point the vista before us is a layered study of darkness and crimson light, fused together with white mist that purls silently in the distance. The light layers with smoking surfaces are a million lakes and distant streams that reflect and redouble subtle hints of dawn glowing on the horizon. The darker layers are this primal land itself into which we have been dumped of our own volition, brooding again, in the absence of daylight. Silhouettes of stout tamarack on the shores of our lake give the scene depth and personality. There is no need to say anything.

The landscape at this moment speaks to my heart. The rock, the land, the trees, the water, the air are bound together in the colour and corona of false dawn. We are outsiders here, but to appreciate, to examine and to celebrate this beauty is to become part of it.

The mist lies over water, but there are patterns too in the air that bathes bare rock, and in that which rises from places of heavy vegetation. For now the land and water have lost their colour. It is the sky's turn to speak.

In the presence of such a crescendo of form and colour, it is the all-encompassing soundlessness of the scene that catches me short. It is an imponderable possibility that something so awesome can be so silent yet so complete. Still puffing from the uphill jaunt, I hold my breath in deference to what lies before us, but this serves only to make me more conscious of my intrusive, pounding heart. We sit down and settle into the irrepressible rhythm of the landscape. At length, the disk of the sun cracks the horizon, and Gail puts her arm around my shoulder and says, "How could anybody sleep through that?"

"Easy," I say, looking at the weathering lines on her face and the joy in her eyes, "as long as nobody wakes them up!"

Scientists know that twenty-four-hour daylight plays havoc with diurnal patterns. Northern plants and animals have evolved strategies to take advantage of the situation, but southerners get confused north of sixty. Rumour has it that, in past days, first-aiders on oil rigs in the Beaufort Sea and elsewhere in the Arctic reported alarming numbers of green roughnecks collapsing from exhaustion. It turns out that the work was no more taxing than it is on any southern oil rig, where people can handle the load without trouble. Without darkness to tell the lads when to sleep, and lacking the discipline to do so on their own, they'd been staying up for far too many hours at a stretch. Rapture of the midnight light had given them rupture of the regular sleeping schedule. No wonder they keeled over. They were beat! The doctors who treated these patients called the condition "arctic fever," and once it was recognized, companies took steps to adapt southern work schedules to twenty-four-hour daylight and, of course, twenty-four-hour darkness.

Gail has caught the dreaded fever. We continue paddling. The next night she is on the prowl again, only this time she just tells me about what she has seen as she slides into her bag for a couple of hours' sleep. The next day, however, we're windbound and spend the day hiking on an esker that stretches to the horizons on both sides of our lake. That night she sleeps, nursing a plugged ear, a plague she blames on the airlines and for which she has taken Chlortripolon–a soporific.

Geographer Yi-Fu Tuan wrote: "The ideas of space and place require each other for definition. From the security and stability of place we are aware of the openness, freedom, and threat of space, and vice versa. Furthermore, if we think of space as that which allows movement, then place is pause; each pause in movement makes it possible for location to be transformed into place."

But, through Gail's and my own recurring bouts of arctic fever, I am beginning to see that a "sense of place" is something that you can have *away* from home too. Slowing down and appreciating the landscape is allowing it to speak to us through strange behaviour. But there is more to the "place" of this canoe adventure than that which is strictly derived from the landscape. After all, we are a group of humans who bring a social context to the environment in which we are travelling. We have in common an allegiance to the simple life-style of canoeing, which gives us all the same advantages and disadvantages, a common lexicon and plenty to talk about. We have our own unique characteristics, but we are all equally powerless before the elements and the other inhabitants of this land. Within this social context, we have forged a sense of security in who we are. We have become insiders in our own little social grouping, which gives great satisfaction.

I'm getting a growing sense that we are responding to an agenda on this trip that has nothing to do with getting from Munn Lake to Bathurst Inlet. It is an agenda that is growing out of common experience in this marvellous landscape that is so different from anything we have ever been attached to before. It is an agenda that makes me wonder, if only for a moment, if there was design behind the rain that kept us put on our first morning on the trail. It is an agenda that seems connected to every part of me except those marked "rational." It is a feeling about being somewhere, or about longing for, or belonging somewhere that I have only *heard* expressed in orchestral pieces like Beethoven's Sixth Symphony or Handel's Water Music, or in popular compositions like "Homeward Bound" by Simon and Garfunkel, "Country Roads" by John Denver or "In My Life" by The Beatles. The landscape is beginning to speak through our actions.

6.
BEAR

CAMPED ON ANOTHER ENDLESS PLAIN OVER THE WATER A COUPLE
of nights later, over our first dinner of freeze-dried steaks, Surprise-
brand peas, fresh puffballs, dried hash-brown potatoes and no-bake
cheesecake, we get around to talking about bears. Most of us have
seen bears in the wild at one time or another: polar bears on the Seal
River, kodiak and grizzly bears in Alaska, barren-ground grizzlies on
the tundra and of course lots of black bears on trips down south in
Ontario. Everybody has heard at least one gruesome tale about
bears, like the one about the grizzly that stalked the cyclist on the
Alaska Highway for 10 miles (16 kilometres) before pulling her
down and eating her. They knew it was a grizzly by the size of the
tracks and the viciousness of the attack, and by the fact that the
organs of the woman had been eaten. Someone added that polar
bears always eat their prey head first. And then there was a student I
had in a first-aid course one time who had been treed by a she-grizzly
in Kluane National Park and had had the good fortune to be rescued
by a photographer/writer team who were working in the same area;
the only problem was they were from *National Geographic* and
published ten million copies of the photos of this guy up a tree.

I go to sleep that night with vapours of my own private bear nightmare. I was in the final year of an undergraduate degree in biology. In summers I had worked as a haematology technician in a marine-mammal lab at the University of Guelph where various types of seals and other marine mammals were studied. But this summer I was given the opportunity to continue a vision experiment with a 750-pound (338-kilogram) male polar bear called "Huxley." It was fantastic experience for a young biologist, simply a matter of following a successful protocol established with the seals.

First, you catch the bear. That was done in Churchill, Manitoba. You build for it a cage with three paddles it can push with its nose. That had been done. You train it to come to the middle paddle and push it and, if a light shines in its eye, to push the paddle to its left; if no light shines or it does not see a light, it pushes the paddle on the right. Correct answers are rewarded with chunks of raw meat. My job was to build the apparatus that would present light to the bear's eye. It was a nifty rig with a xenon-light source that could be filtered to emit individual colours of light at any intensity level. The idea of this experiment–an investigation of the bear's "spectral sensitivity"–is to produce a graph plotting the wavelength of light against how well the bear can see the various colours. Simple enough in principle, except that the bear is not a happy camper in a 10 foot × 16 foot (3 metre × 5 metre) cage. He paces up and down the galvanized metal floor and bangs the bars with his left paw for most of the day, and once a month I have to shoot him at close range with a tranquillizer rifle and take blood samples. I like to feed him vegetable oil and jelly doughnuts when he comes out of the anaesthetic–those, he seems to like.

Polar-bear vision is a compelling biological phenomenon. There is no doubt about that. The fact that these bears can hunt in twenty-four-hour darkness and in the white brilliance of twenty-four-hour daylight on pack-ice, and also see in the monochromatic blue-green light in their dives below the surface of arctic waters makes them optically unusual. But I sat in that small room at the university, trying to get this magnificent animal to push paddles, and wondered what right we have to impound him.

Actually, his presence in my work was more in the sense of using up a bear who was no longer afraid of humans. He'd been caught in Churchill some years earlier and used in an energetics study–running a treadmill to see how far and how fast he could go on various diets and under various conditions. Impressive. He could run at 25 miles (40 kilometres) an hour for four hours without getting overheated. (He had a core-temperature sensor surgically implanted.) But after that extended period of captivity he could not be released back into the wild because he would surely wander back into town and either kill somebody or be shot on the spot. So, he was shipped with the other bears to a zoo. Huxley was a bully, it turns out. He beat up the other bears. Somehow I'm not surprised.

We worked in the dark, Huxley and me. His eyes needed to be dark-adapted to get proper readings on their sensitivity. I sat beside the light-emitting cart that was snugged up in front of the middle paddle, and directly before Huxley. I knew he was there because I could feel and smell his breath 6 inches (15 centimetres) away. I wanted to believe he was trying for me, but it was for food. Most mornings he was not hungry. Often, he bashed the paddles with particular force and resumed pacing, as if frustrated. He would come back and try again, correctly, and get a piece of meat. Sometimes I gave him the meat right through the bars and could feel his soft black lips on my fingers. And some days, in the darkness, I think I felt the presence of this caged bear's wild soul.

He comes to the middle paddle again. I can feel him there. He presses the middle paddle and gets a piece of meat. The round, focused beam of light illuminates his left eye. It's small and intense. I know he can't see me, but all the same I feel as though he's looking through me as if to say "I'm the patient one. I'm just humouring you by being here. I could get out of this any time I choose. You think that every time you give me a piece of meat I push the paddle. Have you ever noticed that every time I push the paddle, you give me a piece of meat? Who's conditioning whom?"

The vet arrived one morning with the drugs that would be loaded into the ⅓-fluid-ounce (10-millilitre) dart that was to be fired at Huxley to sink him into his blood-letting sleep. The bear knew something was up. He was sitting at his water dish with his face against the bars, bashing his right front paw, again, and again, and again against the bars. I pulled the trigger on the rifle, aiming for his buttock. The charge misfired and the dart bounced off the bear. He was angry and made a false charge at the front of the cage, but then resumed his cage routines. A second dart plugged him in the shoulder muscle. In minutes he got sluggish and lay down. I saw contempt in his eyes, still alert, as his body succumbed to the muscle relaxants in the hypnotic mixture–or was what I saw in the bear just a reflection of my own uncertainty about the whole procedure? The vet didn't say much.

We slid up the 3 foot × 5 foot (92 centimetre × 153 centimetre) quarter-inch (0.6 centimetre) galvanized steel door at one end of the cage, propped it open with a piece of two-by-four and went through the process of searching for a vessel in the femoral triangle in the flaccid muscles of his massive inner thigh. But first we rolled the beast onto his back and tied down the head with a piece of inch and a quarter (3 centimetre) manila hawser. We know that the muscles of the neck, mouth and face are the first to come back after anaesthesia with this combination of drugs. Bingo! I hit the femoral artery with the needle and snapped on the first of a series of Vacutainer tubes. The bear's tongue hung out of the side of his mouth and dripped thick saliva on the floor. Save the hushed voices, there was not a shred of dignity in the operation. Waiting for another blood tube to fill, I looked at the propped-open door and wondered if Huxley had any idea that this was the weak point in his cage.

Next morning, one of the mercury switches on top of his cage, part of the paddle mechanism, malfunctioned. Without thinking, I got a step-ladder, put it up against the plate-steel side of his cage and climbed up to change the defective part. In seconds I heard a massive thud below. Peering over the edge and through the top of the bars, I saw the bear's back. He was sitting at the door, punching it with front paws. Quickly I moved over to the door side of the cage and peered down there. Huxley was now punching at regular intervals. I saw the quarter-inch steel starting to bow out from the force and suddenly saw myself trapped in the small space between the top of the cage and the ceiling, 9 feet (3 metres) up in the air, with an angry polar bear pacing below. I leapt from the top of the cage onto the wet cement below, slipped, and slammed my elbow into the wall but kept moving out the exit and locked the room door from the outside. Leaning against the door, panting, and holding my elbow, I stared at the embossed red and white plastic sign my supervisor had earlier placed below the observation window: "Check position of bear before entering." Right on!

In the coffee room that day, there is the usual complement of bad jokes. There's a woman who does cardiac punctures on rabbits to get blood for her immunological work. There's a staff vet whose job it is to euthanize all the stray dogs in the county. And there's the ribald technician from the suite next to Huxley's who skins and then longitudinally halves cadavers for the art students to draw. "Stiffs ain't cheap," he'd always say. "The best the art department can do is half a stiff per group." John Partridge, a zoology graduate student working on seals, is upon me with his persistent, gentle teasing. "Got any numbers yet?" he'd ask. "How's that sample size of one?"

"Hey," says Partridge, with a twinkle in his eye. "I hear you've created a new species in there. Your bear has evolved from *Ursus maritimus* to *Ursus maritimus vet buildingus*." He had a point. After so much time in captivity, there was no way of telling whether this bear in any way reflected the tendencies and behaviours of his wild counterparts. Not that it mattered particularly. We were likely to find out something useful, but at what cost? The bear would only have been "put down" if the zoo had been unable to find a place for him to go. Maybe he'd have been better off, and that was what was gnawing at my gizzard. I felt dirty and abusive and guilty for the angst through which Huxley was being put every day of his miserable confined life. Whatever the virtues of laboratory science, I knew that if I was to continue learning about wild phenomena, including polar bears, it would be as a field observer who would have to live with the uncertainty, and truth, of the real world–and preferably from a canoe. Positivistic experimental science, I discovered, was just one way of trying to understand our fellow earth dwellers. There must be others. A romantic notion perhaps, but I dreamed, like that night in 1980, about meeting animals on *their* terms for a change.

Next day, the water-course between Back Lake and Montours

Lake is troublingly low. We barely make it through one narrow channel filled with boulders without having to get out of the canoes, but are conscious of the paint we have left on a goodly number of boulders.

This was this route's major risk. The flight from Yellowknife was relatively short, but, in addition to having three heights of land to cross, our route choice is predicated on single blue lines on our topographic maps having sufficient water to float the canoes. If that's not the case, we're in trouble. If we are forced to do more portaging or dragging than expected, we could get far behind schedule.

We lunch in canoes stuck between big boulders. Conversation over peanut butter, cheese and crackers is about connections between future lakes.

Jake dips his cup over the side of the boat, takes a long drink and says, "Four."

"Did you just tee off?" asks Norm.

"I bet it'll take four trips to lug all this stuff overland when it comes time for a carry."

Although we know that each crew holds primary responsibility for portaging the gear in their canoe, it is understood that portaging is a collective concern. We are in this together and if one person can carry a little extra on one trip, that's what will be done. Lorraine is uncharacteristically silent. She knows what "four" means.

After lunch, Cath makes a pit-stop on the shore and comes back reporting moose and bear tracks in the mud exposed by low water. "Maybe we can lasso that moose and get it to do some of the carrying," pipes Lorraine, apparently choosing to ignore mention of the bear.

We press on. In time we're all wet to the knee and have dragged our boats over too many rocks. Finally, after making only about a hundred yards (90 metres) in half an hour, Jake and Lorraine opt to carry. The rest of us press on.

I'm walking in the water, watching Jake and Lorraine drag their canoe to the shore; a rock that takes my weight rolls and traps my other foot–I push with the other leg to free it and slip. Now I'm wet up to the chest. Gail is laughing. Then she slips. Now I'm laughing, but see the strained look on her face and realize she has wrenched her healing back. We'll have to be more careful.

An hour later we're still making progress. Norm and Cath are behind us, but we've lost contact; the two couples are now working as independent teams, solving the immediate problems of dragging over this rock or through that gap, one person straddling the bow, the other riding the stern with legs in the water to get past the occasional deep pools. But, always, both crews are trying to maintain the big picture, attempting to make sure that the canoe and its contents don't get stuck in a dead end in the boulder field, where everything will most surely have to be shouldered to open water.

It's one of the canoe-trip challenges on which a person can thrive–manageable problems with immediate reward. You either get through the gap or you don't. If you do, you anticipate the next configuration of rocks and begin solving that one. If you don't get through, you back up and try plan B. It's slow and tedious, but nobody seems to notice.

While dragging the entire weight over a multitude of hidden rocks, I stop for a breath and glance at the shore where we have seen Jake and Lorraine ferrying their loads. To be sure, I look again.

"There's a bear."

"Where?" Gail replies, with amusement, getting no clue about the urgency of the situation from my tone of voice.

"Over there," I say pointing my finger. "And it's running right toward us! *Right* toward us! Holy shit!"

"What do we do?"

"Grab your paddle, come around and stand on this side of the canoe."

I'm conscious of an argument beginning in the nether regions of my brain. It's just like the physiology profs said: somewhere deep down in the stem, there is a frantic reptilian voice asking, "What the hell good is a paddle going to be against a charging grizzly bear? What's it going to do? Pick its teeth with the paddle when it's finished eating you? Run, you crazy bugger! Survival of the fittest. That's what this encounter is all about. Either you get out of here or you're grizzly-bear food. This is it, this is the one, Gorgons, Hydras and Chimeras Dire–the worst-case scenario, only this sucker isn't imaginary. Unless you're planning on being fillet-of-camper or canoeist tartare, you'd better make tracks. It's your only chance!"

But another voice reminds me of the *Northwest Territories Bear Safety Manual*, which sets out a different course of action. "If a bear persists," it says, "without other options, stay as still as possible. Play dead in a low crouch with your hands over your head. This will protect your head and vital organs."

"Vital organs! That's just it, you fool, they're vital. V-I-T-A-L. Read my lips. You can't get along without them. If you sit here and do nothing, it's going to eat you. It only takes the loss of one of those vital organs to ruin your whole day. That's it, buster. Run!"

But the voice of reason cuts in again, "No . . . listen to me. We're standing among loose boulders in knee-deep water. How far could we run anyway? And besides, scientific studies have shown that bears see running things as prey. You studied bears; you know that running objects are prey."

"Prey! . . . Prey! If you're going to stand there, you dolt, you'd better pray–that's P-R-A-Y!"

Meanwhile, the scene before us has slipped into slow motion. At 200 yards (180 metres) and closing, the bear's frosted sun-gold coat is whirling about its head and shoulders, flinging dust against the sunbeams with each rollicking step. Shadowed hair on the broad chest is flattened by the motion, revealing the sturdy musculature flinging those massive paws forward. Five white claws on each front foot glint in the sun, as if flexed and reaching to cover more ground. The ears are back. The tongue is out. And the eyes, the small red eyes–they're wide open and strangely fearful, or angry.

"It's me again, you little limbic lizard. This is Huxley's Revenge! How *imperceptive* can you be? Look at those eyes. It's anger. ANGER. That bear is not pleased that you're in his territory. Run, while you've still got a chance!"

"Now, Jim," intones the voice of reason, "you know that barren-land grizzlies are solitary-rambling creatures. They don't defend a territory, unless this is a female and you've somehow gotten between it and its cubs, which is highly unlikely under these circumstances. Why don't you just stand still and hope for the best? And be serious; you can't assume that playing-dead posture without drowning."

The bear steps off the edge of the tundra into our bouldered water-course and, without missing a beat, begins its way across. We can hear the slap of its wet feet on the rocks. It slips and splashes, head and shoulders into the water. Up again, it's now throwing water with every step. We can see water flying out of its open mouth and off its whiskers with each laboured breath.

Time has been called a substance of infinite elasticity. There, at the giddy limit of fear, it stretches to every bear joke I've ever heard. There's this guy, see, being charged by a bear. He gets down on his knees and starts to pray. The bear comes up to him and asks, "What are you doing?" The guy says he's making peace with his maker. The bear starts to pray too. The guy is totally befuddled. He looks at the kneeling bear with its front paws folded together, claws like a steeple. "You're supposed to be eating me. What are you doing?" he asks the bear. "Saying grace."

Only moments before the animal is upon us, I get an image in my brain of the great wildlife photographer's last shot. It's on the cover of every nature publication in the country. The bear that ate the shooter. I dive into the pack for a camera.

"A gun, a gun. You've brought a gun!" Gail exclaims. "I thought we agreed not to bring a gun? But you brought a gun! A gun! Are you going to shoot the bear?"

There is no time to focus. I trip one shot, and cock the shutter. At that instant, I realize that we are not on the bear's course. It tears by us on the wet rocks, not 10 feet (3 metres) away. I shoot a couple more pictures of its receding backside and am conscious of a musty animal smell. It dawns that something must have scared that animal within an inch of its life. I wonder if Jake and Lorraine are okay.

We turn in the direction of our portaging pair and see Lorraine and Jake waving vigorously. We wave back and they stop. We turn back and see the bear still running, running. For minutes we watch it diminish in size until it is just a moving dot that disappears over the horizon.

It feels like every blood vessel in my body has doubled in size.

There doesn't seem to be fluid to fill the system. Whatever I've been conscious of in the last hundred seconds, my adrenal system has been working on autopilot. I'm perfused with adrenalin, light-headed and trembling from the tips of my sweat-soaked hair to the soles of my water-logged feet.

Gail, too, is white-faced and can't believe that her partner had gone for his camera. "A *camera*! . . . I thought for sure you'd brought a gun. Did you get any pictures?"

Norm and Cath have also seen the incident. For a while they thought the bear was headed for them, too. And when it ran across the water-course, they had no idea how close it had come to us.

We meet up with Jake and Lorraine at the end of the portage and hear the story from their point of view.

"There I was, humping a huge pack across the tundra," says Lorraine. "I'm following a caribou trail. It dips down into a little thicket and I just about run into this bear lying there sleeping. The bear gets up and stares at me. There's no way I can do anything. I can't get the pack off, and there's no way I can run with it on. The bear looks at me. I look at the bear, and then it takes off. I guess you just happened to be on its escape route."

We stop for a GORP (Good Old Raisins and Peanuts) break on a beach shortly after the shallows. As we're getting out, someone notices fresh bear tracks on the beach. Lorraine chooses to eat, sitting in the canoe. I take a moment after eating mine and measure a track. It's almost human in shape, only wider with claw impressions: 5.2 inches (13 centimetres) across at the ball of the foot and 8 inches (20 centimetres) long. That's about size 10, octuple "E."

7.
AYLMER LAKE

Of all the dragons along our route, the one I fear most is a large lake. Today, the first of these lies before us, Aylmer Lake, and I'm anxious about what is to befall us as we make our way toward the water horizon for 70 miles (112 kilometres). Wind and waves for sure. But it's still early July and there may well still be pack-ice blowing around that will impede progress. It is on the lakes that we are most vulnerable. Storms can rise in minutes and leave you wallowing in curling walls of black water. But, as with most dangers, we can take precautionary steps to ensure we expose ourselves to only as much risk as we can safely handle. You try to stay in control, to work with the elements to create enough uncertainty to make things exciting, but not so much to invite disaster.

This morning on the Lockhart River, a half-day's travel from Aylmer Lake, there is a slight wind in our favour. It's the first time this has been the case, so Cath takes a moment before we embark to call everyone together for ceremonial distribution of hand-made, monogrammed, rip-stop nylon sails for everyone. It's a surprise she has made for the gang this spring in anticipation of a moment just like this one. They're splended–triangular, 8 feet (2.5 metres) high, 6 feet (2 metres) on the boom, and about 25 square feet

(2.25 square metres) with a long sleeve sewn in for a makeshift wooden mast. Ours is yellow with a large "GJ" made of contrasting forest green nylon appliquéd to the upper reaches. Immediately all three crews set to work finding the right dead-spruce pole for a mast. The map says that we're beyond the treeline, but it is apparent here, as it is right across the Arctic, that there thrive pockets of conifers, especially along river corridors and in places where local soil and climate conditions allow, well above the so-called edge of the forest.

I pause for a moment with a small magnifying lens after we have cut a tree for our mast; the tree is 2 inches (5 centimetres) thick at its base and I count 105 rings. A tree of comparable age at home would be easily ten times the size. Cutting this centenarian tree for sailing seems wrong, but only momentarily. In the grand scheme of things, what difference will three trees make? Or is that what the white-pine loggers said?

The next problem in getting the boats rigged for sailing is how to affix the mast in the canoe in such a way as to allow adjustment and control in addition to easy rigging and derigging while we're on the high seas. We realize that it won't be that easy to stand up in the loaded boats to make adjustments en route. Gail and I use the 40-foot (12-metre) lining ropes tied to the ends of our big green canoe to make an "X" to hold up the mast: both ropes tied to the top of the mast with clove hitches, one for front and rear stays and one for side shrouds. Jake and Lorraine go for a three-rope system, which Jake claims will give them more sail area before the wind while on a "beam reach"–whatever that is! It's a colourful and lazy crew that pulls out under full sail toward Aylmer Lake. Lorraine is sitting in front of the bow seat, facing the stern, with her feet in the water, reading. Jake is lying back under full sail, steering with a paddle stuck under his arm. You guys better say anything you have to say to us now because, with this well-tuned rig, you'll be falling behind pretty quickly."

On either side of us, to the north and south, and behind us, to the west, deceptively peaceful cumulus clouds sail with square-rigged majesty on the wind, their massive power visible only in roiling that needs time and concentration to see. I lie back and focus on a localized rainstorm far off to the northwest.

By noon we have reached the eastern end of Aylmer Lake. The wind has dropped, making it impossible to read the monograms on the now limp nylon. But the reflections of canoes and people and masts and coloured sails make new letters in my imagination. The flatness of the water leaves us suspended between earth and sky. Look up, look down to the same cerulean infinity. Look ahead to a bright future; where the water ends and the sky begins is anybody's guess. This moment is as full as it could ever be. To the north, close at hand, and to the south, across the lake, is land sandwiched to a thin green smear between the water and sky. Gail casts her fishing rod. I watch the fluorescent orange lure arc through space (fully expecting it to metamorphose into an untethered kite), pull every inch of line from the reel and launch itself loose into the sky on which we float. But, no. With a metallic plop it punctures the mirrored surface and sets up circles that jiggle reflections of the still-falling line and herald the hole the lure has made in this perfect universe. I wish we had a bamboo rod and dry flies–quieter, less intrusive and less likely to wake Qualupiluit, the lake demons.

By mid-afternoon the sun's heat is oppressive. We strip and jump out of the canoes into water that has been ice-free for perhaps days, probably hours. The urge to gulp a breath is stopped short when my head submerges. Hot skin, cold water. The initial burning sensation submits to cold that presses first on the temples and then on the joints, driving heat from the skin and then from muscles that complain and then stiffen. Taking turns steadying the canoe, we immediately crawl up awkwardly over our respective ends and plop our wet bottoms onto the hot canoe seats. As sensation returns, I'm conscious of tiny hairs on my back and arms drying in the sunshine and springing away from my skin. The fullness of the feeling adds immeasurably to the sense of total freedom I experience within this tranquil scene.

Back in the canoe we resume paddling and continue to dry off. Before us a single cumulus cloud is roiling upward into an anvil shape, flat-topped, graded grey bottom. The cloud draws power from the landscape. This sight adds an element of dynamism to the landscape that has not moved for the last several hours. It is as though we have finally become attuned to the pulse and rhythm of the landscape. There must have been movement around us up until now, but it is only now that the movement is apparent. The swim has awakened our senses.

The paddling rhythm allows us to focus on the here-and-now. Senses are tuned and aware, but not focusing on anything in particular. I'm aware of bodies falling easily into the monotony of the motion. The magic of paddling for hours is the efficiency of the action. For every action, there is a resting phase–the yin of exertion, the yang of rest. For every expenditure of energy, there is renewal of breath and power from the motion of the boat. Resting phase: hands fall forward, shoulders tilt, the blade drops into the water and every part of the body evenly flexes to the task. Exertion: I look down and see my bare toes flex against the sand in the bottom of the boat as the stroke begins. The thigh follows, left more than the right. The demand on the right side of my torso is smooth and even. The demand on the left side–the side I'm paddling on–is wave-like. I look down as the power of the stroke peaks: chest and upper arm flex together and then relax as the paddle swings forward again. Gail's back shows the other side of the effort. Sheets of muscle in her back are a series of delicately shadowed triangles that focus their force toward her spine. Her shoulders glisten in the light and drop slightly as she tips forward and begins a new stroke. Watching the sequence of motion played out through the smooth muscles in Gail's back makes me aware of a high-frequency tingling in the nape of my neck. I daren't tip my head forward for fear of springing a wire. It seems odd that the paddle is the object being powered and the spine is the place from which the power is being dispatched. Our paddles enter the water on opposite sides of the boat, but I'm conscious right now that the power is centralized. It comes from the core. It's motion derived of the soul and of the land whose energy flows in through every sense.

At this moment, simple forward motion is our major concern. It's our only concern. There is no distraction. No noise. No static from beginning or end of this journey. We're immersed in the clean, clear middle of the experience. The airwaves are clear.

All around us, especially to the north and east where we have yet to go, where the most uncertainty lies, we see the earth fall away out of view leaving sky-only sky-on which to build our dreams. Around us, in this boat, in the clothes and fetid packs, is the safety and comfort of home, and before us, over the horizon, is the challenge of adventure-our very own *axis mundi*, our world, caught by one scene in distance, time and opportunity. Secure home and unknown horizon; both have their appeal, both have drawn people since time immemorial. If nothing more, this canoe journey has taken us to a place where both ends of our world axis are visible.

To the east, down the lake where water meets sky, an anvil-shaped cloud is forming before our eyes. We watch its bottom darken and rain start to fall. A rainbow appears below the cloud as if sealing the bond between earth and sky. I wonder for an instant if the rain is falling from the cloud, or if, in fact, the heavens are drawing water from this earthly lake. The Milky Way has always been presented as a mythical mirror of earthly streams. Today, it is easy to imagine that water is cycling through the universe.

Anthropologists maintain that many aboriginal cultures see the boundaries between the celestial and terrestrial-the horizon-as places to move between these two dimensions, simply by travelling to the horizon where one can then move upward to the heavens or downward to the great underworld. The Polynesians, for example, thought that sea was simply a flat surface terminating at the horizon and over which the dome-shaped sky spread like a lid. Souls of their dead, travelling across the sea to the horizon, could pass into the hereafter with ease. Little wonder they thought Europeans arriving by sea were gods. On a day like today, with this spectacle before us, anything seems possible.

Later that day we swing left around a finger of land into the north arm of Aylmer Lake, and take advantage of the still-windless conditions to cross the mouth of a deep bay. Had conditions been more unsettled, we would have kept to the shore, travelling 9 or 10 miles (14 or 16 kilometres) instead of the 4-mile (6-kilometre) crossing we do today. Canoeing on the open water, several miles from the nearest landfall, breeds a palpable vulnerability that awakens every sense. If there was ever a time for sniffing the wind for change or watching for the slightest change in the upper atmosphere, this is it. From the middle of this bay, under ideal paddling conditions, it would take twenty to thirty minutes to get to land; a lot can happen weatherwise in that amount of time. Just like eating brussel sprouts as a ten-year-old, it's an exercise in controlled panic. "Good for your character," my mother would say.

I paddle, remembering another arctic voyage when we timed the onset of a storm; the lake went from dead calm to whitecaps in four minutes. Little wonder anxiety on such a crossing peaks just before the middle. But like so many phenomena, even fear has a cyclical rhythm; beyond the mid-point, like on a bell curve–worry slides quickly down to almost normal level as the likelihood of safe passage to the opposite shore increases. Lorraine and John begin to sing as we approach the shore.

After 21 miles (34 kilometres) in six hours, there is no reason to push our luck against the weather, and feeling full and satisfied by ten sun-alive hours on Alymer Lake, we camp on a sloping rock shore. By now the routine of setting up tents and supper preparation is well established: two on tents, two on wood, two on meal preparation. The flip-side of windlessness is bugs. Bad bugs. This evening, against the angled evening sun, they look like ground fog. Bug jackets and bug hats are the order of the moment, but even still the sheer numbers of midges, black flies and mosquitoes are difficult to ignore. Seamstress Cath decides that this is the moment to unveil a second surprise, sewn over the winter: a 6 foot × 8 foot (2 metre × 2.5 metre) bug tent made of no-see-um netting. Norm has had two telescoping-end poles tied inside the gunwales of their canoe. In seconds, Eureka! a bug-free zone.

Supper that night is a joyous affair. In bugless comfort we toast the day and Cath's ingenuity, and devour a meal of fresh lake trout tetrazzini with cabbage salad, soup and fresh-baked carrot cake for dessert. After a rousing game of cards and a nightcap, it is not long before people head to bed or out for a nightly stroll, leaving a pair of noisy gulls in the stillness bickering at the shore over the entrails of our fish.

Returning from a nearby ridge, I see the bug tent empty and can't resist taking advantage of the absence of bugs to read and to bask in the panoramic view. My book is *Ulysses' Sail: An Ethnographic Odyssey of Power, Knowledge, and Geographical Distance* by anthropologist Mary W. Helms who argues that there may have been more to the travels of long-distance adventurers through time than strictly economic motivation. Helms explains that East appears in medieval Christian thought as the place of origins and was often the cardinal direction favoured at the top of maps at that time. The West, she says, was more elusive, literally veiled in mists. The East, by contrast, was more of a power-filled place to be visited by identifiable heroes and the place that yielded real and tangible gems, spices and silks, as well as intangible fables, monsters and sacred settings.

With a view to the eastern horizon outside the bug tent, I think it ironic that, although Canada is not connected by land, as Europe was, to the East, it was the promise of those same oriental riches that placed the Arctic on contemporary maps. But somehow, in the interim between medieval times and now, our maps, at least, have shifted, favouring the North at the top. And strangely, in looking for passage to the East, explorers found another power-filled land with riches of its own, furs and minerals of every description. It occurs to me that whether it's the East or the North, the important issue is that we have an image of what's over the horizon.

8.
PORTAGE

AYLMER LAKE IS AN INVERTED T, 40 MILES (64 KILOMETRES) ON A SIDE. And although weather on the lake remains uncharacteristically calm, it takes another two days to reach its northern end. Flat water and good feelings of day one on the lake lead to intermittent lakeside rambling and dawdling on the water. By the time we reach Sandhill Bay, however, we are eager to move from the Great Slave Lake watershed over the height of land to Sussex Lake, source of the Arctic-bound Back River.

Divides were places of great significance for Canadian voyageurs, who developed a variety of ceremonies to celebrate an initiand's first crossing. Revelry at Grand Portage was legendary. Similarly, a voyageur crossing for the first time the divide between Atlantic- and Arctic-flowing water was anointed by cedar-switch with water from the next basin, and required to promise never to kiss a confrère's wife without first getting permission, then awarded a black feather to signify passage in the far northwest. Whatever the enduring significance of these rites may be, it's important to remember that they all occurred on portages and may have had as much to do with distracting attention from the load-carrying ahead as they did with any kind of divide mythology. Divides are thresholds to new adventures and invariably spine-shorteningly hard work.

We approach the beach at the northern extent of Sandhill Bay, cutting through a ribbon of floating caribou hair that mirrors the sandy shoreline. Because this crossing is only about two-thirds of a mile (1074 metres), we decide to walk unencumbered, along well-worn caribou trails, up the gently rising tundra slope to a point where we could at least look down onto the waters of the mighty Back River. Cameras swinging, people laughing, we head off in ones and twos to see what the future holds. Marshy spots on the trails reveal the tracks of caribou that have to be pretty close. Everything seems to be going so smoothly. A flawless drop-off by plane, a few problems with low water between the early lakes, but nothing serious–except the bear. We have lucked out with three days' calm on Aylmer Lake, and before us lies what look like an easy walk over the height of land to the Back River. Norm finds an abandoned set of caribou antlers, holds them on top of his head and prances ahead.

No one notices, until we catch up to him, that Norm has stopped. He stands beside hastily dropped antlers, arms limp at his sides. There is reason for disappointment and disbelief.

Just as the map indicated, to the right is Sussex Lake, its main arms stretching out of view to the north and east. Before us, unless we are somewhere else, is supposed to lie a river, the Back. The "mighty" Back River. All we can see is a massive boulder field joining shallow puddles trailing off to the northwest horizon. "So *that's* the Back River, eh," quips Lorraine. The sardonic twang in her voice elicits a few nervous chuckles from the rest of us. "It's only day ten," Norm adds. "We've got lots of time for a leisurely stroll to the Arctic Ocean, before winter."

"There must be a water over there somewhere," says Gail hopefully. "Let's get on with it."

We trudge back to the canoes, each one of us mentally calculating what packs would go on which trip across the portage. With the amount of food and gear we're carrying, it will take three loads per person to move everything over land. Before the actual portaging gets underway though, we all set to work packing every loose item we can find; it's the items that aren't in packs or at least tied to a pack that are in most danger of being lost on a portage, and it is these items that can make portaging even more miserable than it is naturally. So, raincoats, boots, cameras, lining ropes, bailers, life-jackets, paddles and binoculars are stuffed, stowed or tied on. Gail and I have five loads worked out for us to share: (1) canoe and camera pack; (2) food pack with paddles and life-jackets; (3) wanigan, map case and day pack; (4) bedroll pack with day pack and guitar; and (5) a final hundred-pound food pack.

Gail produces a shiny white corset, laces it up and cinches it down over her clothing.

"How's your back?"

"Fine."

"Are you sure you're ready for this?"

"Sure. Put it on my back as if you were getting on a horse," she says. "Settle the weight down gently. Easy does it."

Walking with three-quarters of your body weight shouldered is no easy task. I watch her totter on uneven ground and then stride into a short-stepped rhythm that looks strong. "I'll get there," she shouts over her shoulder, as if she's got a rearview mirror. She joins Lorraine, Jake, Norm and Cathy, who are fanned out in the tundra meadow, each on a separate path. It's the family von Pack, picnicking on the tundra!

The 17-foot (5 metre) Old Town Tripper canoe weighs 84 pounds (38 kilograms), and lounges on the beach, daring me to try to pick it up. It has in it a fibreglass yoke for carrying. Although the weight is substantial, the yoke helps distribute it evenly, or as evenly as possible, over my shoulders. And, unlike packs that tend to pull backwards because their centre of gravity is removed from the body, the canoe's weight is directly over the spine and pelvis, the main springs of the human undercarriage. For short distances, and under ideal weather conditions, carrying a canoe is not much different than walking–in theory, at least.

"Come on, you big green pig, let's get going," I say, as if the conversation might magically reduce the weight. An aluminum or fibreglass canoe would certainly be lighter than this one, which is made of ABS plastic, but acrylonitrile-butadiene-styrene slips easily over rocks and remembers what it's supposed to look like when it gets bashed up in rapids. Fibreglass breaks, aluminum sticks to rocks and is difficult to fix. ABS plastic as a canoe-construction material is a measure of safety all by itself. The only drawback is the weight. Bouncing the boat three times on my thighs, I flip it up and grab the opposite gunwale with one hand, reach under and cradle the bottom of it with my other arm, and then, using a rocking motion, rotate the whole boat upside down and onto my shoulders in one continuous action. You can almost hear the sound of vertebrae clicking like dominoes as they press together under the load. It's a little heavy in the stern. I must remember to stuff a shirt or something light under the bow deck next time I put it down to balance the canoe front to back.

The problem this day is wind. As I join the divide-parade, a gentle breeze from the southeast wants to rotate the canoe clockwise about my head. The turning is stopped by my knees, amazing joints that are able to hinge forward and back to accommodate forward walking *and* counteract the rotational force of the wind-driven canoe. The last thing one worries about on portages in Ontario is wind, because all portages are well treed. (Unless, of course, they're on railway tracks–and every time I pick up a canoe I'm mindful of the unfortunate fellow from another camp who was decapitated, while portaging, by a canoe spinning in the slip-stream of a speeding freight train.) Here on the tundra there is no shelter. The wind today is no train wash, but the constant twisting of the canoe is driving my knees crazy!

Gail was right; portaging is like riding. I end up letting the canoe twist like a weathervane until it is parallel to the breeze. Then, to stay on track, I use a three-quarters-forward, one-quarter-sideways step, like a practising Lippizaner gelding. It makes me think of Monty Python's Flying Circus and their Ministry of Funny Walks–a person with a gait like this would probably be awarded assistant-deputy-minister status on the spot, if anyone was around to appreciate it.

There is a shriek from ahead. I look up in time to see Gail hurrying toward Lorraine, who has fallen with her load. The cry is not pain, or anger; it is Lorraine convulsed with laughter because she is pinned, helpless, like a turtle on its back, by the pack straps. Extra hands lift the pack, resettle it on her back and get Lorraine mobile again. "Thanks, but I needed the rest," she says, still chuckling.

It takes an hour to move two-thirds of a mile (1 kilometre) to a puddle on the other side of the divide. The portage itself is tolerable, and everyone works together and gets through unscathed, all of us unable to shake the sinking feeling that comes with the certain knowledge that we will be carrying again after about 200 yards (180 metres) of paddling. We get back in the canoes and sit for a long time, just chatting and staring at the bouldery scene that lies ahead. "Those trip reports from Travel Arctic never said anything about this," Jake laments.

"Maybe they started somewhere else," says Norm. "Or maybe they had teams of sherpas to do all the heavy lifting."

"There was definitely a river here once," adds Cath. "Look at that esker over there."

"Yeah, but if I'm not mistaken," Jake replies, "it was flowing the other way."

"At least there was water here. There had to be for all that sand to be deposited."

We paddle to the end of the pool, stand up, and from there see another puddle about 50 yards (45 metres) "downstream."

"Let's drag it," Norm suggests.

"Great idea!" (*Tutti.*)

With three people on either side, one by one we drag the loaded canoes over the shrubbery and slide them back into the water at the other end. Norm and Cath's canoe is last in line. They snag the essence of the mood by jumping in and taking paddling positions while the canoe "floats" in a dwarf willow bush. We take a few photographs, the dalliance momentarily eclipsing the hopelessness of our situation. Another pool. Another mile-and-a-quarter (2-kilometre) portage. This time I notice Norm dragging his empty canoe across the tundra. There is a certain purposefulness to his step and a certain hunch of defeat in his posture that speak almost as loudly as his action. Nevertheless, the image of a man with a rope over his shoulder, leaning forward and pulling a canoe over the ground, is a memorable construction in my imagination. I want to laugh, but am afraid that Norm might hear me and get even more angry. He has had it with the wind. It starts to spit rain. Rocks and tundra behind us, boulders before us, we make camp.

Diversion tonight is food. Thank goodness we're not eating a steady diet of cornmeal mush or pemmican.

"Or *tripe de roche* like our buddy John Franklin," adds Jake.

For the past three nights, Cath has been sleeping with a plastic bottle of germinating alfalfa seeds (to keep them warm enough to grow), which she produces, as sprouts, to garnish a salad of red and green cabbage, turnip, carrots and cheese. That is followed by beef-jerky stroganoff, apple volcano cake and coffee tipped with Southern Comfort liqueur. And after a day of portaging that might pull the crew down with depression, Lorraine pulls out Stella and everyone joins with pots and pans, harmonica, anything that might make a semimusical noise, and we boogie until more persistent rain sends us to the tents for shelter.

The next day, the rain continues, so we decide not to move. We're two weeks into the trip now. The intensity of the portaging represents a watershed, of sorts, in our thinking about the trip. Enough has happened in these past thirteen days to cloud the details of our exit from Yellowknife. Bathurst Inlet–350 miles (560 kilometres) north–is too far away to be real. We have crossed from a yesterday-and-tomorrow frame of mind into a here-and-now mentality. We have come down to earth at a place in our journey where beginning and end are out of reach, beyond the horizon. Jake claims that this is the mark of a good canoe trip.

Inside the tent, we read and talk and listen to the gentle patter of rain and bugs on the fly. Sound from farther afield is deadened by the two-layer nylon wall. Sound inside has an intimate, studio-like quality, with mounds of clothes and sleeping bags dampening any resonance. The screens are zipped up on door and window. We feel safe, warm, self-contained and secure in the knowledge that today, at least, we have what we need to be comfortable in this northern place. Inside the sleeping-bag my feet are dry and slippery, feeling almost powdered, against the warm cotton liner. Heaven.

It is only when immediate needs for warmth, love and shelter are met that one can begin to think of more far-reaching notions having to do with life and landscape. What luxury has befallen us to be able to conjure up these circumstances in which we can sift and reorganize constituent parts of our lives in a way that allows us to appreciate the essential configurations and patterns that shape who we are. Belonging *somewhere* is important. And here, in this little tent, we have the rudiments necessary for belonging to begin. We have each other, we have a social context of known limits on speech and behaviour; we have our basic survival needs met. But all of this needs to be nurtured somehow by *where* we are. Even basic needs cannot allow you to feel as if you belong if the place in which you are is a fearful or unknown one. We have come from home over the horizon to this spot on the barrens, but there is much we have learned about this land, such as its ranges of temperature, inhabitants, topography, watersheds, that makes it known to us. We have what we need to travel safely and to get from place to place without getting lost–even if lately we've had to do that travelling on foot. It strikes me that who we are has as much to do with where we are and where we belong, as it has to do with simply what our human needs are and whether or not they're being met.

Sometime in the afternoon, the rain has let up, so Gail and I venture out for a walk. We're both intent on climbing the esker behind our camp to see what lies ahead. Footprints tell us that at least two of the others have had the same idea. Halfway up the steep, gravelly side of the aggregate river, we see the print-makers, who we reocognize by height and colour of rainsuits to be Jake and Lorraine.

The esker rises perhaps 150 feet (46 metres) above the surrounding landscape, and from its top, to the south, we can just make out the waters of Sandhill Bay, to the east, Sussex Lake, and from here we can see that the caribou trails we followed over the divide are, in fact, part of a major highway of smaller paths in the tundra that flow northward up the higher land between Aylmer and Sussex lakes. Even though we are only twenty-five minutes' walk from the campsite, it takes a moment to find our tents in the scene below us, laid out on points of a triangle.

To the northwest unravels the esker itself, remnant of a river in retreating ice, purposefully twisting its way to the limit of our vision. With it, below and to the south, rumbles the boulder field that is the Back River. For the foreseeable future, we will be portaging and puddle-hopping. But that begins tomorrow, or sometime. Right now, we are walking freely toward infinity.

We startle a killdeer that rises on the breeze to meet us, then lands and skulks off, flaring one wing. Must be nesting. We try to pin-point where it first took off to see if we can see any eggs or young. Nothing. They're there somewhere, but too well-camou-flaged to see at a glance. As we look down at the sandy surface of the esker, we realize that the entire expanse is patterned with countless three-toed impressions of little birds' feet. And then, as we let our eyes wander to the surface horizons created by the curved top of the esker, we realize that there are, in fact, dozens of little birds scurrying around among the lichens, bigger stones and tufts of grass. Also beside us, a short distance away, are wolf tracks heading in our direction. It is a revelation to realize that we have been looking at this esker for a day and not seen what is there!

A Russian cosmonaut reported, after five months in the Soviet space station, that, over time above the earth, his colour perception became richer and the sharpness of his vision increased to the point that he could differentiate various seas and even different parts of oceans by their characteristic shades. At first the nuances of colour eluded him, but, like us on the tundra esker perhaps, time to look and the inclination to discover allowed him to really see what lay below him.

Gail walks on the esker, stops and sits down. "There's no such thing as a straight line up here, is there?" she observes. "In my grade-thirteen CanLit course we talk about Margaret Atwood's straight-line/curved-line theory. Atwood has observed that only people make straight lines, and that nature deals only in curves. When it comes to literature about settlers in the great Canadian wilderness, there are really only two motifs: straight line battles curve and wins, but destroys human 'life force' in the process; and straight line deteriorates and curve takes over again, meaning settlement fails. We're not really settlers up here, but I wonder how all that applies to us."

"I wonder. There is a certain linearity to what we're doing here. I mean, we were dropped off by plane, we will paddle–or walk, as the case may be–to our destination, and then we will fly home again. It's not a straight line, but it certainly does not have any of the curves of nature."

"So, we're travelling a deteriorating straight line. That means we're doomed to failure as settlers in this little Shangri-La."

"Right. Good reason to move on and try to discover a way to redefine the restrictive win-or-lose relationship between lines and curves. I guess it's important, too, to remember that the path we are following is not our own, but one laid down by water. Our route may be from A to B, but at least it's following the natural curves of flowing water, or water that flowed once."

"The only thing that comes to mind that has a successful union of lines and curves is music. The lines provide the ordering system for the rounded notes and the curving expression marks. I guess most types of visual art have occasionally happy co-existence of lines and curves, as well as some forms of architecture and maybe maps. But what on earth has that got to do with anything?"

"Nothing."

"Good."

At length, we meet up with Jake and Lorraine who tell us that they have walked well into the distance and still not seen continuous open water. "There are four good carries with little ponds in between," says Jake with a grin, "before we get to do some real paddling."

"Is that so? What do you call 'real' paddling?"

"About half a mile."

We shuffle down the side of the esker and pick our way back to camp along the rocks of the Back River bed, stopping every so often to check out a pretty flower or to look at fresh caribou tracks. Sharp-eyed Jake picks up a redpoll leaving an alder bush, and walks us directly to the bird's nest, where we peek in on four nestlings who seem to think our shadow means more food.

Back at camp, Norm and Cath read most of the day and then busied themselves with the gas stoves–in the drizzle–and have prepared a steaming pot of macaroni and cheese. Everyone is most appreciative, mostly because we're all aware of the time and energy it takes to make something as simple as mac and cheese.

Food on these journeys is such an ordeal to prepare. First you have to find it in a sodden pack. Then you have to root out of the wanigan any necessary staples or spices. Then you have to get water from the lake and find some way to cook it. And, of course, cooking on a fire or on a stove, every dish has to be watched with the utmost care because there is no telling how easily good food can be tipped or burned. That's probably why it tastes so good, but so much the better if somebody else tends to its preparation.

Somewhere about the middle of the second back-to-back mile portage the next day, I get a deep chill that brings with it the first inkling that we might not finish our journey before the food runs out. Nearly two-sevenths, or 30 percent, of our trip time has gone and we have only covered 94 miles (150 kilometres), or 21 percent, of the total distance. At this point we can make up the difference simply by hurrying, but, I fear, it is much easier to hurry while paddling than it is to speed up the painful process of portaging. Step after watery step on the tundra, our situation gets worse, if only in my mind.

Lonely business, this portaging. At any one time you can see the others, little dots on the tundra, bent over and humping their loads down the line. We decided that canoe pairs would work together to move their loads across, but, as it turns out, everyone had a different pace, and we end up spread out across the entire length of a particular carry, helping each other load and unload packs when possible. But, fundamentally, the task of portaging leaves us all captive to the burden that we happen to be carrying at the time. It's an exercise in mental as well as physical discipline. The physical is simply a matter of tolerance: how much pain can you endure before you have to put the load down and take a rest? Of course, unless you can find a big rock or a likely ditch on the tundra on which to rest your pack, taking a rest is no easy task, mostly because it's nearly impossible to get back up again. But generally, while the physical task is laid out in a linear route from one end of the portage to the other, the mental challenge is rather more free-wheeling and serendipitous.

By the time my head is finished puzzling through the timing and route problem–I think it has decided to forgo the Mara River and try the more predictable Burnside instead, but better wait to see what the others are thinking–the tumpstrap has embedded itself in my forehead and fused the vertebrae in my neck. At least this 90-pound (40-kilogram) wooden box has no shoulder straps which would stop its porter from bending over at the waist to get the load centred over the pelvis. No wonder voyageurs were stooped and short little fellows. They didn't have shoulder straps on their loads either. Loads like this could stunt your growth! But didn't they carry *two* and sometimes *three* 90-pound loads? But then, their hearts were sometimes known to burst from exertion on the trail.

The pain builds and subsides as the mind wanders in and out of topics. Sooner or later I make a point of reminding myself that this torture is self-inflicted, and is probably one of the most important ingredients to good memories of a canoe journey. Suffering is an important part of the wilderness experience, partly because it's nice to know you can tolerate hardship if and when you have to, but mostly because it's the great stuff to tell fellow canoeists back home. Today alone, we've portaged nearly 4 miles (6 kilometres) in total and the end is still not in sight. No doubt by the time we get back 4 will be 10 miles (16 kilometres), or 40 (64 kilometres)! Still, I must remember to sign up with a Zen master, or somebody eastern, when we get back. Don't they have contemplative ways of dealing with pain? They sure do. Mental discipline: meaning, change the subject.

How about Chinese geomancy and the significance of the cardinal points of the compass? Good discipline. Why not try to bring that one out of storage? Nothing else to do while you're walking.

North, the direction of purification, is associated with winter, the colour black, water and the great abyss, which is supposed to be a gateway to spiritual rebirth; West, the direction of the setting sun, is associated with autumn, the colour white, and its virtue is decorum; South, the direction of summer and light, is associated with red and fire; and East, the direction of spring, is associated with green, wood and thunder and lightning.

But wait, they have another direction that's not really a direction. The most important direction to the Taoists is the centre. The centre is the mother direction, which is the source and destination of all other directions, like the hub of a wheel. The centre, they say, is where nature is the fullest. Maybe that's where this canoe journey is taking us–to the centre, but it's not an easy place to get to.

On the way back to pick up the next load, the wind is cool on my sweaty face. It smells of lichen and Labrador tea. It's rich and fresh and rejuvenating. It's a refreshing change to look up and breathe deeply without a load.

There is motion in the air. Two long-tailed jaegers, crow-sized, slate-coloured birds with white chests and two-dagger tails, wheel and dive with impressive speed and precision. A Lapland longspur does its best to evade the attackers. The agile hunter birds work as a team. One strikes and knocks the prey out of the air. The other pounces on it as it hits the ground. Together they pull it to bits.

We paddle across the largish pond Jake and Lorraine had seen on their walk, and for the first time there is enough water at its outflow to again drag our loaded boats through the boulder field. The dragging is hell on the bottom of our canoes, but a nice change from back and forth, back and forth, back and forth with house-sized loads on our backs. We know the routine and expect nothing new. Wrong. As we pull in to the shore of the next puddle for a late lunch, Cath shouts, "There's a wolf coming down the shore!" "Jee-zus . . . let's get out of here," whispers Lorraine hoarsely.

Wolves in their own way are migratory animals, following the barren-ground caribou, their main prey species, below the treeline in winter, and north again to the tundra, come spring, stopping off to have cubs. Juveniles will travel with a pack but will wander alone when they're not babysitting. This wolf is wet and seems, by its size, to be a young one. It continues down the shore in a relaxed walk, stopping occasionally to sniff under a rock. Tension, for us at least, builds as the animal ambles closer with not a hint of fear. It's panting, and looks more like Lassie than a wild animal. Slowly, cameras come out. If there is a reason for the wolf to be frightened, it is six telescopic lenses staring it in the face. It stops, half-sits, scratches with a hind leg and carries on. Immediately before us, not 30 feet (9 metres) away, the animal stops again, and, almost deferentially, surveys the human cameras. Noontime sun highlights its white-ish coat. It shakes, and carries on down the shore, leaving a quiet hubbub of "Did you get that?" "What just happened here?" "Did you see how relaxed it was?" "That was no killer." "Do you think it was sick?" "Maybe it had never seen people before?" "I wonder if there's a den in that esker?" "Man, what a sighting!"

We camp after the next mile-long carry, get up the next morning and immediately take on another short boulder-field carry that leads us to yet another endless boulder field. For a long section of this portage I'm conscious of my heartbeat–thu-thump, thu-thump, thu-thump–that complements my little steps, which seem to come in groups of threes. The beat of portaging is a double rhythm this day, the straightforward one-two heartbeat and the one-two-three, one-two-three cadence of tired feet on loose boulders. It is our third full day of portaging on the Back River, not including the day of rain on which we rested. It's time for a change. An advance party reports that there is open water ahead that looks like Muskox Lake. Two miles (3 kilometres) more of portaging and we'll be out of this miserable section of "river."

"Even though we're going to be paddling upstream when we hit the Icy River," says Gail, optimistically, referring to our route plan that will have us swing west up a tributary of the Back River to begin the climb to Contwoyto Lake, "I can't wait to get back on the water, even if we have to go upstream. Paddling against the current is a lot better than walking!"

"You better hope there's water," Norm replies.

"There should be water," Gail adds. "The Icy River is not just one thin blue line like this part of the upper Back. It looks like a real river. There's blue on the map that looks like a wide, wet river."

"No boulders?"

"Who's to know? But it looks good."

The final two are interminable miles. Gail's back is permanently crooked and she is taking codeine. Norm is favouring the knee he had operated on in the winter, but still manages to relieve Gail of her heaviest loads. The rest of us are just sore from head to foot. But the task is clear and there is no other way to complete it than to lug our stuff across, load, after load, after load.

Jake strips and takes a swim in Muskox Lake when he finally gets there and takes it upon himself to brighten Lorraine's day by frolicking back over the tundra to her, clad only in low-cut Converse All-Star sneakers. "Fallis, you're an *asshole!*" is all she can muster after dropping her pack at the end of the portage. "Is there anything to drink?"

Seven miles. Eleven kilometres of portaging.

Anything is better than portaging. Being in a canoe feels like flying.

With a mile to cover down the shore of Muskox Lake to the turn-off to the Icy River, we chat, laugh and muse about how refreshing it will be to do something other than portage. Little do we know what lurks around the corner.

Topographic names are not necessarily random. The realization dawns at different speeds for each of us, but the result is the same. Silence. Abject silence. The Icy River is icy. It's frozen! On July 13, the Icy River is solid ice, thick ice. It's blue and white on the edge and snow-covered on top, and looks more like a glacier than any river ice we've ever seen. The whole situation seems too ridiculous to be true.

On inspection, the ice is made up of thin layers, to a total thickness of 10 feet (3 metres), that covers the shallow mouth of the river and extends "upstream" as far as we can see. We walk up the icefield and estimate that there is at least 2 miles (3 kilometres) of solid ice before a pool and more ice. This, I suspect, is a phenomenon I've only read about, called *Aufeis*, formed by upstream water flowing into the shallow lower river in the fall, when temperatures are well below zero Celsius. This water then freezes in successive sheets that, ultimately, are able to withstand daytime summer temperatures. Walking on the surface of this ice on a 86°F (30°C) July afternoon provides a curious contrast of sensations–hot head from the blazing sun, cold feet from immersion in melting snow and ice crystals, with a mind that's boggled by ice in July and a body tormented by clouds of voracious black flies. The image, however, of a ribbon of white disappearing into the distance, flanked by verdant green tundra smattered with pink and red wildflowers, is one that captures the imagination even more than other sensory impressions. For all the sounds, smells and tactile sensations of this place, I remain a visually oriented person.

The only portaging method that makes sense is to use the canoes as sleds, with one person pulling on a rope out front and one person pushing from the rear, using the spruce mast tied to the stern deck. It reminds us all of Sir John Franklin and his crew on Point Lake, the head of the Coppermine River in late June 1821, pushing their birchbark canoes 117 miles along the ice on makeshift sleds.

Mild disaster strikes, shooting our canoes one by one over a 6-foot (2-metre) wide, 8-foot (2.5-metre) deep melt-water ravine in the ice. Jake and Lorraine's fibreglass Woodstream, which has a sharp prow, is holed when it slams into an ice-wall on the other side of the ravine. While fixing the hole with a piece of cloth and some five-minute epoxy glue, we notice that the ice has seriously abraded the entire bottom surface of their canoe. Jake lays on strips of the canoeists's universal cure-all–duct tape–and we're back in action. The notion of dragging canoes over ice in July is so silly that 3 miles (5 kilometres) of exertion goes by almost without notice. After everyone bathes that night in the waters of the Icy River, removing the grimy vestiges of the Back River portage, we relax in the bug tent over coffee and appreciate anew the pure and liquid music of running water.

During the next days on the water, the cold realities of our situation come crashing in. People are pensive and quiet, all for the same reasons. We're sore, tired and seriously behind schedule. If we continue to run into no water or frozen water or bad weather, there is no way we can take a chance on the unknown Mara River route and serious doubt whether we can even make it down the Burnside to Bathurst Inlet before we run out of time and/or food. But land, it seems, always lifts attention to more important matters.

We're camped on the shore at the base of an esker on Glowworm Lake. Having spent twenty minutes trying to massage some of the pain out of Gail's lower back, I step out into the twilight of late evening and face three wolves, not 10 feet (3 metres) away. It's the strangest of sensations. Perhaps because of the previous encounter, perhaps because, for an instant, we have eye contact, I feel no fear at all. Behind them, the rippled lake and the gilt-tinged nightscape. Between us, the tufted sand where I've seen their prints. This is their home. They belong on this lake shore. The path they walk in front of me and down the shore they have walked before, probably at this same quiet time of the day. As if by magic, they move away and fade into the night air. I want to run after them, to talk to them, to ask them questions, and maybe to say thank you, but that would not be the right thing to do. Brushing my teeth at the shore, I feel a presence and turn, but see nothing. Later that night, in the hazy zone between alertness and sleep, I hear a long, plaintive howl and some dog-like yips from down the lake. It brings to mind an eerie blend of fear and fascination and captures the fundamental trap there is to being human. American conservationist Aldo Leopold said that only a mountain has lived long enough to listen objectively to the howl of a wolf. This night I doze off, exhausted, sated, thinking how little objectivity has had to do with what has just happened.

9.
ARGUMENT

THE NEXT 31 MILES (50 KILOMETRES) WHICH INCLUDE PUDDLE-
hopping over the height of land linking the Icy River basin with the
Contwoyto River, are of sufficient intensity and difficulty to test
everyone to the limit. After the Back River walk and the Icy
River slide, energy stores are down. Emotional reserves are also at
low ebb.

We ready to leave from the wolf campsite on Glowworm Lake
and paddle northward along the shore. Norm decides to head for
the bushes just as we're about to embark and leaves us waiting. No
one says anything, but I'm really steamed. How on earth are we
supposed to catch up time and get any sort of free time if we're so
sluggish getting onto the water, now that we have water! Finally he
turns up and off we go, paddling in silence for hours.

Gail senses my annoyance and we talk about frustration. It's
too easy to accept that this route is beating us down and making us
irritable, or something. In any case, she relates her frustration with
never being able to finish anything around the campfire.

"Cath is like a bloody hawk! She swoops down over the
pot every time I'm doing something and either adds something

that I don't want to add or takes it away from me altogether. It's *frustrating*."

We camp, sleep, get up and repeat the cycle one time before we are mired in an endless tract of puddles and portages. Progress is painfully slow.

On one puddle-to-puddle carry that has more holes, marshes and rocky ups and down than we've come to expect, I step on what I think is an alder bush. It is an alder bush, but it's growing in a steep-sided 5-foot-deep (1.5-metre-deep) depression in the ground. As the canoe and I drop into the hole, the bow and stern catch on either side of the abyss, stopping the boat from further fall. I continue, leaving parts of my ears on the rough edges of the fibreglass yoke. The burning pain emanating from the attachment points of my ears is eclipsed only by a momentary twinge that says I have broken or twisted my knee or ankle in the fall.

"Hey, Raff, are you okay?"

Lorraine pokes her head under the canoe and into the hole. She's laughing.

"I guess so. Why in the hell are we doing this?"

"Good, because that was the funniest thing I've seen in a long time. It looked like you had staged the whole thing, just for me. Come on, let me give you a hand getting out of there."

Her "Far Side" view of my pain is just enough to diffuse a bubble of anger and adrenalin I considered venting by picking up the canoe and flinging it toward the next lake.

"You know, it's a good thing Gail didn't see this. She's such a sadist when it comes to crash-outs. We'd probably be giving her mouth-to-mouth right now because she'd be laughing so hard. It was a great wipe-out. Nice work. And thanks for the comic relief."

Later on the same carry, I see Norm struggling to push through an alder thicket, while carrying a pack and their canoe. The footing is rocky and uncertain. He stumbles. I walk over and ask if he'd like some help.

"NO!"

As he stomps into the distance, I notice he's limping.

Gail is doing her best, but her back is really sore. By now the back brace is everyday apparel for her and it's mud-stained now, not white. Every step she takes, even with the lightest packs, is deliberate and gives the impression of creating pain. Her body is noticeably crooked and she's favouring the left side, where her weakened disks are howling. Fortunately for us, the others have carried parts of our load in addition to their own. In the midst of all this pain and ill humour is the undeniable fact that we are all in this together. If one of us falls behind, we all fall behind.

Finally, we drag and slog our way to the last carry on this divide, one that will take us to Hardy Lake. I want to feel joy about making this point in our journey, but I can't. This is the seventh portage of the day, and I'm not looking forward to it any more than I did the portages yesterday, or the day before, or the day before, or the day before. The last load on this last carry is the wanigan with my camera pack on top.

The wanigan has no straps like a normal backpack. Instead, it is portaged with a leather tumpstrap that is worn across the forehead. The box itself weighs something in the order of 90 pounds (40 kilograms), but because the head strap forces most of this weight directly down one's spine and onto the strong muscles supporting the pelvis, it is surprisingly pleasant to carry, at least for the first 50 feet (15 metres).

Ideally, when the wanigan is in place on one's shoulders, another pack, like, in this case, my waterproof bag containing camera gear, can be balanced on top of the box. One walks holding the sides of the tumpstrap on either side of the face. It's a good system, until you trip.

I can see the end of the portage. The canoes are stuffed into the bushes. Packs are sitting on boulders, waiting to be loaded. But, inside me has built the most consuming anger at the bloody box that refuses to balance itself. I have spent the last thirty minutes trying to compensate for a balance problem in the load by tipping to the left. Now my back is burning, my knees are on fire too, and I'm ready to blast anything that gets between me and the completion of this torture cycle. Steps are small, but hurried. Let's get this over with.

Moments before I am to set the beast down, I falter and fall headlong among the boulders at the edge of the lake. The wanigan crashes down on top of me, pushing my face into the water. The camera pack on top, unattached as it was at the beginning of the walk, is propelled by the fall and sails through the air in a perfect arc and lands with a splash in the lake. Of course, I had forgotten to seal its top. Shit!

"Oh sweet are the uses of adversity," chimes Gail, as she retrieves my dripping camera pack out of the water.

"Yeah," say I, "but that wimpy bastard Shakespeare never carried a wanigan!"

Morning brings spattered riffs of wind-driven rain on the tent fly, and a fight to match the weather. After getting over a second height of land, this should be the time to revel in a dry sleeping-bag and laugh at the weather. But wait, this bag is not all dry. It's wet! It's soaked. And, damn it, wet, too, is my journal and everything else around my head – clothing, bird book and paperback. In fact, we're lying in a veritable lake!

"Did you not roll the edges of the groundsheet under the tent?" I ask angrily.

"Pardon?"

She's still asleep.

"Water. We're soaked. You've got to make sure that you roll the edges of the groundsheet under the tent to make sure that water rolling off the tent doesn't end up coming through the floor!"

"Good morning to you, too," she says sleepily. "Thanks for that little lecture. I thought the groundsheet under the tent was just to stop twigs from poking through the floor. How was I supposed to know it would collect water? If it's such a problem, why don't you fix it?"

"Okay, I will."

I leave and she retreats into her wet bag and harrumphs the whole issue–body and sleeping-bag–onto their sides to face the wall.

Outside, the day is considerably less grey than it seemed from within. In fact, a pearly luminescence in the cotton-textured hanging cloud makes the earthly greens and browns of the tundra more vibrant than we have ever seen them in full sunlight. The air is cold wet and a refreshing change from the tent's dampness. And, to be sure, the outside air has not the spark and tension I have just left.

The groundsheet is rolled under the floor of the tent to ensure that no more water flows from the fly into our sleeping-bags, but the damage has been done. We're wet. Our gear is wet, and if this turns out to be a three-day rain, they could be pretty miserable days with no place to dry out the sleeping-bags. There is nothing worse than a wet bed on a canoe trip, especially when the wetness was totally preventable.

Back inside, the situation bristles. Me angry at unnecessary wetness, fussing to pull books and cameras away from the water. Gail, with face to the wall, incommunicado. At length, we steam in silence, pretending to read.

Slowly, I get a glimmer of this rude awakening from Gail's perspective.

I apologize.

No response.

Back to sodden Ludlum, wondering all the while how amends might be made. If only the wanigan and stoves were closer: I'd nip out and whip up a quick pot of tea. It's such a civilized beverage. If there ever was a time for a reconciliatory "Would you like a cup of tea?," that time is now. Right now things look pretty bleak, maybe beyond tea.

Later I try anew. "Can we be friends again?" I query tentatively, genuinely confused about how things could have deteriorated so far and so fast.

"We're not enemies. I'm just a little hurt." The strain in her face and the redness of her eyes underline what she has said.

Pause.

"Is it just this incident, or is this the result of many incidents?" I ask, struggling to determine the scope of the situation.

Her eyes glaze over again. She turns back to the wall, leaving me staring blankly at the spots on her sleeping-bag cover where tears have bled into the nylon and darkened it from royal blue to navy.

"I'm sorry," comes out, but it sounds hollow.

I've been too hard on her. But not with malicious intentions.

She doesn't realize that. Maybe it is me who has not helped her see the importance of doing things once and doing them well. Up here there are times when you just don't get a second chance. I know that, and I want her to know that, but I have fumbled badly in the process of trying to convey the idea. There is so much to learn out here, especially on this, her first canoe trip.

Whatever happens next, I know for sure that something must be done to break down the barrier. But, at the moment, there is nothing more to be said. I leave. Making breakfast this rainy morning for the crew might give Gail some time to breathe and me some time to think. Activity might also ease my growing feelings of guilt, and fear that we have just lost something.

The stove, too, is sodden. It refuses to light. Rainwater collects in the burner and clogs the gas generator. I finish up, pouring fresh fuel from the reservoir onto the outside of the whole stove and lighting that to heat and dry the unit – dangerous but effective. Poof, the gas explodes into flame.

While the stove heats up in the lee of a canoe, I take a pot and wander down to the lake to fetch water for tea and oatmeal. Raindrops stipple the gun-metal surface of the lake, giving it a special uniformity of colour and texture that happens only on rainy days. No reflections, no echoes. Patter on my hood mixed with the swish and consistency of the rain on land and lake creates a unique white noise that refreshes and relaxes my mind. It clears away the anger and immediacy of the incident and makes way for a dull and constricting ache that winds from my gut into the back part of my throat. We need each other on this journey and I may well have blown that with one thoughtless outburst. With all of the pain Gail has had from her back, and for as hard as she has tried to learn, in days, what I have had the luxury of learning over two decades of canoe-tripping, the last thing she needs is an aggressive reminder of her shortcomings before she's even awake. Now I am hurting, for her. Scooping the water into the bucket is a matter of reflex and habit as my mind focuses on Gail.

Back at the stove, as the water boils, Gail emerges from the tent and moves toward where I'm crouched. She says nothing while she opens the wanigan. I watch as she removes the tray and rummages through the contents below.

"Have you seen the toilet paper?" she says, without making eye contact, and as if she's frustrated by having to make contact on such a trivial matter.

"It's in my pocket," I say, wishing words had come out that might have undone what was said earlier.

"Thanks."

Without further comment, she takes the plastic bag with its flattened roll of toilet paper and walks toward low green shrubbery behind the tents.

On return, she again opens the wanigan and puts back the toilet paper. Normally we would be talking. I want to break the tension, somehow. I was wrong and want to tell her so. Shuffling over, I stand beside her as she straightens again. "Are you really burned about this?"

Rainsuit to rainsuit we embrace. This time the tears are mine.

"I'm sorry."

She extends her arms and looks me in the eye. A bitter hardness in her face ebbs visibly when she sees the tears.

"I know you are. You've got to be more patient with my mistakes. This is the first time I've done all of this stuff. I'm trying my best, but sometimes my best is not good enough."

"But I had to learn by making mistakes. It seems silly to have to make the same mistakes twice when we know there is a right, or at least a better way to do something, like setting up a tent."

"*You* know that, but I don't. You can't deny me the opportunity to learn from mistakes too. You've got to learn to be more sensitive."

"I'm trying to be."

"I know you are, but when it comes to doing stuff around the campsite, there's only one way, and that's your way."

"Yes, but that way is not arbitrary. It's a way that is probably the result of screwing up on an earlier trip. Believe me, I, better than anybody, except maybe you, know that, because you're new at this, you've got more to cope with than anyone else on this trip. Especially with you back-sore most of the time."

"But I can deal with the back. I knew that I would have to deal with it from the beginning. But what I did not expect is to have to deal with you watching over me and giving me lectures as if you were my father and I was a little kid who didn't know any better. Your behaviour this morning was uncalled for. I felt like I was being scolded. Getting treated to little lectures on the whys and hows of rolling the edges of the groundsheet is not what I had in mind for this trip. I want to learn, but I want it to be fun."

"Has it been like this since the beginning of the trip?"

"No. Most of the time you're patient and you try hard to teach me, but sometimes, in the canoe, when we're paddling, and you say something about how I should be holding my paddle, or when Cath takes over something I'm trying to cook, I get frustrated. You guys all know how to do all of these things. I don't."

"I think you're doing great."

"I'm trying."

"I know that. I'll try too."

Between us, we fire up a second stove and prepare steaming pots of tea and oatmeal, which we deliver to the others in their tents. No one is interested in going anywhere. With the two of us as outside intermediaries, we decide to stay put until the rain lets up, and then, regardless of the time, we'll press on. Everyone is conscious of how little time we have left and how much paddling we have still to do to get to Bathurst Inlet.

As I walk away from Jake and Lorraine's tent, Gail stands away from Norm and Cathy's tundra abode. I can feel the pain, watching Gail stiffen slowly. As always, she says nothing. She puts her hands on her hips and arches her back pushing her head back and to the right in an attempt to straighten her ailing back.

"Can I rub your back for a while?"

"Sure. Thanks."

Gail has taught me the manipulations and massage strokes necessary to ease the "kinks," as she calls them, caused by portaging, sleeping on permafrost, and by the rigours of daily living north of sixty. Even still, I often marvel at her ability to deal stoically with pain, and at her strength of character in not letting the back totally dominate her first experience on the tundra. Nevertheless, today's incident has been a turning-point in the sense that, for the first time, she has been stretched to the limit, and has been forced to teach me, in no uncertain terms, that I can be and have been a contributor to her problems, for it seems clear now that stress does nothing to make the back situation any better.

Inside, she pulls out the worn and wrinkled tube of A535 rub, which in no time adds eucalyptus and menthol to the vapours of dampness and old socks already pervading our living space. I warm a healthy dollop in my hands before applying it to her tightened lower-back muscles. The cream feels good on the hands. Black fingernails and tanned knuckles with dirt-stained creases fan out on her skin, pushing down the spine and out on either side where the enflamed nerves are pressed and angered by swollen disks. Slowly, she relaxes. "This the first time I've been pain-free in what seems like weeks," she says. "Thanks, partner." Before too long she's asleep.

10.
DECISION

Still on Hardy Lake, we're going nowhere fast. White streaks on black water is all we can see from the door of the tent on our second morning there. Outside, looking out from the confines of high-necked pile sweater and hooded rainsuit, I watch waves hiss at the overturned tails of our canoes, and sputter back off the gravel beach. Full-skirted clouds sail by one way, with matronly purpose and self-importance. The wind blows another. These are unsettled times. There will be no paddling on a lake like that.

Nothing else to do on a rainy day, I stand and stare out over Hardy Lake. Except the lake, the pink granite rocks and us, no one in the world knows that we are here right now. Eyes focus for a moment on a point deep in the lake, rendering the grey surface patina to a silver-sparked expanse of the finest black silk, square-etched by wave crests and wind streaks.

The colour beyond and around my feet is without the brassy reflections and black shadows of a sunny day and simply glows restorative green with tan and rust accents. Delicate pink zithers of mountain sorrel have visual integrity and identity that tundra flowers never have in sunshine, or maybe I'm just paying attention like never before. Perhaps this pause in our travel has a purpose.

Beside the scraped and battered canoes, bobbing in the wind, are luminescent pink and white petals of river beauty, that low-growing northern relative of ubiquitous fireweed. Still, though, I wish the wind would change. It's day twenty-two, the half-way point in our anticipated trip schedule, and of the 438 original miles (700 kilometres) we have yet to cover 275 (440 kilometres) of them. We're at least 56 miles (90 kilometres) off schedule.

Cathy emerges from their flapping green Timberline with its catchy red vestibule. Their tent looks pretty, but it's no match for barren-land wind. She and Norm have been awake for some time and have cooked up a rainy-day program for the gang.

"How about cards with cheese and crackers a little later on?" she asks.

"Great idea. It's been a while since we got together for a rousing game of 'Oh Hell.' I can't wait to lose."

"Don't forget the Drambuie."

Later, we leave the damp confines of our tent and make our way over to the Timberline. Dumping our wet shoes and rainsuits in the red vestibule, we congregate for a lunch of tinned oysters, Triscuits, Plum Hollow cheese and GORP. The tent is ripe with the smell of smoked oysters, wet wool sweaters, bug juice and old socks but no one seems to notice until a few vestigial whispers of last night's dried onions are added to the mix.

Jake has brought his maps and wonders aloud if the Mara River is still a workable route. We chat and meander through our situation as it presents itself this rainy mid-trip day.

Fifty-six miles (90 kilometres) ahead, at the 219-mile (350-kilometre) mark, which happens to fall at the southern extent of Contwoyto Lake, we must decide whether to go with our planned route, overland to the Mara River, or to branch out down Contwoyto Lake to the Burnside River, which we know, from trip reports, is paddleable.

The Mara has never been paddled, as far as we know. This fact alone makes it an attractive alternative. The problem with the Mara River route, is that there is a 19-mile (30-kilometre) height of land that looks suspiciously like the last one. For this one we have stereoscopic air photos that show water in most of the little creeks, but based on hard lessons with similar situations this summer, we have no reason to think that there will *still* be water when we get there. In fact, consensus is that, as fate will have it, there *will not* be water and we'll be subjected to more of the dreaded drag-and-grind. Last winter, when we scouted this route on the maps, the route looked possible, but now, in the heat of the action, lugging our gear down the waterless Back River, we're even beginning to wonder if the Mara River itself might be dry.

A complicating factor is the benevolence of the people at the Pacific Western Airlines weather station, 25 miles (40 kilometres) down Contwoyto Lake, who agreed to fly in our food cache with their regular bi-weekly grocery drop. Even though the turn-off to the Mara River route is at the near-end of Contwoyto Lake, we must paddle to the weather station–25 miles (40 kilometres) into plan B, the Burnside route–to get our food for the second half of the trip. And who knows what big Contwoyto Lake will have in store for us? It's 75 miles (120 kilometres) of big-lake unpredictability. We could get hung up there, too, for days, or weeks. Actually, there's a good chance we'll run out of food before we even get to the cache, to say nothing of running out before we get to Bathurst Inlet! Wouldn't *that* be grand!

There are other factors at play in making this decision we seem to be making. Lorraine wants time to photograph wildflowers and is not interested in racing to get to the end of the trip. Norm says he's game for anything, but he's worried, too, about rushing. His knee, he fears, will not make it through another ordeal like the Back River. Cathy doesn't care either way, but is conscious of the fact that our food cache is half-way down Contwoyto Lake, forcing us to backtrack for at least a day to get back onto the Mara River route. Logic and common sense, says Cath, would favour going down the Burnside. Gail doesn't want to race either and wonders which route might be best for seeing wildlife.

"All we need," Jake adds, "is to have no water in the crossing between Contwoyto Lake and Nose Lake, and we'd be walking again for as long as, or longer than, we did on the Back. We can better predict what life will be like, and how long that route might take, if we go down the Burnside. We can only guess for the Mara."

This decision-making process we have just been through is a curious phenomenon that may occur only in situations where friends are forced to choose a course of action. It's not democratic; it's not really consensus–it's a strange and subtle recognition of various types of expertise and a bringing to the surface of various patterns of influence that exist between and among people. Rarely, under any circumstances, at home do we engage in such a process, and even if we did–as a sixsome–there would be external factors at play that would change the decision-making dynamic and probably occlude even more its inner workings. Decisions are never really made. Tendencies and inclination are just uncovered, and the group then seems to let circumstances push the tendencies and inclinations to conclusions and concrete courses of action.

Our decision-making process–if you can call it that–is actually as much a measure of what the group values as a tool to shape the course of events. We value democracy, everyone getting a chance to say what he or she thinks, and stay well away from management by edict or autocracy. We seem to value not stepping on other people's toes, either by coming out with a hard-and-fast opinion about something we'd like done, or by stepping on someone else's idea. What we value most of all, it seems, is lack of structure. We're intent on making decisions with as little overt structure as possible. It's a horribly inefficient system that may have only the pretense of being egalitarian, but it's a system that is different and less structured than the ones the six of us encounter in our daily work lives, and that, it seems, is, in the end, what's important.

"Raff! Deal the cards!" And on it goes.

The rain stops by evening, and predictably, as the sun drops low in the northwest, the temperature drops and the wind abates. Differential heating of the air around us by the sun as it moves through the sky from morning to night is a big factor in controlling the winds in this place. It's usually calmer at night than it is during the day.

Clad in long underwear, turtlenecks, sweaters, rainsuits and life-jackets, we pack up on the shores of Hardy Lake and head out, a group resolved–I think–to forgo the Mara River. Optimism is slashed not three hours later when a new frontal system blusters through from the northwest and blows us back off the lake. As we're packing up and battening down for another onslaught, the sun peeks through the cloud system and spreads a hand of white fingers that dance and drum on the Contwoyto Plateau. Arctic fever is gone. This scene seems only to mock our helplessness before the wind.

"Go when we can?" Norm yells to the rest of us.

"Twenty-four-hour clock," adds Lorraine. "We've done enough hanging around in the tents for one week. It's time to get on with this trip."

11.
COLLAPSE

IT IS NOT UNTIL THE SAME TIME THE NEXT NIGHT THAT THE weather system blows itself clean. People's preoccupation now is with moving, getting on with the trip. It's a very real possibility now, and a prospect that grows by the minute, that we will miss the last flight out of Bathurst Inlet Lodge. We're counting on the lodge transportation system to get us back to Yellowknife. We have the emergency locater transmitter and that would get us attention, but not the kind we had in mind. We have no other radio and, should we get to the coast after the lodge people have left, we would have to see what help we could get from the local people or wait for our RCMP check-in to stale-date itself, or we could set off the transmitter. All of those prospects sound embarrassing and potentially very expensive. But, the sky has cleared and the wind has dropped. We'll have to paddle through the darkest part of the night.

This departure is unsettlingly reminiscent of a winter trek on James Bay during which, because we had encountered deep snow that had slowed us down, we were hopelessly behind schedule. We had to snowshoe farther on the last day of our trek than we had done on any two of the previous ten days, which forced us to travel the last 10 miles (16 kilometres) of the journey in winter darkness.

Hunger, cold, fear, fatigue and broken equipment comprised that journey's Gethsemane. We survived and made the distance, but not without angst and physical pain.

We bundle up as the daylight wanes. Underwear; long-johns; two pairs of socks; pants; rainpants; T-shirt; turtleneck; long-sleeved, collared wool shirt; pile sweater; anorak; raincoat; gloves and toque. It's all a bit constricting, but damp cold is what we're fighting, and that's the worst kind. Gail suggests we leave out our sleeping-pads to put on the canoe seats to stop the lake cold from seeping into our backs. The last thing I see her do before we close up our toilet kit is take two codeine tablets.

It is cold, but the night scene is magical. The sky hangs on the edge of darkness, always blue, gradually shifting to black overhead, with a rotating kaleidoscope of colour on the horizon as the sun moves under the pole star toward daybreak in the northeast. Twilight has drained all colour from the landscape, leaving a thin-line silhouette that undulates along the mirrored surface of the lake. Cold night air against the day-warmed surface water creates a light fog at eye level that plays havoc with our ability to estimate distance. We stop for a rest at a recognizable point along the way, and Cath produces a round of hard candies. We suck them in silence.

At the outflow of Hardy Lake we scout and prepare to shoot an easy rapid by moonlight. The white water is blue, all colours are muted, we're bundled up in multilayers of clothes that restrict our ability to move and our ability to sense the world, especially the sounds, around us. We decide to take turns shooting and acting as safety people on the shore. When it is our turn, Gail and I settle into the boat and sweep the canoe's motion into the movement of the river. Everything in our perception is speeded and intensified by the dimly lit shoreline slipping by against the night sky. The light and the motion and the feeling of being inside a cocoon of clothing lend a surreal, movie-like quality to the experience.

The colour and texture of the night-paddling experience, which includes lying on the cold rock in wait with the throw line, kindles memories of the film version of James Dickey's novel,

Deliverance, especially the night that one of the characters spent lying on a river ledge with an open fracture of the thick bone in his thigh, predicated by a nasty tangle with a rapid. I wonder if we're pushing things a bit by shooting rapids at night. That scene epitomized the consequences of a macho-men-against-nature theme. It doesn't take more than a couple of rocks and a gentle current to break a canoe in half, much less a person's leg, even if the character was played by Burt Reynolds. To suggest, as Dickey's characters did, and maybe as we're doing right now, that people can enter into some kind of win/lose competition with nature is a dangerous premise. This could well be fearful thinking bred by darkness and cold. If nothing more, this night-time rapid shooting has my complete and undivided attention. My senses are on high because I'm in fear for my life.

By 1:00 A.M. we have made nearly 10 miles (16 kilometres) on the calm waters of Pellatt Lake, but a dark line of cloud moving in surely from the southwest is etched menacingly against the lightening sky. A light breeze comes up from behind as we begin a 2-mile (3-kilometre) crossing to the west shore of the lake. By the time we are three-quarters of the way across, it has strengthened considerably and shifted a little to the west. Gail puts down her paddle, turns stiffly, and says, "I need a little rest."

The cold, dim light; growing swells; and deteriorating weather conditions have me on the edge of fear and keep the paddle moving. Gail's back is sore, but I wonder if she is aware of the danger swirling around us. As she rests, we fall behind and out of contact with the other two canoes. In waves like this, two paddlers keep the momentum necessary to stop the canoe from wallowing between the crests. She begins paddling again and we head toward the others. I can tell by the jerkiness of her stroke that she is angry and very sore.

To our surprise, the others are heading into what looks on the map to be a dead-end bay instead of down the west shore of the main body of the lake. We are out of calling range. Staying together in conditions like this is important, so we follow them past the point, now surfing on the occasional breaking wave. We are only a couple of hundred yards past the point when they realize what's happened and about-face. We hold position in the water as they beat their way upwind to where we are. Then the six of us head for the point, where we will again be able to go with the wind, only this time keeping very close to shore.

Quickly the others pull ahead of us. Gail is stopping every five or six strokes now and trying to straighten out her back. I pull as hard as I can, but it just doesn't seem to move the boat. We need two paddlers with this load, under these conditions, to make significant headway. Gail stops again, puts her paddle across the gunwales and drops her head, this time for several strokes.

"Come on," I say as encouragingly as possible. "You're doing great. As soon as we get around the corner we'll be able to drift with the wind for a while. Come on, try to paddle; we're losing ground. Do the best you can!"

She makes a valiant effort, reaches as far forward as she can and begins a massive pull. Mid-stroke, she stops and doubles over. "I'm taking a rest," she yells at the bottom of the canoe in front of her. Somehow she manages to begin again. We eventually make the point and turn again with the wind.

Several hundred yards down the shore, the others have pulled in to camp. By now the sky is light, and green has returned to the landscape. We drift slowly in the wind and waves toward them and Gail uses the time to sit up straight, arch her back, and do what she can to make the pain go away. By the time we land she's able to get out of the canoe by herself, but barely.

"If you get the tent out of the blue pack, I'll go and start that while you unload the rest of the stuff," she says blithely, as if–at about 3:00 A.M.–we had just finished a nice afternoon paddle on a calm lake. She takes the tent and shuffles away from the shore to find a tent site.

By the time the canoe is unloaded and the other packs secured on the shore, it is really quite a nice morning. The sun has broken over the horizon across the lake and it is beginning to scare away the cold and dampness. I look around to share this with Gail and see her crumpled over a half-set-up tent. Going over to her, she manages to stand, but tears are falling. "I need to lie down for a while," she says bravely.

"Would a hug help?"

"Probably."

12.
CARIBOU

WE ARE WOKEN BY HEAT BUILD-UP IN OUR DOME-SHAPED SOLAR cooker. Outside we hear the plaintive call of a loon. Gail is feeling much better, still stiff and sore but in a better frame of mind.

"I could have stood some of this heat a few hours ago," she laments.

We talk about the implications of changing our route from the Mara to the Burnside River, and agree that the predictability of the Burnside is preferable, now that we're running behind schedule, to the unpredictability of the Mara River route.

"I don't want to have to go through that again. I don't think it was the length of time we were paddling, or the conditions," she says, managing a smile. "It was the cold and dampness that cut right through every bit of clothing I had on. My back just can't function when it's cold. It's just not flexible. And when you have to try to keep your balance and paddle in waves like those last night, especially when the light is dim and it's hard to know which way is up anyway . . ."

Today, the whole enterprise has a different feel to it. The notion of schedule, which has been poking at us all as we've got progressively farther behind with every portage and low-water setback, seems less pressing. Time has loosened our grip on distance and given over our notions of where we should be, and when, to the wind and existing water levels.

"There is no point in rushing," adds Gail with renewed confidence. "We'll get there when we get there. I think if we push it again, somebody is going to end up getting hurt, I mean really hurt. The costs are too high. Besides, there's so much to see up here, I'd hate to end this trip thinking we didn't see something because we were in such a damn hurry to get home."

"Interested in a coffee in bed?" I ask.

"Sure thing. The heat in this little dome sauna feels good on the old back."

Stepping outside, the heat and closeness of tent air in my clothing is replaced by an infusion of the coolness and possibility-of-morning air. The sun that saw us to bed is high overhead, highlighting Cath and Lorraine in pink and yellow turtlenecks out on the tundra with rose clippers, snipping dead twigs to make a breakfast fire. Norm, it appears, is still in bed. Jake is casting at the shore.

The lake sparkles this morning and gives no clue whatsoever of its black mood the night before. Flashes of wind and water snap into the serene consciousness of this new day. Whatever weather system riled Pellatt Lake last night has passed to the east, leaving behind it ripples, not waves, and a full-circle cloudless sky. Even the bugs have taken the morning off, or perhaps they're still just a little bit slow from the coolness of the night. There is a sniff of renewal that only morning can bring. I walk down the shore to see what Jake has caught, and notice a line of hollow caribou hair marking the place on the shore rock where the waves reached at their peak the night before. We're getting closer to seeing caribou, I hope.

"Caught anything yet?"

Jake turns from where he is standing. His once-white Malvern Collegiate T-shirt, the one he proudly told us came from the lost-and-found box at his school, hangs over the top of matching filthy tan workpants. His black Converse sneakers, "Limos" he calls them, are frayed and worn from hard days on the trail. A lime green baseball hat with the Ontario Farmers' Cooperative corn-cob logo is bent, worn and stained with a delicate mixture of sweat, bug juice and the smeared carcasses of the bugs themselves. The peak of his cap shades a tensionless face. This is a man in his element. He takes another cast, begins winding his reel and replies: "No fish, but it looks like if we'd been here a few days earlier, we might have caught a few thousand caribou swimming around! We're getting close. There are tracks and droppings everywhere, but still no animals."

"You're just dodging the issue. You don't know how to catch fish. That's the problem."

"What kind would you like? How many? And how big? Actually, you're going to have to make do with whatever I catch in the next couple of casts because we've got to get moving while the lake's right. How's Gail? Is she ready to travel again?"

The answer to that is a positive maybe. But travel is getting to the urgent stage. The route we have chosen to get to the southeast end of Contwoyto Lake involves passing through a series of lakes and ponds, and at least another eight short carries. There is no talk of what lies ahead as we breakfast on double-smoked bacon and pancakes, but people waste no time in getting packed up and back onto the water.

Packing down is now a steady routine. Dishes are done using soap and hot water in a plastic dishpan. The dish-washer usually loads the wanigan with staples, spices, cutlery and dishes, along with the grill, pots and other cooking equipment.

Gail and I, like the others, also have a well-established pack-up routine inside the tent that by now happens automatically. Our sleeping-bags go in one green-garbage-bag-lined stuff sack, which, when closed, is compressed with three nylon straps sewn to its outside. Clothes for the day, hats, gloves, extra sweaters and rainsuits, are left out; all of our other personal apparel is kept in one stuff sack each. Green garbage bags, the all-purpose water-proofer, are kept handy for any extra items that might need to be kept dry. Books, cameras, insect repellent and other personal toiletry items are kept in specially water-proofed smaller packs that sit in front of each of us in the canoe for easy access. Our Thermarest sleeping-pads, which provide protection from the cold in the ground as well as unevenness, are deflated and rolled. The tent is shaken and rolled. All of this fits in one Duluth pack, which is carried down to the canoe and dumped. It always gives me a tickle that this pack contains, with the exception of food, all of the necessary comfort and security to make a home-away-from-home for two people.

Days on the water and hours carrying our gear on one portage after another fall in, one on top of the other, each one with its own character created by the blend of what we see, what we do and how we feel. Each cycle of sleep and activity is fundamentally the same–we eat, we travel, we explore the land and aspects of each other, we sleep and then get up and do it all over again–but each day is laid down on top of the one before and becomes part of the journey in my imagination that will be the enduring legacy of this physical odyssey from Munn Lake to Bathurst Inlet. In this sense, photographs and journal entries, charged with the images and energy of the moment, will become windows to this store of memories and impressions of this journey as etched in my head.

We make our way into the upper reaches of the Contwoyto River. By now the line of caribou hair along the shore is visible from some distance.

"Hey!" I shout to Gail. "There's a wolf, over there at ten o'clock."

She turns quickly in her seat to have a look and inadvertently knocks her glasses into the water. One pair is all she brought, but they were a light prescription and only for distance vision. However, even without the glasses, she says, "Are you sure that's a wolf? It looks too low to the ground."

"Sure it's a wolf. Or if it's not a wolf, it's a caribou. I wish the heck I'd brought those old binoculars, even if there was a bit of permanent condensation inside the lenses."

Norm and Cathy have heard my outcry and are scanning the shore with their field-glasses. We jockey our boat up beside theirs.

"What did you say that was, Raff?"

"A wolf."

"A wolf, eh?"

"Here, take a look at your wolf."

He hands over his binoculars. I train them on the shore. There, to my surprise and slight embarrassment is a pair of Canada geese and a line of six little grey and yellow goslings trundling along the bank. The adults are moulting at this time of year and are unable to fly, which forces them to resort to running as an escape technique.

"It's an honest mistake. Maybe I just wanted to see another wolf."

"Maybe," says Norm wryly, "you should go for a dive back there, fish out those glasses, and *you* use them for the rest of the trip."

To no one's surprise, the Contwoyto River flowing out of Contwoyto Lake has so little water in it as to make it impassable in canoes. The map indicates a deep little bay in the lake that can be accessed with a portage that would begin about a mile back from where the outflow rapid is supposed to be. We drift back along the shore and are caught by a light green swathe across the tundra that seems to head toward the bay we've earmarked for our carry.

"That must be the remains of the winter road that they pushed through here to get to the mine site on Contwoyto Lake," says Cath. "A guy was telling me in Yellowknife that they came up here last winter and the winter before with a huge bulldozer that scrapes a path in the snow. The road takes mostly lakes from here to Yellowknife, and when the bulldozer has done its work to smooth over the rough spots, they drive ordinary tractor-trailers right over the tundra."

"So, why is the road light green like that?" someone asks.

"Who knows?"

We pull in the boats and lay out a lunch to give us energy with which to mount yet another portage. Gail busies herself with our bedroll pack. It's an unusual thing for her to do at this time of day.

"Forget something this morning?" I ask.

"Don't be nosey. Why don't you go and have some lunch?"

Minutes later she sidles up beside me and presses a brown paper bag into my hand.

"Here," she says, grinning. "I was going to save this gift until your birthday, but after what's happened today I think you could use them now."

Inside the package is a brand new pair of 7 × 20 mini-binoculars.

"You mentioned on the plane that you didn't bring your old binos because they were no good any more, so I picked these up in Yellowknife. I hope you like them. I *know* you can use them."

After lunch we begin the portage on the winter road. It extends to the horizon on the low-rising hill that separates this portion of the Contwoyto River from the lake that feeds it. Just as we're getting settled into carrying mode, Gail shrieks with delight, "*Caribou!*"

An ungainly-looking creature with stubby little velvet antlers, big bulging eyes and knobby knees approaches on feet that look too big for its body. We stand on the road and watch as the animal moves closer and closer, finally stopping about 30 yards (27 metres) away. Its coat, in summer moult, looks like the work of a one-armed barber using dull scissors. As if it has only now noticed us, its head comes up and its whole body flexes attentively. It steps back one leg away from its normal standing position, as if getting ready to wheel and flee, and then just stares. One of us lifts a camera, it blinks, turns and prances off the road, stopping almost immediately to begin grazing again.

Location says that this is likely a member of the 350,000-strong Bathurst herd, probably a juvenile left behind earlier in the spring as the main herd moved northeast, toward Bathurst Inlet. Probably born east of the Inlet last summer, it will have migrated below the treeline for the winter. This spring the animal may well begin its journey in the trees closer to Yellowknife, at Ghost Lake, Drybones Lake or Lake of the Enemy.

The migratory rhythm of the barren-ground caribou is one of the great spectacles of the North. Crossing paths with this animal is like crossing paths with the lifeblood of the North. Each year thousands upon thousands of these animals make their way to the treeline from refuges in the Coppermine River valley south, and as far east as Lake of the Enemy, just 5 miles (8 kilometres) away from Munn Lake. They reach the treeline and inexorably latch onto a compass bearing roughly thirty-five degrees east of north that takes them to the southern end of Bathurst Inlet. Males and immatures may stay behind or head up the west shore of the Inlet, perhaps into the valley of the Hood River, while the females continue northeast to land bisected by the remote Ellice River where they give birth to the year's crop of delicate new calves. And in autumn, they cycle back to the shelter of the trees and scratch a living until lengthening April days begin the cycle all over again.

The life of a caribou seems purposeful, unadorned and highly rhythmic. The cost of the irrepressible urge to move is calves that are born on the run and left because they can't keep up with their mothers, and animals that are suffocated or drowned while travelling in a big herd. The benefit of a life pulsed with a fragile tundra ecology is a phenomenal number of animals that rarely deplete a food source because they are rarely in one location long enough. The omnipresent trails, worn by thousands of years of migration, are the only sign that these animals have passed the south end of Contwoyto Lake. By contrast, the cat train to the new mine on Contwoyto Lake passes through once or twice, and already there is a mark on the landscape that will likely not fade. Walking back, to begin portaging, we pass an empty 5-gallon (22-litre) can of hydraulic fluid. It's full of bullet holes.

At the time we have no way of knowing that this road will be the scene of much activity in the future. The gold-mine on Contwoyto Lake will be the northern-most in the non-Soviet world and one of the largest and highest-grade gold-producers in North America. From late January to early April each year, this road will be travelled by 700 to 900 semi trucks, making the twenty-four hour one-way journey over 360 icy miles (576 kilometres) from highway end in Yellowknife to Contwoyto Lake. To meet the mine's annual supply needs, they'll draw 5 million gallons (22.5 million litres) of diesel fuel and 15 million pounds (6.75 million kilograms) of chemical reagents, steel-grinding media, explosives and other bulk supplies.

We notice the strangest thing. In much the same way as we

have traversed the tundra on portages and turned to follow caribou trails when we've encountered them travelling in roughly our direction, so too the caribou we encounter stop on reaching the lighter green path where the trucks have driven, then turn and follow the road. The parallel paths of migration–made by the trucks and the animals–are plain to see. The question is, who's following whom?

During the course of the 2-mile (3-kilometre) carry to the southeast end of Contwoyto Lake, we encounter more animals, on the road and elsewhere, who pay us little attention. Some of these are bulls with impressive antlers. They seem wary at first, but as we go about our business, they relax and return to grazing. Treeless green landscape punctuated by grazing caribou and portaging canoeists has a peaceful, almost bucolic feel to it. I am glad the Contwoyto River was dry.

From the shore of Contwoyto Lake, we watch in awe as several dozen more caribou filter south around the end of the lake. The only human construct that comes close to explaining the movement of the caribou is Bruce Chatwin's explanation of the Australian Aborigines' "songlines." Their totemic ancestors were thought to have scattered a trail of words or musical notes along the line of their footprints across the outback of Australia. These so-called dreaming-tracks provided communication between even the most far-flung tribes. A "song" was both a map and a direction-finder. Provided you knew the song, you could find your way across the country. Listening to the click, click, click of the caribou's leg tendons from close range, watching the spring and balance in their steps, is more like watching dancers.

Biologist friends have told me that they can recognize caribou from the various herds across the North. "Don't show slides of the Beverly herd and slip in Bathurst animals because the photographs are better. Anybody who knows will call your bluff." How they do that is anybody's guess; could be size, antler configuration or colour patterning. It could also be a figment of an office biologist's imagination to give the impression of rich field experience. In any case, we are among them and for the first time on this trip I feel the curiosity cycle completed. I came here hoping to encounter these animals. I will leave this landscape feeling blessed by the encounter. Maybe the land gives each group a different song?

The land and its many factors have shaped the behaviour, anatomy and rhythms of these animals until it is a near-perfect fit. Their sharp two-toed hooves are webbed with a small piece of skin, making them excellent for swimming, walking on snow, cutting through icy crust and digging for food in winter. Their hair is hollow, which provides flotation for long swims in summer and insulation against −40° temperatures in winter. Their migratory path and preference for tundra vegetation take them away from competition and predators in the forest to a place where they can calve in relative peace, and even their herding tendency minimizes losses from the wolves who follow them out onto the barrens.

Jake notices maybe thirty animals swimming toward us from a point across the bottom of the lake. I take a camera to the shore and lie down among the alders to await their arrival. The ground is cold and wet. I think of the permafrost 3 feet (1 metre) below my wet navel. I think of being within touching range of these magnificent wild animals. First, I hear the sound of their antlers knocking together as they jockey together in the water, then the rhythmic sound of measured breathing. Their nostrils are flared. Their heads, backs and rumps are well out of the water. They touch bottom, take a step or two and shake, while their legs are still in the water. They walk up onto the land directly in front of me and shake again, throwing a flurry of water droplets against the bright sky. Without sensing anything amiss, one by one they set their heads back and move smartly away from the lake. Their heads and antlers stay relatively quiet while their lower bodies reach and recoil in fluid motion below. They fart, jostle and move on.

The pictures I take today are at close range and will probably rekindle the excitement of being in such close proximity to these caribou, but they won't be technically very astute because pieces of the animals will be out of focus or out of frame, and there will certainly appear in many of them pieces of the bushes that conceal me. But they will be different, happier, less consumptive pictures than ones taken on Point Lake at the head of the Coppermine River some years earlier. That was a horrific, but nevertheless instructive encounter with caribou.

IT WAS THE YEAR AFTER MY FIRST COPPERMINE TRIP. I WAS A GUIDE on a commercial canoe expedition. Eight of us were paddling down Point Lake, heading for the Coppermine River, when we encountered many thousands of caribou crossing the lake. It was early August and we watched as cows, calves, yearlings, adolescents and bulls streamed down over the rocky north shore of Point Lake and into the water, five abreast. We sat in our canoes off the south shore of the lake and marvelled at the spectacle. That much life moving in concert was captivating. They swam past us, up to the shore and disappeared to the south.

There was a break in the procession, but shortly thereafter we saw another herd moving down toward the lake. This time we moved closer to the crossing path, to get better pictures. Just as the lead animals in this swimming line approached, two people in the party began paddling across the front of the line, presumably to photograph the animals head on, or from the opposite side. Without warning, the front animals turned 180 degrees and began swimming right into the face of the animals that followed them. We had cut off all options for escape, and created a mêlée of splashing, kicking, bellowing, antler-bashing and who-knows-what-else for these unsuspecting caribou. People in the group cried. Others just stared in shocked silence.

Had we just watched, instead of trying to master the scene with camera, things might have been different. Taking pictures doesn't have anything to do with learning to see. In fact, as we so graphically demonstrated to ourselves and the caribou, a camera can be an impediment to vision and understanding.

But photography doesn't have to be that way. Although calendar pictures and full-frame television images give us the notion that animals are there to run up to and photograph, I am beginning to comprehend that this act is a selfish one, of control, of domination over the animal. Our domination of caribou on the

Coppermine resulted in death. But there is an alternative. If one learns to move in synchrony with the animals, using the eyes and the senses to learn and to understand, the camera can then become a device to celebrate a harmonious moment, a relationship, between person and animal, or, for that matter, person and plant, bird, rock or landscape.

13.
STORM

THERE IS A RULE OF WILDERNESS PADDLING THAT MUST NEVER BE contravened: Beware large lakes! Contwoyto Lake: 77 miles (123 kilometres) long, 15 miles wide (24 kilometres), is of ample magnitude to be considered worthy of extreme caution. By now, though, we have been out for twenty-seven days, covered 200 miles (320 kilometres) on foot and in our boats, including the broad expanse of Aylmer Lake; we're behind schedule and looking to make some quick, easy miles on big Contwoyto Lake. As if nature needs to chip off the impetuous edge, we're windbound on an island in the lake by two o'clock on our first day out. We're lucky to be there.

I remember only too well deciding to cut a corner in Damant Lake in the headwaters of the Elk River system en route from Lynn Lake, Manitoba, to Baker Lake. A following wind has been pushing us along steadily, and the sky has looked the same all morning. To save a few miles, my partner and I opt to cut across the mouth of a large bay instead of doing the right thing and following the shore. All is well until the moment we make our turn to port and head out into open water.

The wind rises almost imperceptibly, but it's from behind and difficult to gauge because there is no tell-tale whistling in our ears that comes with a head wind. Before long, however, the waves have doubled in size from 6 inches to a foot (15 centimetres to 30). In another twenty minutes they have doubled again, and our canoe is starting to spin on the crests and get funnelled along the watery troughs. Broadside, we are vulnerable to waves breaking over the side, but it's too rough to bail. Getting to the other side looks impossible.

To our left appears a tiny island that didn't even figure in the equation to cross. But there it is, less than an acre in size, a little oasis with a green top; one, lone, stunted spruce tree; and enough shelter for three canoes! It was there we stayed for two days and a night, marooned, and intensely glad to be so.

The same thing happens on Contwoyto Lake while we are making our way through islands, heading for the main body of the lake. The difference this time is that the wind is coming toward us and builds less quickly. Gail and I are last in line, and this proves to be a drawback because we are also in the shortest and least seaworthy of the three canoes. Jake and Lorraine in their 18.5-foot (5.6-metre) Woodstream are out in front, cutting through the waves and enjoying a fine day of paddling. Norm and Cathy in their high-sided Miller canoe are rocking a bit in the waves, but are making good progress. The two of us in the Old Town, with its flat bottom and lower sidewalls, are getting close to panic. The boat rides up one wave and crashes down into the next, showering Gail with water. Even when she braces her paddle out flat in front of the boat to stop it from cutting into the next wave, the water still pours in occasionally behind the bow seat. This time there is a moment to bail, while thoughts of immersion death from hypothermia flash through my head. What a way to die! And on a sunny day, after all the miserable weather we've been through!

The others pull in behind an island and it is only when they turn around to see where we are that they realize our plight. But it's one of those situations about which they can do very little. If they were to paddle with the wind toward us, they might be able to break some of the wind and waves, but they would be putting themselves at almost equal risk, and one of the worst things that can be done by two boats in big waves is get too close together. All we would need to happen is for one gunwale to catch on the other and one, or both, of our boats would be over for sure. And if one boat went over, it would only be a matter of time, in any kind of rescue we could conceive, before all of us were in the water.

Paddling those last few hundred yards I contemplate how it is that we have put ourselves in this silly predicament. The answer, I tell myself, is that we have gotten cocky. Our guard was down, and now this. I promise myself that it won't happen again, but who's to say it won't? That would mean that we were in total control of what goes on out here, and I'm pretty sure that we're not. That's what we're here for. Simply setting a date by which to get to a particular place against the caprice of weather generates a good measure of uncertainty. But, I remind myself, it is uncertainty–risk–that is one of the principal reasons for taking this trip in the first place. These last couple of hundred strokes in the waves of Contwoyto Lake are taken at the edge of my tolerance level for fear–fear of the unpredictability of nature and of our vulnerability before it.

The fear breeds a total-body response to a situation: head, heart, hand and viscera, all pumping together like they've only done once or twice before. When the panic is over, the lingering feeling is good. It takes an afternoon of being perched on the island in Contwoyto Lake to let the adrenalin seep away, while appreciating the raw edge of my fear and focusing on the importance of leaving the comfortable middle of my existence from time to time to explore the limits of what I know and hold to be true.

At its simplest level this journey we have cast for ourselves is really just a set of contrived circumstances, its course determined by where we've chosen to travel, whom we've chosen to travel with and the equipment we've chosen to use to ensure certain comfort and safety levels. Without intentionally putting ourselves in dire danger, the probability of something like a wave-wrestle happening is higher than it is in our daily lives. That's why we're surprised when something does happen, and relieved when it is resolved happily, and ultimately pleased, especially after the fact, if the emotion-charged event, whatever it might be, involves momentary contemplation of a cold and unnatural death.

Having had a good long snooze in the sunshine, waiting for the wind to settle, the six of us sit on the edge of an island bluff, looking northwest toward the main body of the lake. Jake spies a bull caribou on another island to the north. We all watch as it wades into the waves and swims doggedly southward.

By late afternoon, spittle-white wind-streaks settle into the lake, the waves relax and we're back on the water, cautiously making our way up the north shore of Contwoyto Lake, the difference now being that we have agreed to crawl back onto the "twenty-four-hour clock," meaning we'll paddle whenever it is calm enough to do so. The sky is awash with cloud and colour and far from settled but, for the moment, the lake is calm enough to embark. We make 11¼ miles (18 kilometres) before another storm strikes, this time from the southeast, and again we're on hold–this time on a sheltered crescent beach on an island toward the north shore of the lake.

It's spitting rain as the slate cloud approaches. Sun burning through the western sky shatters into a massive double rainbow against the low angry clouds. The outer bow's colours are reversed from those on the primary arch: inside, violet through red; outside, red through violet. "The rainbow is the sign of the bond," said God to Noah, when the flood began to subside. Locked in this spectacle, as sure now as it was then, is almost everything you'd ever want to know about the structure of matter. But there's a mystical side to rainbows, too: without exception, even before this pending storm, every one of the six of us pauses for several minutes to savour the sight.

The next day the wind, if anything, is stronger. Norm and Cathy go for a long walk, returning with news of a radio mast they've seen on an island in the middle of the lake. This, they figure, is the weather station where our cache of food is supposed to be. If only we could cover the final 12 miles (19 kilometres) to pick it up. Fortunately we have been catching fish whenever it's needed and have spices and staples enough to do us for a few more days. It is the schedule, not the threat of hunger, that's gnawing away in my stomach.

The only way to deal with the problem is to accept that, for the moment, there is absolutely nothing that can be done to make the situation any better. Until the wind abates, we will be pinned on this windy point. It's a situation that calls for a suitable diversion. Take a walk and check out the tower. Maybe there will be some caribou along the way.

In a protected hollow behind our campsite, I slide down a rock face encrusted with a profusion of multicoloured lichens. Stopping to look at these plants I've heard could be hundreds, perhaps thousands, of years old, I'm met by an upwelling of a deliciously savoury smell of brimstone and freshly cut flowers. Leaning down to the rock surface, I breathe deeply and learn that it is the broken rock and bruised lichens that give off this heady essence.

The lichens are a study of shape, texture and colour. There are smooth, grey ones that stick to the rock like a gentleman's glove; black ones with regular yellow dots that look like pieces of Mactac no-skid tape you might put on a front-porch step; there are layered and circular lichens reminiscent of broken-yolk eggs cooked hard in the frying pan; there are patches of vermilion lichen that seem to grow especially well on splashes of bird droppings on rock faces; and, of course, there are great patches of leafy black rock tripe–or *tripe de roche*, as Franklin called it on his starvation menu of 1821–the only plant material on the face that is in any way moved by the wind.

It's a pity that more of the world is not aware of the lowly lichen, partly because any organism that has lived a millennium or so has a story to tell, but also because this living entity is comprised of not one but two living organisms living in symbiotic harmony. And they are a study of colour, a form of adaptation.

There are three types: crusty, as in map lichen–the yellow and black lichen that makes interesting map-like patterns on rocks; bushy, as in green-beard lichen or reindeer moss, which occurs in grey-white busy patches or singly among mosses and on soil; and leafy, as in white rock tripe, which is found on exposed vertical rock faces and is easy to recognize because of the white colour and the single attaching point, and brown rock tripe, which has small ridged fruit sunken into its surface. Green-beard lichen is a bushy yellow-green lichen with fine grey spotted tips. Sunburst lichen has very tiny yellow leaves, which are attached to rock in sunburst patterns. This is the one I have called fried-egg lichen.

These antique members of the floral community are the result of an adaptive combination of an alga and a fungus growing together as one, an ecological partnership, and a hugely successful one at that. The mycelium of the fungus provides the structure and support for the photosynthetic algae cells, while the alga in return provides converted solar energy in the form of sugar to nourish the couple. Somehow, between the two of them, an acid is produced that weathers the rock substrate, providing grips in the rock for the tiny fungal fingers, and releases nutrients from the rock, which then become available for uptake into the plant. The lichen is one of the first living beings in the soil-making process, thereby gaining the distinction of being a colonizer species. And not only can this unusual combination of plants grow on rock, where no other plant can find enough nourishment, these plants in the Arctic are able to survive harsh winter conditions without aid or insulation or any kind of shelter or covering whatsoever–and without the aid of psychologists, analysts or marriage counsellors of any kind. Human relationships should be so durable!

I turn from the rock face and continue scanning the tundra-scape that stretches to the horizon. By now, in the short arctic summer season, the greens are well tinged with sprinkles of the rainbow. Short ferns grow only in the shelter of south-facing rocks. Expanses of flat, marshy land–areas of the most delicate light green–are home to sedges and the white-tufted arctic cotton grass. Better-drained sloping soils nurture thick carpets of reindeer moss that, in turn, give rise to harder green dells of bilberry, blueberry, ground birch and the occasional alder thicket. Ropy arctic heather, great white-flowering clumps of it, do well next to the rocky outcroppings of granite on the highest points of land. And among all these shrubby perennials, each in their own time during the short summer season, and each within their own set of biotic and geographical parameters, thrive wildflowers–purple saxifrage, yellow arctic poppies, pink moss campion, white mountain avens, red fireweed, and my favourite, river beauty, the ground-hugging northern cousin of ubiquitous fireweed that sometimes reshuffles its genetic deck and comes up white among fields of electric pink.

Flowering plants, like the spruce trees and shrubbery, have ingenious strategies to allow them to survive in this northern desert. Winter abrasion, from flying sand and snow, and drying are problems for flowering plants too, but generally these problems are simplified by the fact that these plants all grow close to the ground, and often in hollows, where snow protects, and where wind velocities are less severe than they are at even 3 feet (1 metre) off the ground. One might expect that all flowering plants would have thick scales protecting their buds over winter; curiously, however, scientists have found this not to be the case. Thick scales, they think, would be a hindrance to rapid development in spring. Instead, flowering plants tend to grow in clumps that give individuals protection from the cooling effects of wind.

Clumping is not the only way that flowering plants make sure they can produce seed in the short arctic summer. Dense matting and dark pigmentation in many cases allow temperatures in the immediate vicinity of these plants to rise well above the temperature of the surrounding air. On a spring day, when the air temperature was 10°F (−12°C), temperatures surrounding a light-coloured purple saxifrage plant have been observed as high as 38°F (3.5°C). Temperatures on that same day among the tendrils of a very dark-coloured clump of moss were recorded as high as 50°F (10°C)–fully twenty-two degrees higher than the ambient temperature!

This dark colouring, mostly red photosynthetic pigments, allows some plants to absorb enough light to begin growth in the spring while still beneath a cover of snow. This heating of the plant occurs at a time in the spring when the incoming solar radiation changes the crystalline structure of the snow to a translucent layer of ice that allows for excellent transmission of light from the top down. The same crystals somehow trap almost all of the reflecting outgoing infrared radiation, which creates a mini-greenhouse effect ideal for plants to get a jump on summer growth.

Arctic plants are hardy and opportunistic in the sense that many of them can withstand summer freezing, going brittle with frost, being sheathed in ice or buried in snow, even during periods of rapid growth, and yet resume growth without injury as soon as weather permits. Whatever the physiological or morphological reason for this, it is obvious to people who investigate such matters that these plants can freeze with impunity.

The fuzzy white willow catkins we saw on the early days of our journey are an example of another intriguing adaptation to northern living. The hairs on plants, such as the arctic willow, are transparent and function like a greenhouse, allowing all wavelengths of light into the developing seeds, but trapping the outgoing infrared waves. This speeds leaf and catkin development early in the season, while the air temperature is still very low. It's important to keep in mind, in the case of the arctic willow, that the catkin elements are deeply pigmented with anthocyanin, which also assists in heat absorption. However, when there is dense hair on the undersurface of leaves, this probably functions principally in limiting water loss by reducing air circulation close to the stomata.

The fresh-faced yellow arctic poppies we have seen twisting their way out of seemingly soil-less boulder fields have yet another strategy to make the most of a short growing season. Scientists have shown that they rotate their parabolic-shaped flowers to follow the sun. Temperatures at the focus of the parabola, where the seeds are developing, are always higher than they are elsewhere, owing to concentration of the sun's rays. These solar heaters, which combine controlled shape and a sun-tracking mechanism, also provide warmth that attracts insects, which in turn, by rubbing the stamens of many poppies, provide a cross-pollination service.

THE WALKING CLEARS THE MIND AND AWAKENS THE SOUL. I THANK the lichens and flowers for that, but suspect that the land and the rhythm of walking have had as much to do with dispensing with the niggle of time and distance. The walk has certainly provided an opportunity to forget pragmatics for a while and concentrate instead on this vast, enveloping, harsh-yet-compelling world that is the tundra. Steps on the tundra have brought thoughts into synchrony with action. I'm bothered though, by a west-coast Indian teaching that says, "When a man abandons his home ground, he loses his soul." I'm away from "home ground" but only now seem to be finding my soul. Strange. One of us is wrong.

More steps dredge words from memory that focus feelings of the moment. It was an article, I think, by environmentalist Brian Fawcett in which he said something like "the soul is a relationship between consciousness and material objects, a sensibility created by familiarity and loyalty to places and things." My soul tells me that I'm beginning to feel a sense of belonging in this place: it is becoming familiar–I know its smells, its sounds and its many faces and moods in the shifting light of summer, and I know that something deep down was jarred by the dead-straight scar of the winter mine road on which we walked. These days of helplessness here on the shore of Contwoyto Lake, and elsewhere on this journey, hours for walking and thinking and talking, have had an important purpose. Just choosing to come here, I suppose, reveals a certain disposition to finding a sense of belonging here, but almost in spite of who we are and what we think, these wind-bound hours have helped us settle into the landscape.

Lorraine takes a couple of casts off the point and lands a 9-pound (4-kilogram) lake trout, which she fillets for supper. The blaze-orange slabs of fresh flesh lie glistening on a paddle blade as Norm and I attempt to light the Coleman Peak I stoves in the wind. Once one of the stoves is going, we put it in the largest pot to protect the flame from the wind and use the wanigan and its lid as further shelter. First order of the meal is soup, making a pot of water the first item to be heated on the stove.

The stove seems to be taking forever to heat the water, primarily because the wind is stealing the bulk of the heat away from the bottom of the pot. But, suddenly, there is a percussive "POP" and the little mountaineering stove tips over inside its large, aluminum housing.

"Jee-zus! What the heck was that?" asks Norm, backing away from the stove. To which I reply flippantly, "Oh well, we've probably built up so much heat in the pot that the fuel has expanded and rounded out the bottom of the fuel tank."

"Turn that sucker OFF or we'll all be killed!"

That, to our horror, is exactly what has happened. The concave bottom of the green Peak I stove fuel tank, designed to withstand the pressure of normal operating temperatures, has popped out like an over-inflated beachball, leaving the seams stretched and puckered like plastic, not hard metal.

"Let's get away from that thing and let it cool off," says Norm excitedly. "It's turned into a Coleman hand-grenade, and we're not even at war with anybody!"

Returning cautiously several minutes later, we examine the stove more closely and appreciate how lucky we have just been. Norm adjusts his glasses, turns up the red label with the stove's operating instructions and begins to read: "Caution: Consumes air. To prevent health and safety hazards provide at least eight square inches of ventilation. Always fill and light stove outdoors. Here it is. 'MINIMUM CLEARANCES-SIDES SIX INCHES. Do not use as space heater.' That's it, Raff, we forgot to read the instructions. We've got to learn to read the labels or we'll all be killed."

"Right on."

In a frying pan on a second stove–this one in a protected cove created by packs and one canoe–the trout fillets spit and sizzle quietly in their light dusting of flour, garlic, tarragon and dill. The yellow light of evening intensifies the rich rosy colour in Lorraine's face, neck and hands as she sits on her haunches, tending the fish. Jake busies himself chopping carrot, onion and cabbage, while Gail and Norm empty the contents of the wanigan spice shelf into a mixture of olive oil and wine vinegar.

Cath has pounded out a margarine-and-graham-cracker crust in a rusty baking pan, and poured into it self-setting "cheesecake," made from a long list of space-age polymers, that she sets into a pool at water's edge for extra cooling. I ponder the stove problem with a wrench, trying to determine if the "hand-grenade" will again ever heat food for us.

We chat and putter as the meal takes shape–about home, about work, about the state of the universe. We could have opted, as some paddlers do, for boil-in-a-bag meals, but we would never have been able to carry enough to do us for even half the trip; or, we could have gone for instant freeze-dried meals, which would have been light, but very likely would have put us on the rough edge of nausea for most of the trip (not to mention filling our tents with noxious fumes on a regular basis); or, we could have opted for cornmeal mush and bannock, which, along with a few supplementary items, would have sustained us nutritionally, but been no fun to eat. And for sure, that diet would have denied us this kind of group banter around the details of preparation. Instead, we opted for the rather more elaborate eight-day menu, which hits the middle on taste, weight, palatability and, unless someone adds too many dried onions, gets a low average score on the flatus index as well.

Food preparation is one of the boons of self-contained travel such as this. When people say that food tastes better on camping trips, they're really saying that they were hungrier than they might otherwise have been, and that they enjoyed the labour of preparing it under Spartan conditions. Camp food tends to taste like its packages, but camp cooking brings people together in the shared simple pleasure of preparing, cooking, serving and cleaning up after a meal. You know where the food comes from, how it was cooked, who prepared it and where the uneaten portion goes, if there happens to be one, which is a rare event on this journey. Preparing our journey meals is an important social binder, a time to lift everyone's spirits and attentions back to the common cause.

On a one-to-one level, the simple act of making a cup of tea captures the same co-operative spirit. Robert Perkins, author of *Against Straight Lines*, one of the best books about canoe-tripping ever, tells a wonderfully instructive story about the social value of tea, which in many ways is representative of all food preparation on the trail. He and his partner fight, but learn to reconnect with a simple set of words, "Would you like some tea?" This works whether you've just finished tea or are in the middle of a portage or wherever. What is really meant in making the tea suggestion is: I'm so tired or grumpy or thirsty or whatever *you* think, I want to stop and reconnect with you.

By evening the wind has picked up. We must stay in our tents to stop them from blowing away. The parachute-cord guy-lines to windward are humming. Jake and Lorraine turn their Deer Creek dome side-on to the wind and open both windows to relieve pressure on their guy-lines. The idea works; the wind flows under the fly and in one window, equalizing the pressure inside and outside of the tent. The design of our dome does not allow this to happen. Our guys and wands bow and creak with the blow.

Norm and Cath's Timberline tent is not a dome and has been flapping madly all day. They have done their utmost to peg down, tie down and otherwise secure it to the ground. Front corner into the wind minimizes pressure on the poles and seams, but this exposes the non-waterproof fabric of the under-tent to the weather. For now, it's wind, not rain, that we have to worry about.

There is a lull around midnight, during which we gather up the plastic water jug, crackers, cheese, peanut butter, salami and GORP and congregate in the Timberline for a meal. Inside the tent, the wind sounds ferocious because it is worrying every loose bit of fabric it can find, but Cath, cool Cath, seems unbothered. Norm has out the duct tape and sewing kit–just in case.

When we return to our tent later, the sky is a swirling mixture of deepest orange and black, and against it, proudly silhouetted, stands the most magnificent caribou buck we have seen to date. The animal stands for many minutes, then disappears over the hill. It is a moment of total calm in what are otherwise busy, noisy and unsettled circumstances.

Plants and animals, living as and where they do, always seem so well adapted to the full range of conditions in their home territory. We seem to spend our lives trying to predict what will happen, to maintain some kind of consistency, but end up getting confused in the process. Peace and harmony with the environment are fathomable concepts when defined by a caribou–this caribou, or any of the others we have seen in the last couple of days. This flicker of calm, the image of one caribou against a fiery night sky, is a moment to be treasured, mostly because what the animal is doing cannot be counted, weighed, measured or charted. It is just there, and we just happened to be there to see it. Scientifically, it's a non-event. But this tiny moment in time has been good for my soul. Huxley would have enjoyed this too, poor bastard bear.

In the dying light, when Gail and I return to the tent, the wind is again building in intensity. The door zipper on the fly is pulling away from the material. Although it is a perfect job for Captain Duct Tape, our fix-all superhero, I remember a package of pre-glued rip-stop nylon strips in the first-aid kit and ply one of those to the task. We settle in and try to get used to the sounds of nylon under stress. We sleep.

The sound of a hollow canoe scaping on rocks jars my consciousness. In a panic, I rummage around for a raincoat, stick bare feet into cold boots and dive headlong out the door to see if the canoes are blowing away. It's not the canoes; it's a tent failure.

Norm is moving his canoe to form a windbreak for their fatiguing tent. Together we rock the canoe down and duck back inside. It feels good to be able to work toward a common end without having to say very much. The two of us seem to be able to sense each other and what needs to be done without stepping on each other's toes. The wind knocks me off balance. It's reminiscent of a night on the Elk River when two of us actually discussed the possibility of being rolled willy-nilly across the tundra inside our tent. We've done what we can.

I lie awake for the longest time, listening to the Timberline flap and chatter in the wind. Fitful sleep is cut by the clank of aluminum tent-poles. But it's the middle of the night! There is more rustling, some rocks are moved, the canoe is shifted again and the sounds stop.

"PSSST. Can I come in?"

It's Norm. Cathy has gone to bunk in with Jake and Lorraine. Their Timberline has disintegrated in the wind. A pole broke, which resulted in general failure of the whole suspension system of their tent. They've put canoes over the remains and will look at it in the morning.

14.
LUPIN

NEXT DAY, THE TENT IS REPAIRED WITH STITCHES, DUCT TAPE AND creative lashing on the poles, but the wind shows no sign of letting up. Another day ticks by. The average distance we will have to make per day to get to Bathurst Inlet is up to nearly 19 miles (30 kilometres). We play cards until it's too dark to see. Norm is the only one with a working watch, so we agree that he will wake us at 3:00 A.M. if conditions are right for travelling.

It seems like we've been asleep for just a couple of hours when Norm sticks his head in and rouses us.

"Jeez, Norm, it feels like about one o'clock in the morning, not three."

"Wakie, wakie, rise and shine. The GORP is ready, and the water's fine!"

"Okay, okay. We'll be ready in a couple of minutes."

Out on the water, it seems darker than it should be for 3:30, but we dig in and make miles while conditions allow. That's the beauty of the twenty-four-hour clock. The wind builds gradually as the sun rises in the sky and after three hours' paddling we pull in for a rest.

"Boy, I'm hungry," says Lorraine. "Is it time for breakfast, Norm?"

"Sure, why not?" he says with a smile.

We pull in to a cove just up the shore and step out on the beach where we'll heat up water on the stove for tea and hot chocolate, and mix up a batch of powdered milk for a quick granola breakfast.

"What time is it, Norm?" someone asks.

He looks for a lingering moment at his watch, as if he is having difficulty reading it, and says, finally, "Quarter to five."

"Quarter to five! You bastard! You got us up at one-thirty, not three-thirty! I told you it felt like I'd been asleep only for a couple of hours! I was right. We all had been asleep only for a couple of hours!"

"I just wanted to make sure we didn't miss some good paddling time," replies Norm, with a sadistic grin. "Besides, it's clear from the fine-looking hat-heads in front of me that none of you needs beauty sleep anyway, so quit whining!"

Visibility through a low morning mist is 2 miles (3 kilometres) maximum at 6:00 A.M. when we settle back into our canoes. We island-hop to the south shore of the lake, from where today's breeze is building, and then, little by little, make our way up the shore. Fog on the water makes points of land look farther away than they really are, giving the illusion of great speed in our canoes.

By mid-morning we have travelled to the point due west of the radio mast and our cache. We're at the widest point in the lake now, and our destination is an island in the middle. There is a 2-mile (3-kilometre) stretch of open water to span to reach another island midway between us and our destination. The wind is rising, but it's at our backs. It's a rough crossing on following waves. Partly for effect and partly because we're tired, we stop on the near island, tie up our masts for the first time in weeks, and set sail around the island and then straight to our cache and the first people we've seen in five weeks.

It's a triumphal-approach scene of the type common in Holly-wood re-creations of historic conquests by sea. Three brilliant yellow sails bulge before the wind. A Nova Scotia flag Gail has had hidden away in her personal pack is hoisted on a paddle lashed to the top of our mast. Welcoming flights of ringbills and arctic terns wheel overhead. All that's missing is a grand Wagnerian orchestral theme to usher us in. There is a man standing on the beach.

"By Jesus, boys, I didn't know what was happening." The fellow in red T-shirt, jeans and lambskin slippers scratches his head as he smiles and looks us up and down. "It looked like some kind of invasion happening right here at Lupin. It wasn't until you got close that I saw those green and yellow things as sails. They *were* sails! What the hell are you doing with sails? I was expecting a bunch of canoeists to show up here. But the pack says you were to be here nearly ten days ago now. What was the hold up? Did you run out of food? You better come in here, ladies, and have a cup of coffee while the guys get these boats secured. Come on in when you're done," he says, beckoning Cath, Lorraine and Gail to follow him through a vivid patch of pink fireweed to an assemblage of freshly stained shacks.

This is Steve Garrison, Contwoyto Lake radio operator, weather observer and our convivial host. He's an old hand at working in this outpost–"the only speck of human habitation in all the hundreds of miles between Yellowknife and Bathurst Inlet"–but he is not used to visitors, especially female ones.

The structure at the base of the tall, triangular radio towers is actually a conglomeration of three buildings, that, like many buildings in the North, show a history of development. The original building is a half-round Quonset hut about 20 feet (6 metres) in diameter and 50 feet (15.25 metres) long, to which has been added a lean-to on the back and a rectangular frame addition on the front, all clad in red asphalt and rolled shingle material of differing ages, and tacked on with long, crooked rows of big-headed shingle nails.

Behind a white-painted, insulated-steel front door, which one might find on any house in suburbia, is a vestibule containing a home-made bench and barbell set and a wall of high-powered rifles. Beyond that, through another door, is the radio room-cum-living-room where we meet Steve's partner, Peter Wolfe, who is still in his first year of work at the station. Lanky Peter is in his mid-twenties and already an ex-soldier. He pulls back long dark hair from his face, and lights a cigarette at the operator's table, in front of banks of radio equipment, weather instruments, stationery supplies, and an old, black manual typewriter with the duty log of radio transmissions and weather notes rolled part-way around the platen. Mid-sentence, he answers a call, courteously responding to a pilot's request for weather information. "That's the sked [scheduled flight] to Cambridge Bay checking in," he says, for our benefit, not Steve's.

From the operator's desk, the room opens to the right, revealing nondescript walls, functional carpet, a ping-pong table and two deep, thick easy chairs situated strategically in relation to speakers from an elaborate quadraphonic stereo system whose command-post sits at the opposite end of the chamber. Doors to Ron's ham-radio cubby and a storage area-cum-dark room flank the stereo. Three smallish windows and six bare hundred-watt bulbs reflect light off the white plywood ceiling and give the room a light and cheery feel.

A double door kitty-corner to the operator's table opens into the original Quonset hut, which is one-third kitchen and one-third pin-up-papered lounge, the final third split into side-by-side bed-rooms for two operators. What was the radio room off the kitchen, when the place was originally built, is now a workroom/bathroom combined and a room full of stand-up freezers.

"It ain't much, but we call it home," says Steve proudly as he shows us through. "Yeah, there are four of us who man this station. We all work for Pacific Western Airlines, and they're under contract with the federal government to provide weather information from here and to provide flight services for pilots in the area. We're four weeks on and four weeks off–not bad, eh? We're staggered, so that when the plane comes in here every two weeks with supplies from Yellowknife, somebody's always going out and somebody's always coming in. That way you always work with two different guys in a month . . . keeps us from driving each other crazy or wrecking the place. We're each on twelve hours and off twelve hours. There's lots of work to do, but we do find time to get a few other things done around here."

Then he adds, as if he's just remembered that we're guests in his home, "You'll stay for supper, won't you?"

"Peter," Steve yells from the kitchen, "are there any of those lobster tails left in that box in the back freezer?"

Lobster tails! We can't believe it. We were all pretty sure we'd died and gone to grocery heaven when Steve offered us glasses of cold, fresh, homogenized milk. But now lobster tails, cooked in an Amana Radar Range! This is bizarre.

"Those tails will go great with T-bone steaks. I know there's a box of those out back we've been trying to use up before the next big food order comes in. Do you like steak? Sorry, there's no wine. We're not allowed to bring booze up here."

Gail laughs out loud.

That night, with eight of us seated around the green-topped ping-pong table, four on each side of the net-less foul line, we dine in fine style. Our contribution to the meal is a Sigg bottle of brandy out of the cache; it's the least we can do.

"What's it like here in the winter?" Lorraine asks.

"Cold and dark. I spend a lot of time listening to music and talking to people around the world on my ham set over there in the corner," Steve says, pointing to a radio set-up that is as elaborate, if not more so, than the government installation.

"Do you ever go outside?"

"Only when we have to, to check the instruments. There's nothing to see out there."

Except for marvelling at the fact that we had been out for nearly five weeks, the radio men had few questions about what we were up to or why. Instead they tell us about life at Lupin; as the night wears on, and the Sigg gets lighter, Steve begins telling a tale of northern terror.

"There are lots of animals that go through here. We see tons of caribou in the spring and fall, foxes pretty well all year round, and wolves, but this spring we had a bear. We dump our garbage a ways out back, beside the esker where the Twin Otter lands. We pour gas on it from time to time and try to burn the smell out of it, but that doesn't always work. The dump sometimes attracts a passing grizzly.

"But this spring the bear wasn't content with just the dump. He was coming around the buildings. We were scared shitless to go outside to check readings in the Stevenson screen (that's that white louvered box on the post out front). It stayed around for a couple of days and we were trapped inside. I even went out and fired a couple of shots to try to scare it away, but it kept coming back. Finally, enough was enough.

"We drew straws to see who would shoot it. My partner and I went up on the roof one day with the .303 and waited. Sure enough, it came back and we had to shoot it. Shot it three times, and just to make sure it was dead, after a while we went down and chopped its head off with the axe. Not an easy job, you know, chopping off a bear's head. He took one swing and the axe didn't do anything. We had to get a big block of wood to put under the neck to get the axe to work. It was too heavy to move, so we poured gas on it and burned it. The foxes and wolves got the rest."

Our bear story was next. Before long Stella was out and we were playing and singing and dancing up a storm. Peter, who was still on duty, cocked an ear to the radio over the din of thumping feet on the hollow plywood floor. He strode over to the operator's table and picked up the microphone: "Radio Contwoyto, go ahead please."

It was the cross-Canada synoptic weather check. Six times a day a synoptic weather reading is taken from every weather observatory in the country. This time, Peter has been too busy dancing and carrying on to make the necessary readings, but he rattles off pressure, temperature, wind details, relative humidity and other pertinent information. He concludes with "Thank you and good night," and hangs up the mike.

"Nice work, Peter. You're becoming a pro !" says Steve, with a smile.

"Where *did* those weather readings come from?" I ask.

"I made them up," he says, with a grin, and adds, "we do our best to report the weather. We're one hundred percent accurate most of the time, but if there's a bear outside, or we happen to sleep through the hourly reading–we estimate. Normally we're not too far off. But if you happen to check the paper and see a big dip in the weather map at Contwoyto Lake, you'll know we had a party the night before."

After the radio call we say good night and fade out into the twilight to set up our tents. Steve directs us to a flat area on a small point well away from the weather station where we find level gravel tent sites but also scads of two-stroke-oil containers, half-chewed caribou legs, faded red five-gallon gas jugs, old Ski-Doos, broken komatiks and three bare wolf skeletons gleaming white in the dying light. Too much has happened in the last few hours; we're too tired and befuddled to find a more suitable place to set up, so we camp. The bellyfull of fried meat doesn't sit well, and I feel flushed from being in a heated space. Sleep takes a long time to take hold of my consciousness and even then it is fitful, with dreams that whirl with images of bears and axes, and wolves with their skins on.

15.
MINE

WE ARE AWAKENED BY THE SOUND OF A CESSNA 185 TAXIING UP TO the beach between us and the weather station. The young pilot jumps out, walks along the pontoon, picks up the painter rope, hops onto the shore, ties the plane to a full forty-five-gallon (200-litre) fuel drum sitting upright on the beach and disappears through the white door.

Jake has been inside, checking the cache, and comes down excitedly to the tent to let us know that Dwayne, the twenty-one-year-old pilot, will fly us to the mouth of the Burnside, if we're interested. With now just thirteen days left to go, the prospect of jumping over 45 miles (72 kilometres) of lake may be morally bankrupt but, practically, it is a superb option. Sure we're interested. How much?

"Three round trips, ninety miles each, at $1.30 a mile, with $0.17 per mile with an external load (the canoes) and a $3-per-gallon surcharge on thirty gallons of aviation fuel. That's $464–$77.33 each."

"We'll take it."

The problem is that Dwayne has no way of determining how much each canoe party weighs. He must take one canoe, its contents and two people on each round trip to the end of the lake. That seems a prodigious load for a four-seater, single-engined aircraft. Dwayne is left on the beach, lifting packs, trying to estimate their weight. He's quiet and maybe even a little apprehensive. And no wonder! Even on choppy water it takes a near-endless take-off run to get the plane into the air, and even then, the plane only waddles off the water with Dwayne in a concentrated hunch over the wheel, and Jake and Cathy waving madly from the windows. Norm and Lorraine will be next.

Left to wait, I can't help pondering these curious trappings of humanity. On the one hand is garrison "Lupin" and its occupants, who seem to derive nothing except fear from the landscape and fast cash from the experience. On the other is the squalor of a native spring hunting camp whose occupants have long since returned home, presumably, to "Dynasty," "Dallas" and Schneider's deep-fried chicken, the kind of settlement life we've seen elsewhere in the North. Then there's Dwayne, in his element, doing what he loves to do, even though, through talking with him, we learn that he seems not to care what's below him as long as there's air lifting the wings. And then there is us, just passing through on a northern quest, who, without second thought, dump the noble self-propelled quest for a quick-fix flight that is all part of the adventure. Strange that four such different northern realities have overlapped at this outpost. But are they so different?

Wally Maclean said that the North is the "land of the possible," where people exercise "the playing out of two great human dreams: Eldorado and Utopia." To some extent the idea of finding riches and or true happiness is a motivator for Ron and Stan, for Dwayne, and for us too. In light of twenty-five linear miles (40 kilometres) of portaging, we may be closer to living out the myth of Sisyphus. At the very least, this north is a place for all of us to live out some kind of dream.

The plane lands. Dwayne refuels while Gail and I pack in the last of the group's gear. We bid goodbye to Steve and Peter, taxi out and feel Dwayne wrestle the gravid plane off the water and into a painfully slow angle of climb. Caribou graze on the dusty green tundra below us. They are frightened by the noise. Fields of tundra polygons look more regular from the air; up to now we've only known these pentagonal and hexagonal frost-heave patterns as shallow ditches that must be negotiated with great care lest an ankle be turned, on portages. The mine site–final destination of the winter road–jars the landscape, even its infancy. Roads and a 5000-foot (1525-metre) runway can be seen from 20 miles (32 kilometres) away. How they'll get the gold out from here is anybody's guess.

There was no way we could have predicted at that time the enormity of what was going on here. On this 26-square-mile (68-square-kilometre) lease of land on Contwoyto Lake, 56 miles (90 kilometres) south of the Arctic Circle and 250 miles (400 kilometres) northeast of Yellowknife, would be one of North America's largest and highest-grade-gold production facilities. By 1988 the shaft of this mine would penetrate to nearly 3000 feet (915 metres), even below the 1775-foot (540-metre) extent of the permafrost. Hard-rock miners working in heated air pumped underground, using electric hydraulic drills, would have removed enough rock with gold concentrations of three-tenths of an ounce per ton for workers above ground, using conventional milling and chemical recovery methods, to smelt a million ounces of gold in the first eight years. On site would be a living and recreation complex for the mine employees that would rival the West Edmonton Mall for choice of foods, comfort and entertainment. Workers would spend two weeks at the mine site and two weeks off, hopping the thrice-weekly Boeing 727 shuttle from Edmonton to the mine site. Costs of production for an ounce of this precious metal would be $220 US, but would not include the energy cost for caribou that would have to take more circuitous routes in the area to avoid contact with the noise and disruption of the mining and milling process, nor would it include the long-term environmental cost of chemical leached onto the land surface by a 1.2-square-mile (3-square-kilometre) settling pond, or the other intangible local impacts at the Contwoyto Lake site.

How blind we are to development of this kind. We celebrate INCO's achievements in the North with tourist exhibits like the Big Nickel, and somehow know that all of that is going on, but we never stop long enough to consider why or whether this kind of development is necessary. We could not have flown in a twin Otter without nickel as an alloy in aircraft components. But somehow *gold* represents evil in a more pure form. It is the world's great symbol of value, and yet it is intrinsically worthless. Gold generates all kinds of economic activity and jobs, but for what?

When confronted with the tip of the development iceberg in a place like the heart of the NWT, somehow the idea of development is different. The change is more dramatic. We never saw the land around Sudbury before it was developed. But we can see the land at Contwoyto Lake. There's the difference. Historical photographs of how things were are not enough to move us to action. It seems to take personal connection to the land for the non-economic costs of development to sink in. That's one reason why wilderness travel is important. Maybe, just maybe, if more of us were confronted by sites under construction like the Lupine mine site–after developing some sense of connection to that piece of land–then maybe, just maybe, we'd think about buying inconsequential items derived from the industrial process. It's a gradual process, but it's a process of reduction and of rationalized consumption–thoughtful consumption–being aware of the contradictions that might, ultimately, bring development of our last remaining wild spaces into check. Or maybe economics is a fact of our lives. Maybe we should assign a value to caribou, clean air and undeveloped land. Maybe then we'll come to see that some projects are too expensive.

In thirty minutes, Dwayne drops the nose and lands beside a stone inukshuk at the outflow of Contwoyto Lake. We stand with the others as he takes off. He wheels around and dives down over us like a Zero on a South Pacific strafing run. Moving away from us with developing speed, suddenly he jerks the plane into a vertical climb and travels from 10 feet (3 metres) off the water to 200 or 300 feet (61 to 92 metres) in the air in a matter of seconds. He's glad to have an empty plane again. A waggle of wings and he's gone.

16.
INUKSHUK

DWAYNE HAS DUMPED US AT THE BASE OF THE WILLINGHAM HILLS. The 500-foot (153-metre) vertical cliffs here are the first real relief of this kind we have seen since leaving Yellowknife. Using my new binoculars, I scan the cliffs for patches of vermillion lichen, sure sign that eagles or falcons are nesting. There is nothing I can see, but it's certain that this is not sufficient reason to think there are no raptors in the area. I wish there was time to explore these magnificent faces.

The flight has brought with it a sense of renewal in our trip. In some ways it feels as if we have started our canoe trip now at the source of the Burnside River. The previous thirty days have been a warm-up for the main event.

The map says we're at 1460 feet (445 metres) above sea level. That is the distance we have got to slide to get to arctic tidewater. But it is impossible to deny the strong sense that we have worked hard to get here. We began at 1315 feet (400 metres) at Munn Lake and dropped to 1200 feet (306 metres) at Aylmer Lake. The height of land to Sussex Lake, headwaters of the Back River, represented a climb of 58 feet (18 metres). Over those gruelling days on the Back River, although most of the climb seemed to be uphill, we actually dropped to 1105 feet (337 metres) before climbing again, up the Icy River, to eventually make Contwoyto Lake at 1460 feet (445 metres).

This place is marked with a classical stone inukshuk. It is more like a cliché than any I've seen before. It stands about 5 feet (1.5 metres) tall and has protruding rock arms and a recognizable head. The first idea that comes to mind with the sight of this Inuit landscape marker is one of pilot Ted Allen's midnight tales about a pilot pal of his (probably Allen himself) who dropped down, whenever he got the chance, and built a hasty inukshuk "just to confuse those damn archaeologists."

Close inspection reveals that this structure has well-developed lichens growing between component rocks as well as on their upper and lower surfaces, which tell us that it has been here for some time, and therefore is probably authentic. But whatever this particular inukshuk signifies–maybe the Burnside River's rising–we're hot on the trail of a cache of books and instruments left near this spot by Captain John Franklin on his tortuous and death-ridden return from the arctic coast in 1821. Under order from the British Admiralty, Franklin set out from England in 1819 to map North America's unknown arctic seaboard. He descended the turbulent and supposedly unnavigable Coppermine River in birchbark canoes. It was on our Coppermine River journey some years before this one that Jake, Norm, Cathy and I really became aware of the immensity of what Franklin and his party had set out to do. Where we stopped at the village of Coppermine on Coronation Gulf, Franklin turned east and surveyed about 200 miles (320 kilometres) of intricate and ice-clogged shoreline. By the end of August, Franklin set out to make his way back to Fort Enterprise before winter, and that's when his troubles began in earnest. Jake has brought along an excerpt from Franklin's journal to spice up our journey. He tells us that, by mid-September of that year, fatigued by cold and hunger, Franklin was forced to leave behind his dipping needle, azimuth compass, magnet, thermometer and several books that they could no longer carry.

Having no idea what a 160-year-old cache might look like, we are satisfied to find nothing in two hours of looking. One of the puzzling things about this particular chapter in our history is how scholars and popular-history buffs alike call Franklin the greatest explorer in the British-American Arctic, when this man, in life and beyond, was responsible for the deaths of more people than any other northern rambler, ever.

In the weeks after the items were cached at the head of the Burnside River (named by Franklin after Matthew Burnside, a Royal Navy Surgeon), Franklin littered the tundra with human fox fodder. There was Junius, an Inuit translator and canoeist, who vanished on September 27; Mathew Pelonquin, a voyageur who, when he was unable to keep up, was left behind after a chilly crossing of Obstruction Rapids on the the Coppermine River; Registe Vaillant, another voyageur who collapsed hours after Pelonquin and was left behind; Ignace Perrault, voyageur, left behind on October 8; and five others–Antonio Fontano, Gabriel Beauparlant, Michel Tero-haute, Joseph Peltier and François Samandre–who all died in one way or another, getting Franklin back to safety. Four of five Englishman on the journey survived, but the cost in natives and voyageurs was steep: only three of thirteen lived to tell the tale of unspeakable hardship.

And the irony of all this is that it was only by slowly dispensing with the ways of the silver tea service and adopting native methods of clothing themselves, building shelter, hunting and navigating that Franklin and his officers survived at all on this journey.

My boyhood hero, Robert Falcon Scott, on his ill-fated slog to the South Pole, also studiously ignored native wisdom, to his detriment and ultimate demise. His victorious rival Roald Amundsen boldly proclaimed before the big race that "the English have loudly and openly told the world that skis and dogs are unusable in these regions and that fur clothes are rubbish. We will see–we will see." His comment was low on humility and high on accuracy.

The inukshuk gives me an inkling that the Inuit might have a different way of looking at landscape than those of us who follow the European tradition. To them it is "home," but instead of viewing any particular place as a set of co-ordinates on the earth grid, it occurs to me, they might, in fact, see their interaction with the land as a series of invisible tracks criss-crossing the barren lands, all leading to somewhere or something, and marked, from time to time with these stone statues.

I can't help thinking of sitting on the steps of the Hudson's Bay Store in Fort McPherson, on the Peel River, listening to Andrew Kuneesi–a Loucheaux Indian elder and former native guide on Corporal Dempster's RCMP Yukon patrol–relate to me, from memory, and in graphic detail, the entire route from Dawson City, Yukon, to Herschel Island in the Beaufort Sea. The only white person I know who can do anything like that is canoeist and map-maker Craig Macdonald, and he has spent most of his adult life interviewing Cree elders about their winter and summer travel routes across northern Quebec, Ontario and eastern Manitoba.

And then images come back of chatting with Inuk Mike Alerk in the hamlet of Baker Lake. He told me how he navigates to one of his favourite fishing spots in winter without map or compass. He said he heads toward the light part of the sky until he comes to a big rock. Beside that rock is a river that he follows until he gets to a big hill. He goes around that hill and goes straight until he gets to the lake. "I get lost sometimes," he told me with a big grin, "but not for too long."

Back on task, repacking food from the cache and reshuffling the rest of our gear for the final run to the ocean, I look again at the inukshuk and think of travelling north, up the coast of Baffin Island, in a freighter canoe, through dense fog, dodging ice-pans, with Inuit friend Theo Ikkummaq. Today this inukshuk is a symbol for that about the land which we have never learned to see.

Geographer Yi-fu Tuan has been more successful than I in understanding the Aivilik Inuit of Southhampton Island. He says: "To the Eskimo, space is not pictorial or boxed in, but something always in flux, creating its own dimensions moment by moment. He learns to orient himself with all senses alert. He has to during times in winter when sky and earth merge and appear made of the same substance. There is then 'no middle distance, no perspective, no outline, nothing that the eye can cling to except thousands of smokey plumes of snow running along the ground before the wind–a land without bottom or edge.' Under such conditions the

Eskimo cannot rely on the points of reference given by permanent landmarks: he must depend on the shifting relationships of snow contours, on the types of snow, wind, salt, air, and ice crack. The direction and smell of the wind is a guide, together with the feel of ice and snow under his feet. The invisible wind plays a large role in the life of the Aivilik Eskimos. His language includes at least twelve unrelated terms for various winds. He learns to orient himself by them. On horizonless days he lives in an acoustic-olfactory space."

Whatever the real significance of the Burnside inukshuk, it is a marker that speaks of an orienting system, derived of the landscape, and silently dignifies a very important turning-point in our journey. Finally, after five weeks and a lion's share of portaging and uphill struggle, we have reached the brink of the continent's north slope, the slide down to tidewater at Bathurst Inlet! We will drop 1460 feet (445 metres) in only 160 miles (256 kilometres). We will paddle to the sea. And, as a special bonus, there is water in the river!

The setting for this important moment in the journey is appropriately dramatic. For the first time, we have the feeling of being in a river valley. Up until now, especially in the days since Icy River, we have been on a plateau that dominates the east-central barren lands, but now, instead of waves and fog, shadowed hills foreshorten our vision to the east and to the west and force us to look north, forward and downriver.

For the first time on the trip we put on life-jackets because of their buoyancy in white water rather than just for extra warmth. Throw ropes, bailers and sponges are given more prominent positions in the canoes. And the packs, which up to now have been water-proofed, but mostly against splash and rain, are tightened with special care to ensure that their contents will stay dry in the event of a dump. River-paddling will present new challenges for working together, and it will take a few strokes to get the boats manoeuvring the way they should. Using first a pair of draw strokes with the paddles and then two pry strokes used in combination, Gail and I turn the canoe, first one way and then the other, each time ending up with the bow facing the inukshuk. The others have done the same. They're ready too, and we're off.

The long-awaited sight of river dropping out of sight is ours soon after embarking. Occasional flips of white water that jump above the greasy blue-water horizon are the only indication that the river doesn't just end here by dropping into the earth. Several more strokes and the sound of rushing water comes our way on the breeze. More strokes and we can feel the pull of the current.

Rivers with their contemplative flat sections and passages of heart-stopping, moving water have been my most influential teachers. The riparian world is a world that breeds in journeyers, humility, knowledge and enduring principles about the fragility and sanctity of all life. These lessons came later. It was the thrill of white water that first took me to back country rivers. The sheer joy and physical fun of crashing down a wild-water rapid can never be oversold.

"This is it," shouts Gail excitedly. "This is what we practised for all spring! Are we going to stop and take a look?"

"You bet!"

We step out on the shore and, with the others, make our way to a high point on the bank from which the entire length of the rapid can be seen. It's not much to be negotiated really, a narrow chute with a tongue of deep water in the middle that drops 3 or 4 feet (92 to 122 centimetres) in a couple of hundred yards. Where the faster water in the chute runs into the pool below, energy in the moving water is transformed into a regular series of standing waves that are decreasing in size. Rocks near the surface of the water always make some type of wave that can be seen, and although we see nothing to indicate there might be a lurking rock waiting to capsize our boats, Norm throws a rock into one questionable spot just to make sure. On either side of the tongue are frothy sheer zones between the river water flowing downstream and the back-eddy water circling upstream. These are potentially the biggest hazards of the chute. Should we decide to pull into one of the back eddies, crossing the sheer zone will make the canoe very unstable; a gunwale could easily be caught and pulled below the surface by the fast-flowing eddy current. It looks like a straightforward, down-the-middle shoot; perfect, for the first real rapid of the trip. I turn, and notice three people ensconced in the powdery green alder shrubs responding in unison to an urgent physiological need to relieve bladder pressure. Easy rapid or not, it's the first, and that is giving us all cause for concern.

Everything is stowed and ready to go. We have tied nothing to the canoe except our personal packs containing cameras, books and journals. Everything else will float, one hopes long enough for it to be rescued. The reason even the big food packs are not tied in has to do with a rescue manoeuvre we have all learned, called canoe-over-canoe, that requires an upset boat to be emptied midstream by dragging it upside-down in a T configuration over the centre of another canoe; this rescue is impossible with 90-pound (40-kilogram) food packs tied inside the swamped canoe. Our personal packs are small and likely to be missed floating half-submerged in a rapid, so, on the assumption that the canoe will never be lost (a catastrophic event that *has* happened several times on northern rivers), we loop their straps around thwarts in the canoe. Losing film or a journal at this point would be heart-breaking. We take no chances.

Gail is kneeling, her bottom on the bow seat. She takes a moment to unzip her personal pack and reroll the plastic bag inside.

"Ready?"

"Ready," she says, pushing off the shore with the duct-taped tip of her paddle. I can tell by the way she uses her arms to push, thereby protecting her lower back, that the portaging and late-night paddling marathons have taken their toll. She'll never complain–I know that now–but we'll still have to be careful. Now that the decision to run the rapid has been made, the actual act of shooting it is quiet and uncomplicated. We paddle out into the river, lining up our canoe just to the right of the middle of the V, and take easy strokes while the canoe picks up speed with the current. I stand to make a quick check that we're where we want to be. At this point we could back-paddle lightly to hold the canoe against the current, and by angling the boat one way or the other relative to the cur-rent, execute a "ferry" manoeuvre that would move us laterally to where we want to be on the river. No ferry necessary. We're on-line. We resist paddling too vigorously, because the last thing we want to do is drive the bow into the standing waves at the bottom–we've had enough of big waves! Slowly, inevitably, we are sucked over the brink by the current and take the long, smooth ride to the end of the black water, at which point the canoe jostles and bobs into the standing waves below. In less than a minute the ride is over. It's a dead-easy shoot, but it's our first and we feel great; everybody feels great. It's wonderful to be going downhill. "Owooooo!"

"Onward and downward!" is Norm's cry as we pick up a regular stroke again and continue downstream.

A second marked rapid gives way to a third, much longer and technically more difficult than either of the first two. This is "Belanger Rapids," named after Solomon Belanger–Belanger *le gros*, to differentiate him from J.B. Belanger *le rouge*–perhaps the hardiest of Franklin's voyageurs. On September 14, 1821, this rapid was the site of great drama and tragedy. Among other things, it is the place where John Franklin lost his journal. In an account reconstructed from the notes of his officers–Dr. Richardson, Mr. Back and Mr. Hood–Franklin tells the story of his baptism in Belanger Rapids. Jake has photocopied the pertinent section, and reads aloud:

"Having searched for a part where the current was most smooth, the canoe was placed in the water at the head of a rapid, and St. Germain [a Métis and Yellowknife Indian interpreter, and the only native member of the Franklin expedition to survive], Solomon Belanger, and I, embarked in order to cross. We went from the shore very well, but in mid-channel the canoe became difficult to manage under our burthen as the breeze was fresh. The current drove us to the edge of the rapid, when Belanger unfortunately applied his paddle to avert the apparent danger of being forced down it, and lost his balance. The canoe was overset in consequence in the middle of the rapid. We fortunately kept hold of it, until we touched a rock where the water did not reach higher than our waists; here we kept our footing notwithstanding the strength of the current, until the water was emptied out of the canoe. Belanger then held the canoe steady whilst St. Germain placed me in it, and afterwards embarked himself in a very dexterous manner. It was impossible, however, to embark Belanger, as the canoe would have been hurried down the rapid, the moment he should have raised his foot from the rock on which he stood. We were, therefore, compelled to leave him in this perilous situation."

By this point in the reading I am standing on the east shore of the river, about half-way down the first cascade of Belanger's rapid. The noise of water is crashing about in my head with the image of Belanger waist-deep and abandoned in the middle of this rapid. Even on a bright sunny day like this one, it must have been excruciatingly painful to be in such a predicament. It occurs to me as well that Belanger might not have been able to swim, adding another layer of fear to an already dreadful situation. We spend a moment trying to imagine exactly where the unfortunate Belanger might have been. Then, Jake continues:

"We [Franklin and St. Germain] had not gone twenty yards before the canoe, striking a sunken rock, went down. The place being shallow, we were again enabled to empty it, and the third attempt brought us to shore. In the meantime Belanger was suffering extremely, immersed to his middle in the centre of a rapid, the temperature of which was very little above the freezing point, and the upper part of his body covered with wet clothes, exposed in a temperature not much above zero, to a strong breeze. He called piteously for relief, and St. Germain on his return endeavoured to embark him, but in vain. . . . At length, when Belanger's strength seemed almost exhausted, the canoe reached him with a small cord belonging to one of the nets, and he was dragged perfectly senseless through the rapid. By the direction of Dr. Richardson, he was instantly stripped, and being rolled up in blankets, two men undressed themselves and went to bed with him; but it was some hours before he recovered his warmth and sensations."

Standing at the site of this near-disaster, years later, is a palpable encounter with history, of a kind I have had only on canoe trips. I recall a powerful and empathetic connection made to the tragic end of John Hornby, Harold Adlar, and nineteen-year-old Edgar Christian made while I was reading a published version of Christian's diary, standing in the remains of their death cabin in the Thelon River Game Sanctuary. Our experience on the river is immeasurably enlarged, enlivened and enriched by the reading. "Every country has its own hagiography of dead people and spooks lurking behind rocks and trees in their history," Margaret Atwood has written: there is no denying that the macabre, the uncomfortable aspects of the story are the most titillating because they vivify an intellectually appealing level of risk, but one that we have worked hard to avoid.

But I ponder Franklin and the others at this point in their journey. There's Franklin, standing all alone on the other bank, thirty-five years old, and divested of his captain's authority by a serendipitous dunking in the river. The landscape, it seems, is doing its utmost to teach him a lesson. He and the others began with a prodigious amount of gear: Hood detailed this at the outset of the expedition: "We gave guns, ammunition, tobacco, blankets and cloth, to the Indians. Our remaining stores were a few unserviceable guns, eight pistols, 24 broad daggers, two barrels of power, and balls for ⅔ of that quantity, nails and fastenings for a boat, some knives, chisels, files, axes, and a hand saw; six nets, with meshes of different sizes; some cloth, needles, looking glasses, blankets, and beads. Our provision was two barrels of flour, two cases of chocolate, two canisters of tea, 200 dried reindeer tongues, and portable soups, arrowroot, and dried moosemeat for ten days." And now, having run out of food, he is left wet, cold and hungry on the shore of the Burnside River, facing the prospect of getting to his destination without aid of a dipping needle, aximuth compass and the other instruments he has to leave behind. I suddenly get an image of the tools and books wrapped carefully in oilcloth and placed under a small cairn somewhere near the inukshuk to be digested over time by the landscape from which they were wrought. I am glad we found nothing. And this day I see bitter irony in the fact that, on the day when Franklin must baldly face the barren lands on their terms, not his, the river washes away his journal and all of the recorded readings he has made with those instruments.

But we can't help laughing at the characteristic British never-say-die, stiff-upper-lip resolve with which Franklin handles the loss. Jake reads on and we imagine what a mere mortal might have said under the circumstances.

"I had the misfortune [to] lose my port-folio [SHHEEEEE-IT!], containing my journal from Fort Enterprise, together with all the astronomical and meteorological observations made during the descent of the Copper-Mine River, and along the sea-coast [EVERY-THING! I LOST EVERYTHING!]. I was in the habit of carrying it strapped across my shoulders, but had taken it off on entering the canoe, to reduce the upper weight. The results of most of the observations for latitude and longitude had been registered in the sketch books, so that we preserved the requisites for the construction of the chart. [THANK GOODNESS FOR THAT!] The meteorological observations, not having been copied, were lost. [DAMN!] My companions, Dr. Richardson, Mr. Back, and Mr. Hood, had been so careful in noting every occurrence in their journals, that the loss of mine could fortunately be well supplied. These friends immediately offered me their documents, and every assistance in drawing up another narrative, of which kindness I availed myself at the earliest opportunity afterwards." [THANK THE NAVY THAT THOSE GUYS ARE STILL OBEYING ORDERS!]

Although not packed to provide balance to Franklin's unstated account of terror at the outflow of Contwoyto Lake, I have with me Farley Mowat's 1958 editing of Samuel Hearne's journal describing his experiences in the region fifty-two years earlier. Even through the gloss of editing, Hearne's experience of crossing the river at this point is dramatically different from Franklin's, probably because he is one white man travelling with dozens of Indians, in Indian style. It occurs to me, reading Hearne back-to-back with Franklin, that Hearne's journal may be one of the most literary of all written accounts of exploration.

In the previous three days, Hearne and his band of Indians had walked 80 miles (128 kilometres) on the ice of Cogead (Contwoyto) Lake, the part we had just overflown. I pick up the account there.

"On the 22nd [of June, 1770], we arrived at the banks of Congecathawhachaga (Burnside) River where we meet some Copper Indians who were assembled, according to their annual custom, to kill the deer which cross the river there.

"The ice now being broken, we were obliged to make use of our canoes for the first time, to ferry across this river; which would have proved very tedious had it not been for the kindness of the

Copper Indians who sent their own canoes to our assistance. For, though our number was nearly 150, we had only three canoes, and these could only carry two persons each, without baggage. In some cases the Northern Indians lash three or four canoes together to make a raft which will carry a much greater weight, but this can only be done when the water is quite smooth.

"Having arrived on the north side, we discovered that Maton-abbee [Hearne's Chippewyan guide] and several others of our company were acquainted with most of the Copper Indians whom we found there. The latter seemed highly pleased by our presence and assured us of their readiness to serve to the utmost. By the time we had our tents pitched, the strangers had provided a large quantity of dry meat and fat, by way of a feast."

Although Franklin and Dr. Richardson are in their thirties, midshipmen Back and Hood were twenty-four. Hearne was twenty-five. It is fantastic that men of such few years have become icons in northern history. But, nevertheless, it is being able to ground their tales in the landscape of which they speak and in our experiences with the same weather and lakes and rivers that elevates the simple act of scouting Belanger Rapids into a meaningful encounter with a part of our history that leaves to ponder how two British sailers – Franklin and Hearne – could have had such different experiences at the same geographical location.

Hearne is there in June, Franklin in September; they both run into cold weather and ice. They are both walking, and have been for some time and for many miles. But, the operating principles governing Franklin's travel are those of the Admiralty; Hearne is travelling light, the native way. Although Franklin seems to be learning slowly (and painfully) that there are other ways of navigating, he is locked to the earth grid by his need to plot latitude and longitude. Hearne, however, with his native guide Matonabbee, is locked directly to the earth by the lore and travelling mythology of his Indian host. Hearne is a guest of people in their homeland. Franklin is a stranger in unknown country.

17.
WOLVERINE

RAPIDS BELOW BELANGER RUN INTO EACH OTHER AND PROVIDE AN exhilarating experience in which to celebrate teamwork, partnership and the joy of shared physical and mental exertion. At times Gail and I fight each other, one wanting to go one way, the other with a different idea, both able to manipulate the orientation of the canoe, and both suffering the splashing cold consequences of straying from the driest route. But at the best of times, nothing is said; we anticipate each other's moves and flow with a purpose through haystacks, V's, rip currents, around rocks, and invariably, for a rest, into back eddies where the downstream force of the main current and the equally strong upstream push of the back eddy spins the canoe with a force and feeling that rival the very best of combination snow skiing, banked corners on Highway 401 and the Wild Mouse roller coaster at the Canadian National Exhibition!

We pause for a moment in an eddy, to catch our breath, and look up to the steep cream-clay banks that now flank the river, edged, as they are, by intermittent layers of undulating green hills and endless peacock blue. The river has taken hold of our perceptions and our experiences, because it is only at times like this, when we can divert attention from the whitewater obstacles, that we are able to give this changing colourscape the attention it deserves.

Back in the river, we find ourselves in an unmarked set of rapids on a long sweeping curve in the river. There could be unspeakable danger ahead, so we quickly pull over and walk down for a look. There are two large rocks at the bottom with canoe-eating souse-holes attached, but there seems to be a workable route around them if we stay first to the left of the river, until the corner, and then ferry right across to the opposite shore. Passing the souse-holes at water level reveals waves 6 feet (2 metres) high. It makes me think that, if the water were much higher, parts of this river would be impassable in canoes.

Fifteen miles (24 kilometres) down from Contwoyto Lake, the Burnside opens into a 20-mile-long (32-kilometre-long) widening marked "Kathawachaga Lake" on the map. Rapid after rapid, we hoot and ride our way toward it, arriving much sooner than expected. Predictably, the wind is blowing right in our faces, so before heading out into those waves, and almost as an afterthought, we pull in to the shore to bail excess water from our canoes. A brown animal hunkers up the bouldery shore.

"Hey, look at that," says Jake between bailer loads. "Will you look at that! It's a wolverine!"

What a lucky sighting! This is the animal that will move 20 miles (32 kilometres) in a day of foraging. The home range of single animals can be 500 square miles (1300 square kilometres), or more. It marks its territory by wiping its anal scent glands on prominent features and, like bears, scarring plants and the ground with its massive claws.

We scramble as quietly as possible to get out of the canoes. Walking toward this animal is a strange sensation. It appears to be totally unfazed by our presence. It appears to be the size of a big male golden retriever, but in actual fact most of what we're looking at is a thick coat of underfur and sable guard hairs that give the animal a thicker and stronger impression. A 35-pound (16-kilogram) wolverine can bring down an adult caribou. Its feet look especially menacing and disproportionately large. No-nonsense yellow claws catch the sunlight. It is a glistening chocolate brown colour, with blond-ish highlights. Its head is rounded, more like a cat's than a dog's, with little peaked ears visible from the distance. Its eyes are black and sparkling. There may even be a swagger in its step created by the curving swing its forelegs make in the recovery phase of its natural gait.

There is nothing but diminishing space between that animal and me. It is as if we are on either end of a balance beam, walking toward the centre. The first one to break concentration must step down. My eyes etch a portrait of an unbothered animal strolling along the shore of a river, but my brain cries out, "That animal is a known killer!"

I look down, for only a second, and lose the game. The animal is gone. Vanished, as if into thin air. Where this Muppet-like creature had been is now nothing more than a beach of rounded pink and grey granite boulders. To the right, a rising tundra plane with no sign of movement. To the left, the sinewy waters of the Burnside. An animal in that water would be obvious by its wake. It's gone. Simply gone. We walk to the place where we last saw it walking and examine the boulders for any sign of a den or hiding place. Nothing.

We return to the canoes. In the excitement my paddle has fallen into the water and drifted to the other shore. Beside the paddle, someone points out, another wolverine is walking!

"Could that be the same animal?"

"How could it be? We have been sitting here the whole time and would have seen it swim across the river."

"Maybe they can hold their breath and swim underwater?"

"Maybe, they're supposed to be known for their elusive nature. And they're supposed to have dens in rocks. Maybe that one has tunnelled under the river with those big feet; for handy access to the other side!"

"There are strange things done in the land of the midnight sun," Gail begins, in the eeriest tone she can muster.

What a sighting!

This encounter with the largest member of the weasel family-the one called "the animal of superlatives" because its character-istics are the strongest, longest and most powerful of its kind-reminds me how lucky we are to encounter such animals on their home ranges. The wolves, the caribou, the birds, and even the little Arctic ground squirrels that have chirped their characteristic "Sic-Sic" at us from sandy burrows in the riverbank have all helped us to see that this so-called barren land is full of dynamism, of the rhythm of life, and death, all shaped, informed and bound together by the landscape.

In a time when Marlin Perkins and Walt Disney and the glossy nature magazines would have us believe that nature is clean, simple and available for human recreation, this journey has given us animal experiences that involve us fully with the lives of the animals and not just with the sanitized, anthropomorphized versions of nature presented by the mass media.

In the wind, we're back to the old grind, but now the river valley surrounds us, instead of the vast flat expanses of the Contwoyto Plateau. We paddle without thinking, each of us searching the shore for more wildlife. The wolverine has renewed our interest in the landscape.

For a while, at least, the fact that we are making only minuscule progress against the wind doesn't seem to matter. But enough is enough, it's time for lunch.

Back on the water, with bellies full of crackers, peanut butter, jam and slabs of fresh cheese and dried sausage from the cache, we slog against the wind for another two hours, making less than a mile, and call it quits. On solid ground again, with recharged packs and a sense that the land's harshest lessons are behind us, we spread out in ones and twos to explore the sun-filled valley.

For the first time in a long while, Gail and I walk for hours, exploring a stream-bed. Picking our way through the rocks, we wonder now and then what's to come in our lives. The journey-within-a-journey quietly celebrates the growing bond between us. The edges of our nature as individuals have been blurred and meshed into a zone of shared adversity, common adventure and trust. More often than not, now, we enter the experiences of this journey through that zone that includes the other. There is still private time and individual experience, but most often we are drawn to share the never-ending series of surprises that is this incredible journey.

A family of rock ptarmigan scurries through the undergrowth. We are drawn to the flurry of feathers and sound that is one of the adults leading us away from the brood. It stops beside a rock, right out in the open. We approach slowly, until we are standing right over the crouching bird. Blink and it disappears into the mixture of greens and browns. Look again, and focus for that little band of red and white over its eye, the only part of the bird's outer surface that is not perfectly camouflaged. We wonder if the bird thinks we can't see it, and walk away and sit on the side of the hill. In several minutes, the young ptarmigan fall in behind the invincible adult and continue on their procession, as if we weren't there at all.

Gail tells me of another family of ptarmigan she followed on another walk, days earlier. She brings up her hands to demonstrate just how small the chicks were, and I can't help noticing her brown fingers with chipped and dirty fingernails. Her face is weather-creased and radiantly tanned. As a result of our paddling and walking against the wind, streaks of salt have dusted the corners of her laughing eyes. Her hair is a tangle under the brim of her battered green felt crusher, loose ends dancing around her mouth and ears. She had gone to an alder thicket with the express intent of finding birds of some kind, and then she had discovered the ptarmigan. She had followed the family for the better part of an hour, she says, and that was a first for her. Never before had she actually gone out looking for something in nature. And never before had she taken such joy in just watching and following birds.

"I don't feel so much like a stranger here anymore," she says with easy confidence. "I had no idea that there would be so much to see up here. And I had no idea I would ever begin to feel comfortable. Everything here is so connected to everything else, and I'm beginning to feel a part of it all."

"That's cause for celebration!"

We arrive back at camp to find Jake studying a black dot centred on a rising slope across the bay on which we're camped.

"I've been watching the dot for an hour now," he says. "I can't tell for sure if it's moving. If it is, it's a musk-ox."

We all take turns with the binoculars, studying the dot, and agree that it looks more like a rock than a musk-ox.

Over steaming bowlfuls of Lipton's stroganoff laced with reconstituted chunks of Lorraine's fiery, homemade barbequed beef jerky, Norm and Cathy ask for rental accommodation because they're afraid that their taped-and-sewn tent won't withstand tonight's wind. We're quick to invite them in, although secretly four of us have a quick finger raffle to see who will get Norman, the sleeping foghorn. Norm catches on good-naturedly and calls back, "With the amount of spices on this jerky we could all be outside blowing out the pipes most of the night, so I wouldn't worry about the snoring if I were you."

Reaching for another shot of East Indian Hot Sauce (the ultimate secret to palatable food on canoe trips), Jake puts down his bowl and again picks up the binoculars.

"I thought that rock was moving. It *is* a musk-ox!"

I marvel at Jake and his ability to see. On the Coppermine, we would always be looking, trying to outdo one another with the observations of the minutiae of nature drifting by. Jake always won, because he was so attuned to what was going on around him. He, like me, looked for what was there, but he also, I think, had taught himself to look for what wasn't there, and patterns of shape and movement. Ptarmigan running on a hillside, for example, would cause Jake to look up, and invariably he would pick out a soaring golden eagle or a gyrfalcon that had given the ground birds a start.

In this case, he has been sitting at the fire, stirring a pot, but instead of drifting back into his own head, or focusing on the immediate surroundings in the kitchen area, his eyes are prowling the surrounding countryside. He has learned to take joy in the smallest observations, whether it is a fish jumping across the lake, a fight between sic-sics on the beach, a shooting star, a miniature flower on moss beside the fire, a nearly invisible crimson fruiting body on a lichen or a black dot that turns out to be a musk-ox. One of Jake's great gifts is his insatiable curiosity. The result is not simple knowledge about the world, but *understanding*.

"You game for a skulk?" he asks with a grin.

"Sure thing."

We slurp down the rest of the meal, grab cameras and charge off to have a look. It take us an hour or more to get around the bottom of the bay and into proximity of the magnificent animal, but all the while we are energized and driven by frequent stops to have a look through binoculars.

From a distance the animal gives an impression of being bigger than it is. At 200 yards (180 metres), we can see from horns that are joined into a boney "boss" on the top of the head that this is a lone bull, but even at that, the bigger of the sexes, this animal is still only the size of a smallish Holstein heifer. it is the long shaggy hair that gives the impression of grandeur and size. We circle around to windward, to give the animal every chance to know what and who we are, and see that when the wind mats the hair down, the animal's physique is rather more delicate than it first appeared. Nevertheless, the recurved scimitar horns look menacing, and like something *not* to be trifled with.

We watch as the animal grazes and slowly plods along through the heath, clods of qiviut, its dense underfur, catching, from time to time, on branches of alder and dwarf willow. Its legs are light brown, almost white, and give the impression of socks or leggings. Its long guard hairs form a curtain from which the legs protrude. The hump behind the head looks sun-bleached. Everything, except the animal's lips and nostrils, is furred, well furred. But the overall impression, at least from a distance, is comical. "Looks like two guys and a blanket on the way home from a Hallowe'en party," says Jake wryly.

We separate and crawl through the cold wet tussocks to get closer to the animal. Jake has his camera and a 300-millimetre lens before him, but most of the time he just watches the animal, no doubt soaking up every detail. It is a peaceful and satisfying encounter. At length the musk-ox ambles up the valley and disappears over a clay terrace. We stand and begin the long walk back to camp.

There is something about a fenceless encounter with a wild animal that is spiritually instructive and meaningful. We have felt it this day, just as I did with a rather more intense encounter with a bull musk-ox in the Thelon River valley.

On that occasion we saw several animals not far off the left bank of the river. While three of that canoe trip stumbled up the steep till bank and disappeared over the rise, I carried on down the shore, thinking there might be something different to see there. I heard resulting noises atop the bank, but saw nothing. Suddenly a bull vaulted over the edge on its way to the river. I was right in the way. Front legs straight out, hind legs bent, broad hooves back-pedalling madly in the gravel, the animal came to a halt not 30 feet (9 metres) away.

It was the strangest sensation. I looked at the animal. We made eye contact. It was just as afraid as me! I *knew* that. I could see fear in its eyes. But what could I possibly know about musk-oxen feelings as expressed through their eyes? Nothing. Everything. We are both animals. Both scared. Both cornered. It's not a matter of who knows what or how. We are communicating with our eyes.

I took a peek through the lens. It's a skyless image, of wet nostrils, mouth, nose, horns and liquid bovine eyes, one of which blinks when a fly lands near. I bowed and backed away slowly, this time keeping eye contact with the beast. With equal deference, the animal stepped slowly forward on a curving path toward the river.

Two hours later Jake and I straggle back to camp. The rest of the crew has gone to bed.

The following morning, we awake to south-wind smoke that reduces the sun to a luminous red disk in the daytime sky. It's a haunting scene that leaves us speculating from where it might have come. Fires from lightning are common in the Arctic–there are even reports of caribou who have been killed by lightning–but this smoke has divested itself of blackness and odour, and leaves us guessing that it has come from far afield, perhaps below Great Slave Lake or even as far south as northern Saskatchewan.

After we have packed up and got back onto the water, ever conscious of dwindling time, the smoke spawns a realization that these long canoe journeys across the country have created a strong sense of the geography of the watersheds in which we've paddled but also of the country as a whole. Northern Saskatchewan is sunshine, tail winds and pelicans on the Churchill River; forest fires and fast water on the Fond-du-Lac. What the smoke seems to indicate is that all these separate and distinct experiences on the land have coalesced in our minds, creating a strong sense of the spatial relationships between and among the places where we have paddled. Now, as I turn and look at the sun in the southeast, I see images of caribou on Contwoyto Lake, of the Icy River, of the majesty and spiritual stillness of Aylmer Lake, and of our bear rooting out some unsuspecting sic-sic on the highlands west of Margaret Lake. Open spaces and nameless lakes have become treasured places and bright waters in my imagination. These images are blending, day by day, to an understanding of geographic relationships, a mental map, that is beginning to eclipse any lingering feelings of alienation.

But more than that, this idea of map in one's imagination is an integrative phenomenon built of experience on the land itself that side-steps the intellectual dualism that exists in some other part of people's brains between maps and landscape, between people and place. Science and the urge to collect knowledge has cooked up hard-edged dichotomies–mind/body, subject/object, sky/water– that, ultimately, get in the way of understanding the world in which we live.

The map in my head that plots matters of the spirit and of the heart, in addition to all the facts, figures and observations that still get teased from the whole, provides a sense of belonging here in the barrens. This mental map features the substantial and ephemeral feelings and sensations of being on the land, here or there. As long as memory allows, this map can never be studied, viewed or explored without those sensory and personal connections to the landscape.

Late that afternoon, the shadowy figures of several thousand caribou line the ridge to the west of Kathawachaga Lake–moving, always moving, to the south. Their purpose in coming north is done. No time for us to stop; our season is running short too, but so is our need to run up to these animals and quantify their existence or justify it with our cameras. Today, we share this landscape with these animals. We travel one way. They travel the other. We both use the river corridor. Their presence is with the rock and with the lake and with us, as ours is with them. Finally, that is enough.

18.
LINK TO THE STARS

SEVERAL MILES DOWNSTREAM, WE COME TO A LONG POINT IN Kathawachaga Lake that is marked with a circle containing a cross–an "Astronomical Monument," the map legend says. It's aroused our curiosity, so we pull up to the promontory, tie up our canoes and scale the rock, where we find nothing, absolutely nothing, except the lichens, hare droppings, saxifrage and other plants that we have come to expect in places that look like this. We look skyward, half expecting to see a satellite or a spaceship or something to give us a clue about the significance of the map designation. Nothing.

"Maybe it's a recognizable place on the earth that can be picked up on satellite imagery," suggests someone.

"Maybe it's the site of a classified UFO landing?"

"Maybe it's the place where Franklin lost a few more of his instruments?"

It was not until long after the trip that I learned from geodetic surveyor Bill Brooks, with Energy, Mines and Resources Canada, that this was one of a series of horizontal reference points hastily established during the Second World War by sighting stars in the four quadrants of the sky. These astro points were then used in pairs to compute distances on the ground that were used in turn to calibrate maps made from air photos of uncertain scale. The maps were used by pilots ferrying bombers across the North to points in Russia and Europe. At that time there weren't reliable maps of the North. Dominion land surveyors did a real blitz, said Brooks, over a couple of summers to provide a position astronomically for the map-makers. These astro points provided the ground control to make the maps from the available aerial photographs shot by the airforce. Sometimes the surveyor would put a tablet in the rock or build a small monument to mark the spot from which they worked, but this didn't always happen. Brooks also noted that the sixtieth parallel, the one that defines the southern border of the Northwest Territories, existed for many years on paper in definition, but it was only in the 1950s that they actually went out on the ground and set markers, using the same astronomical techniques that put Kathawachaga Lake's exact position on a map for the first time. A subsequent letter from the department of Energy, Mines and Resources revealed that this exact spot was called Control Point #7, and was established on August 13, 1947. In a report filed by the surveyor, G. Martens, it says: "This astronomic control point is located in unmapped territory about 100 miles southwesterly from Bathurst Inlet Post and is situated on the northern shore of a narrows between two lakes which are probably part of the Burnside River system. The site of the observing station is on the beach below a plateau rising 150 feet from the water level. The surrounding country is quite hilly. The station mark is a bronze Geodetic Survey reference tablet set in a rock cairn." If it was still there–we missed it!

Back in the canoes, we stroke along, unconscious of repetition and physical monotony, our bodies taking their cues from the ebbing and surging motion of the boat. We paddle now from the centre of our bodies. We are an extension of the canoe and it of us. Adjustments are made without thought, without word. My eyes concentrate on a point on the far end of the lake. Without passing information through my conscious mind, I convey the line of our course to muscles that steer the boat. Teamwork, harmony and direction are bound up in our duality, moving through space and time. Motion is a unified blend of body, mind and spirit. Paddling, today, is self-propelled meditation–rhythmic, purposeful and liberating.

Perhaps Wally Maclean built this invisible astronomical monument. He'd be old enough. For him, riding *The Muskeg Express* from Winnipeg to Fort Churchill was a form of meditation, rhythmic, purposeful and liberating. Surveying is a science of the land. Glenn Gould said that Maclean parlayed surveying into a literary tool. Maclean could read the signs of the land and find in the most minute measurement a suggestion of the infinite. A suggestion of the infinite. Stroke, stroke, stroke.

Glenn Gould also had a grasp of the infinite, but he was a musician, not a surveyor.

A flight of oldsquaw duck zooms in from the right and crosses our bow, taking with them my concentration. They drop off the background of sky and disappear against the landscape. Gail shifts a little in the bow seat without missing a beat.

Gould, then, must himself have come to the idea of north through his music, just as Maclean had internalized the North through the lens of his surveyor's transit. The combination of these two men's conceptions of north was what made the program so powerful. Stroke, stroke, stroke.

Our method of travel, even as we make our way, slowly, rhythmically, along the north shore of Kathawachaga Lake, is more like that of a surveyor than it is of a musician. It is our business, if only to stay on track and stay alive, to read the signs of this land. But how we make sense of these signs is mostly a matter of choice. We could, if we so choose, try to understand the land through a series of co-ordinates, or through an array of physical principles–biological, geological, ecological–through art as did the Group of Seven, or, as Glenn Gould did, through music.

My paddle exits the water roughly and catches the surface, sending a rainbow burst of droplets onto Gail's back. She turns and smiles, and we continue.

Stroke, stroke, stroke, stroke. But it was Gould, the musician, who happened to team up with Maclean, the surveyor. This is such an odd combination of talents and interests.

We pass through a school of giant lake trout surfacing lazily in the lake, their dorsal fins cutting the surface like those of a school of miniature freshwater sharks. One fish near the canoe is startled and leaves a serrated ripple on the surface of the water as it wiggles to build speed.

Music does make sense as a way to understand the land. Music is rhythm, music is waves, music is order. Music is the harmony of heaven and earth.

A pale white full moon has arisen on the eastern horizon. Today is day thirty-three on our journey. The moon was waxing full at this time. Lunar rhythm. When this moon wanes to nothing, our trip will be over.

Thirty-two strokes per minute we continue. One octave of strokes every fifteen seconds. The recovery of our paddle tips over the water is a sine-wave pattern I'd never noticed before: first close to the canoe as the power phase of the stroke is completed and then swung out, like a pendulum, and back to the gunwale to begin again.

"Hark, the Herald Angels sing," their singing is the link between earthly chaos and godly order. Music is number, and number is the fundamental principle from which the whole objective world proceeds; it is origin of all things and the underlying harmony of the universe.

"Glory to the newborn king . . ." This carol is going to be going through my head the next couple of days. That's what always happens when you're paddling. Music is order. Music is number.

What are the numbers that inform this trip? One. One is primordial unity, the beginning, the centre, the essence, and it is all around this place we are in, excluding no rock, no drop of water, no being. One is God, the great spirit, omnipotent–the land, the water, the animals, the plants. Stroke, stroke, stroke.

Two. Two is duality, the root of the canoe partnership; mutuality, dependence, otherness, balance, stability, ying and yang, opposites, polarity. As One represents space or area, Two signifies length, the beginning and the end.

Three. Three canoes, three pairs of people; atmosphere,

biosphere, hydrosphere; the triad is the whole in as much as it is beginning, middle and end; Three is the phases of the moon, birth, life, death; body, soul and spirit.

Four winds, four directions, four seasons. Four is completion. Five. Stroke, stroke, stroke. Six paddlers. Seven. All good canoeists go to heaven. Huh? Eight. Eight is paradise regained, regeneration, perfect rhythm.

A lone arctic loon, its head bowed, overtakes us from the rear, passes through the space directly above our boats, curves ahead into the distance and disappears into the river valley. We follow Mookwa.

This *has* to be the life. To be out here in the sunshine, with good friends, on calm water, on a river flowing to the sea, with no one around in a world filled with caribou and musk-oxen and wolves and birds and flowers and wolverines, with nothing to do but sit and think to the rhythm of self-propelled motion. There's nothing like it.

So, if there is music to this journey, it must be derived of the numbers One, Two, Three, Four, Six and Eight. This is so contrived, it's silly. But puzzling it through is the ultimate luxury. There is nowhere else on earth right now better suited to such a task. Stroke, stroke, stroke.

Gail and I have adopted a scheme, common to paddlers, whereby when one person gets tired of paddling on one side, all that person has to do is call "Hut," and both paddlers switch sides. She looks quite comfortable up there. Normally, when her back is really bad, she'll be changing position about every five strokes. I'm ready for a switch, but maybe Gail should decide when she needs a break.

Music in six/eight time can accommodate all of those numbers. It's duple time with a one-two-three, one-two-three beat underlying a one-two, one-two rhythm that one might hear in any small-town parade. When Johnny comes marching home again, hurrah, hurrah; when Johnny comes marching home again, hurrah, hurrah. I think that's a song in six/eight time. It matches beautifully with the paddling.

Other songs in six/eight time fit too. Hey, even that famous

Canadien voyageur song "En Roulent, Ma Boule Roulent." Come to think of it "Row, Row, Row, Your Boat" is written in six/eight time. It's great travelling music, full of beat and infused with the feeling of motion. Stroke, stroke, stroke.

We get up, we travel, we go to sleep. We get up, we travel, we go to sleep. Who's to say that there isn't rhythm to our journey? Who's to say that we haven't worked our way into snychrony with the land? That's it. That's it! This, at least at some level, is a musical journey, a journey in six/eight time!

The six/eight aspect of this idea may be hare-brained, but it does make some sense. The numerology ideas could be contrived, I dare say, to justify any time signature, but there's an old Highland piper around home who always says that soldiers can march all day to music written in six/eight time. I've even heard of a long-distance swimmer, who is also a musician, who claims she swims her daily lengths in six/eight time. Stroke, stroke, stroke.

Music from the land. What an intriguing notion! A journey in six/eight time whose travellers learn to listen to the music of the land, the music that allows them to see and to feel the spiritual elements of the experience. The barrier to this way of thinking for those of us who live in cities, where the natural world is neatly packed and marketed in tidy, uncomplicated chunks, is the fact that we have lost touch with the fundamental experience of what it is like to live a life shaped by the landscape itself. If this canoe journey has done nothing else, so far, it has brought us into tune with the cycles of the earth. Stroke, stroke, stroke.

My own ancestors, the Celts, and the Druids, considered the earth a living, breathing being. They believed that there were sacred places on the landscape where heaven, earth and the underworld, all came together. It was at these places they built megalithic stone circles, as at Stonehenge, where they sang and chanted their pagan celebrations of their kinship with the earth. They knew about music and the power of the natural world. "Hut."

How wrong we Christians have been in denigrating the God-centred, earth-bound religions of first peoples around the globe. Our terms for such ritualistic worshippers all have such a pejorative ring to them. There is great wisdom in such teaching, and more than we might think. "Heathen" means simply the one who lives life on the heath. "Pagan" means the one who lives in the country. And "savage" comes from the French verb *savoir*, which means to know deeply. We need more savages.

"Do you want to take a break?" asks Gail.

"Sure, let's raft up with the others."

19.
BIRD ISLAND

WE DUCKED OUT OF THE WIND AND INTO THE PROTECTION OF THE Peacock Hills at the outflow of Kathawachaga Lake and drifted happily through the narrows. But upon turning north out of the narrows, we again faced a stiff breeze that forced us to dig deep and to take short rests every half-hour. One of those rests was on a most remarkable island within this widening of the river.

There is a rich and penetrating cacophony of birdsong, which rises to a crescendo as we eddy in behind a trailing sandbar. Within seconds, a flight of angry ring-billed gulls swoop down and open the bomb doors at the strategically correct moment. It's a fetid mixture of fish and dead meat. Bombs spent, they wheel and attack again, this time snatching Gail's wool toque and dropping it in the water. It is all we can do to find twigs to stick in the necks of our jacket that stick up a foot or so above the tops of our heads. This keeps those beaks from hitting our heads until we can run along the beach and out of range.

On the island itself is a profusion of wildflowers growing on the thick coating of nitrogen-rich bird droppings. In every available niche on the entire island, there are nesting birds. Terns, plovers, sandpipers, gulls, redpolls, phalaropes, even a couple of families of mergansers nesting under the dwarf birches at the upstream end of the island. In the centre of the island is a variety of caribou antlers. Either they were stranded here one spring by high water or we're standing on a pretty substantial archaeological site.

Perhaps the birds are here because the island protects them from foxes, and other egg-pillaging wanderers. What we have happened on is a compact little interactive community, filled in every way with colour and life and sound.

A dark shape moves through the edge of my vision. I see the tail of a loon slide silently into the water. Moving over quickly to investigate, without taking eyes off the exact spot where the bird was on the land, I walk, trying hard not to step on other nests. Ah-ha! There, sitting on a volcano-shaped mound of dried yellow grasses, are two brown-mottled green eggs, the size of medium chicken eggs. Out on the water, saying nothing is Mookwa, a yellow-billed loon. This is no time to have these eggs uncovered. They need incubation, and with adults off the nest, they're susceptible to raiding of every kind. Gulls, ravens, other birds, or, today, the great foot of a two-legged paddler could snuff the germ of life. Just by being here, we are invaders in this place. Back to the boats.

Every North American culture, including our own, has mythologized the loon in one way or another. The Inuit have a legend about how, at the beginning of time, loons and ravens were both white. One day loon and raven got together, gathered sticks from the beach and built a fire to make charcoal. That day, they would tattoo each other with charcoal dust to make beautiful patterns for all the world to see. First, raven was the artist. Loon stood still for a very long time while raven painted loon's head black, leaving a stunning necklace of white and a white belly. On loon's sides raven worked carefully around white dots and then made a delicate black-and-white checkerboard across loon's wings and back. Loon sat very still.

By the time it was raven's turn to be tattooed, she couldn't sit still for a moment. Loon began trying to do the same for raven by creating elaborate patterns of black soot on raven's beautiful white feathers. Raven moved to scratch under her wing, and loon's bill smeared black across raven's tail. Not to worry, said loon, I can work around that and you will still be the envy of all the other birds. But raven couldn't stand still. She moved and moved again. Loon smeared and smeared again until, in a fit of frustration, loon picked up all the charcoal dust she could on her powerful swimming wings and flung it over raven who was transformed instantly into the blackest of all birds.

Raven, the scavenger, tends to follow the herds of caribou, knowing that there will always be carrion spoils from wolf kills. Perhaps if raven was really hungry and happened by this little island in the Burnside River, she might be able to feast on a few tasty eggs. She might, on the other hand, be so pestered by the diving attacks of gulls and terns as to make by-passing a better thing to do. But, I know for sure, even if the other birds on this island have no long-standing grudge against loon, as does raven, that if those eggs are left untended for too long, it will not be good.

Back in the boats, the terns come at us another time. These images of feathered wings and fanned white tails linger on the breeze. Ahead, the river is squeezed down by the surrounding hills into a narrow water-course. The birds are behind us. Now we must tend to the river. For the next few miles it will drop at an average over 11 feet per mile (5 metres per kilometre).

The drop is gradual. The ride is smooth and cathartic. Today's meditation is visual and physical. Sometimes we drive forward to get to the inside of corners where the water is smoothest. Sometimes we back-paddle in a ferry manoeuvre, angling the boat and using the current to move us from side to side. Sometimes the water is like a river of flowing glass. We zip over rounded boulders and ripples of white sand, not 3 feet (92 centimetres) below the keel, conscious always of sunlight and shadow on shifting patterns of pink and black, taupe on stippled green. Air, water, land and motion; blue, white, green and magic. Today's music sings through the boat.

Canoe, the ultimate craft. Light, symmetrical and balanced. It moves in the river, and leaves no track. It runs on hard work and the cycles of nature. It supports independence, but teaches duality. It carries what we need to survive with no room for extras. It is strong but bends to wild water and big waves. It can move with the water or against it, but only for so long. It counsels care and moderation. It can be blown away by the wind, and it can provide shelter when all else is gone. But best of all, this canoe takes us to the land, into the land, to places we would never be without it. We can take it up the mountain to where the river rises. It can take us to the sea.

That evening it is time for a derby. We spread out along the shore, everyone wearing blue bibs that Cath has made to keep our clothes "clean." Good therapy, is fishing. One gets to make all manner of individual decisions about where to stand, what kind of lure to use, where to cast, how to cast, when to start, when to stop and what to do with the fish when it gets caught. But the true magic of fishing comes from the repeated cycles of throwing and winding the line, and from standing within the beating waters of the river.

Brain scientists have determined that our brain waves tend toward the frequencies in our environment. The rhythm of the river is slow and steady. The alpha rhythm of a person in deep meditation is eight cycles per second. The frequency of fluorescent light–the music of Ontario Hydro that plays in every school and office in our home province–is sixty cycles per second. No wonder we go snakey inside and mellow out beside a river. Whether or not that is the case, the ultimate proof that fishing is rewarding is, as they say, in the pudding. There is absolutely nothing–raw or cooked–that tastes quite as good as arctic char or grayling pulled from 50°F (10°C) waters.

The following morning, I awake to the familiar smell of outside and old socks. A small bird lands and skitters off the taut tent fly. Angular morning sun filters through the nylon and falls softly on Gail, who is invisible in a heap of blue-on-blue sleeping bag. A toque sticks out of the top like a Thermos stopper. The only sign of life is the rhythmic rise and fall of the bag's outer cover. Delaying the daily torment of putting warm, dry feet into cold, wet boots, I sit up, pull on my pile sweater, unzip the door quietly and savour what has to be one of the best-kept secrets of wilderness–morning.

Outside, the enticing smell of fire, coffee and sizzling double-smoked bacon reveals Lorraine, down the bluff, rolling out cinnamon buns on the wanigan lid. A tern flies over, its head down, as if looking for something. I follow its motion until it disappears down the valley. Movement on the opposite shore replaces that of the tern. It's a grizzly bear!

Lorraine is understandably nervous. But we stand and watch as the bear ambles its way up the shore. It stops beside a big rock and gives its hind end a good scratch on the rough, granite surface. The bear gets to a point almost directly across from our camp before it stops and rears up onto its hind legs.

"Can it see us?" Lorraine asks quietly.

"Hard to say, but I bet it can smell that bacon," I say, realizing immediately that we may have a problem on our hands. I have never forgotten the square-ended cedar-canvas canoe old Charlie Haltain had on Lake Temagami: he said he cut bacon on it one time and a hungry bear ripped the end right off, looking for something to eat. "But maybe he's just curious."

Then, just like the other bear, this one set down on all fours and bolted for the hills, stopping once to look to see if we were following.

This kind of chance encounter, and the sense of fear, satisfaction and of simply being alive it brings, goes far beyond any hope or expectations I had for this journey. It seems to be taking us places we never thought possible, and showing us things that humans were not meant to see.

The physical journey Gail and I anticipated in the spring months of this year, as we marked our maps and pulled together our kit, was one whose bounds I knew about, one whose limits I could understand. But this journey in my imagination that has been evolving in parallel–the journey in six/eight time–is new, unexpected, unpredictable and more like the "journey in pursuit of itself," described by Esau Gillingham in Harold Horwood's book. Everything now seems to be happening too quickly.

The blond sun-drenched sand hills downstream from the bear campsite prompt Jake to remark that "it feels like we're paddling in Afghanistan" as we continue on the river. Lingering adrenalin from the encounter with the bear only adds to the feeling of other-worldliness that this experience breeds.

We pass more desert hills and arrive at an outcropping of the

Canadian Shield that forms the backbone of Bellanca Rapids. Stopping to scout, Cath lets on that she figures Bellanca was the half-sister of the ill-fated Belanger. It was not until after the trip that it came to light that Bellanca Rapid was named after a workhorse aircraft of the north called a Bellanca CH-300 Pacemaker which crashed near this site in the early 1940s. Among attributes such as superb load carrying capacity, economic design and long range, the Bellanca was used extensively in the north on skis, wheels and floats. Bellanca aircraft of similar design and performance bettered Lindbergh's New York to Paris distance record in 1931. And Bellancas were popular planes for use in aerial photography in the early days of Canadian map-making.

Bellanca is the first rapid we decide is too difficult to shoot, in entirety, in our open canoes, so we paddle the first third, lift over the main ledge and ride out the remaining white water with hoots and cheers that celebrate the fine day and the rollicking power of the river.

That enthusiasm is carried over in a naked frolic on a white-sand beach, just downstream, where we swim, for the first time since the top of the Icy River, cavort on clay flats and ski down steep sandbanks to the edge of the river.

After a quick lunch, we press on with washed socks and underwear drying on top of the sun-warmed packs. The river speeds up and whisks us between now towering hills of post-glacial sand and gravel. We reckon at one point that we're breezing along at 7 or 8 miles (11 or 12 kilometres) an hour! After thirty-odd days of hard grind, this laid-back rapid shooting is like the answer to a prayer.

As I lie back in the canoe, drifting along with the current, the contrails of a polar jet etch the sky. It's too high up to see what airline, but it could be one of many, on any number of great circle routes: Chicago to Tokyo; Toronto to Singapore; Honolulu to Frankfurt; San Francisco to Moscow. The white streaks bring to mind Canada's greatest (if not most controversial) Arctic explorer, Vilhjalmur Stefansson–the "prophet of the North" and commander of the 1913-18 Canadian Arctic Expedition–who remarked in the early years of this century that "in the future, the Canadian Arctic will most certainly lie at the crossroads of the world."

But the plane also makes me realize how few people we have seen - two, to be precise - and how far we are from the experience of being in that airplane, and how good that feels. I think of a night at the Arctic Circle Club in Ottawa back in the spring when Gail and I were invited to see a slide lecture by a prominent politician who had paddled the Burnside River. It was an interesting presentation, but unremarkable except for the fact that this group had with them a radio that allowed them to communicate with commercial jets flying overhead. They would raise the jets on a known cross-country radio frequency and ask the pilot to relay a message of their well-being to the control tower in Yellowknife, or somewhere, who, in turn would pass the message on to family or friends of the paddlers. Our emergency locater transmitter, stuffed away in the bottom of a pack, would wail on that plane's international distress frequency if we needed it, so we are not exactly holier than the safety-conscious politician, but today, the thought of making a bi-weekly link with the world that we have worked so hard to leave for a while is the last thing I would do without dire reason!

It is clear to me now that we are not escaping society on this journey. While some people may go to unmanaged landscapes as part of an organized scheme to avoid the central issues of the day, the time we are spending out here has just the opposite result. Only at this distance from our high-tech lives can we begin to get a glimpse at what the issues of the day really are. The main issue that comes to mind is the fact that we have systematically alienated ourselves from the land, and that, I'm afraid, is catching up with us. What we have lost is a meshing of the human spirit and the land that engenders a sense of fit, of belonging. Maybe that's what journeys in search of themselves are about.

For the first time on the trip, a raptor soars into view. It's a golden eagle, a magnificent bird, high overhead. We camp immediately at a right-angled turn in the river, several miles on to the Mara River topographic sheet, and notice a series of lichen-encrusted cliffs nearby. Binoculars reveal streaks of vermillion lichen, which, with more careful scrutiny of the cliff face, lead to sighting first one, then two, and then a third stick nest perched among the rocks. We hike back immediately to a point from which we can observe a two-foot-high (60-centimetre-high) eaglet standing amid what looks to be a sea of half-eaten sic-sics.

How well-adapted and -tuned to the landscape is the golden eagle! Its nest is built on a cliff face, protected from predators and sheltered from at least some of the weather. It rotates use of the various nest sights year to year, some think, to allow parasites from one year to be cleared before the next use of the site. Two eggs are laid and often the stronger of the two hatchlings kills the weaker, leaving the adults to devote all their time to raising just one young. Up here there is little competition for nesting space or for food, with plenty of sic-sics, arctic hare, ptarmigan and other sources of meat. The summer season is just long enough for the young to fledge in time to fly south to warmer climes for the winter. The bird cries *kyriea-kyriea* and beats its wings with whispers of a valley-spun wind.

20.
NATIVITY

THE FOLLOWING DAY WE WEAVE THROUGH SHALLOW BRAIDED channels in the river, each boat taking a different course, and everyone laughing loudly when others get accidentally beached on a shoal. It is the best of river-running: the water is not technically difficult and we're working together and relating as a group; we're alert and paying attention to what's around us and making good time, and exceptional mileage, in the current, that is slowly putting to rest our worries about not getting to the coast in time. It's a sunny day on which the darkness of toil crossing divides to get to this place is all but forgotten, except, of course, to the extent that our joy of river-running is heightened by the great difficulty encountered in getting to the head of the river. Kibitzing in the river stops when a most remarkable sight materializes before our eyes.

A wolf and two cubs are running in the shallow water on the sand island ahead of us. The young ones stop to look at our canoes, but the adult keeps on, turning occasionally, as if to say "Come now, children, there is danger there." We watch as the three of them work their way to the shore of the river and then up the steep hillside. Now, they stop regularly and look down over us. And on they go, disappearing occasionally into the similarly coloured backdrop of sand and boulders. Eventually all three animals are silhouetted against the sky high on the ridge. They trot purposefully to what seems to be the highest point of land, then stop and sit down. The adult's head tips back in classic fashion and seconds later the haunting howl touches us all.

Not much farther downriver, we're caught off guard by a man standing on the shore. We pull in and learn that he has been staking a plot of land along the river for a company contracted by a big mining interest to do this on-the-ground work. He's from Yellowknife and thinks the company is interested in large deposits of copper-zinc and silver/lead-zinc. A chopper is to pick him up any minute and move him to another site farther inland. While we're standing there, the percussive thump of an approaching turbine helicopter overpowers our voices and the sound of the river. It lands, we say goodbye, and leave the staker and the pilot to load up. It takes a long time to get the smell of jet fuel out of our hair and clothes.

The paddling continues. We round corners, always on the inside, not knowing the exact configuration of rock and water that lies ahead, and down straightaways, through quick narrow stretches and wide, slower patches of water, arriving eventually at the confluence of the Burnside and Mara rivers. If things had been different, if the Back River had had water in it, for instance, or if the Icy River had been unfrozen, this would have been the place where we would have first seen the valley of Burnside River.

In deference to what might have been, and in spite of needing to put in miles to get to Bathurst Inlet on time, we hike high into the hills of the Mara River valley. From a vantage-point nearly 1000 feet (300 metres) over the Mara River, it looks peaceful, almost pastoral, as it switches back and forth through the deeply dissected landscape. The river and the classical U-shaped valley are a study of interconnected power and possibility, cause and effect. A look at the river through binoculars reveals rocks and wild, shallow rapids. "Maybe too shallow to shoot," says Jake.

We walk and talk, separate and recombine in different groups, as we make our way through the hills. For this experience with the river we might have paddled to be authentic we must suspend our schedule to properly honour the twist of chance that showed us the magic of the Burnside instead. There is no question in anyone's mind, at least to my knowledge, as to the "rightness" of breaking passage to tidewater to walk the Mara. The thought makes me think of the Czechoslovakian writer Erazim Kohak, author of *The Embers and the Stars: A Philosophical Inquiry into the Moral Sense of Nature*, who says we experience a loss in "morality" when we come to believe in our own models. But what intrigues me about Kohak's perspective is that he includes *time*–I presume linear, scheduled time, as we know it in our work worlds–as nothing more than a human construct, a type of technology that should not *automatically* be given credence. "Good physics makes bad metaphysics," he writes, implying that there is no reason to think the technical reason that produces the machine (and, in this context, I believe he considers time to be a "machine") is also a valid reason for humans to use it. "We can speak of a *right* time," he writes, "only in the matrix of natural time, the rhythm of life and the cycle of the seasons."

That time–non-linear, one-minute-doesn't-have-to-be-as-long-as-the-next-time, natural time, the time of the pulsing seasons–was the time of the people who placed rocks in circles at the confluence of the Mara and Burnside rivers to hold down tents made of caribou skin. On a triangular promontory, backed by the green hills and flanked on one side by the Mara River, and on the other by the Burnside, we walk among dozens of such tent rings and ponder the people who made this awe-inspiring place their summer home.

The rocks, some of which look too big to lift, are covered with lichen of all types and colours. Some, nearly buried in the tundra, are dressed with a uniform constellation of lichens, and appear to have been at this site for many, many years. Other rings have a disparate look to them; the stones evidently from different places up and down the bank, each coloured differently with moss and lichens. These, we imagine, have been put to use more recently, maybe even with cotton canvas tents.

Inside one of the larger, and older-looking rings is a squarish structure, also made of rock. Speculation that this is a hearth connects the site to our own experience. Skin tents seem a long way off and far removed from our enterprise on the Burnside, but in that hearth, the people who camped here very likely cooked up the same fat char, fiesty grayling, and lake trout that we have been catching on our way down the river. The thought is enough to send us farther, trying to imagine what an encampment here might have looked like.

Walking among the rings makes me wonder what we have missed in the way of evidence of habitation since the inukshuk on Contwoyto Lake. Surely, if there were Inuit people there, they would, at some time or another, have lived close to the river, or at least in the river valley where the wildlife is drawn in summer. Were there rock fish, weirs, caribou hunting blinds, meat caches and more stone tent rings? Our focus on the river has made us oblivious to these. Or was it that we wanted to feel as if we were the "first ones" to walk on places in this river valley, to think that it was "pristine," unsullied, virgin land–all ideas present in society, and certainly in the literature of exploration, that would have us ignore the fact that this has been homeland to native people for as long as 4000 years and maybe longer. Somehow I think not. Even the concept of "wilderness" doesn't really seem to fit as one stands in the centre of an Inuit tent ring. This land is only "wild" to those who don't live here, and even at that, as we have paddled and portaged and listened to the music of the land, it doesn't seem "wild," in the sense of forbidding and unpredictable and in need of having its head chopped off, at all.

I wish suddenly for the winds to conjure up the skin-clad keeper of this place in the barrens to take us all down to the river and show us where the fish spawn, to take us up into the valley of the Mara River and teach us the ways of the caribou and the tracks of the bear. I wish for that person to tell us that the land really does have music and that by journeying across the barren lands there is a sense of belonging and kinship between people and with the land that grows and settles and abides just as strongly as love or hate or compassion or envy or any of our other spiritual and emotional ties we have at our disposal. This place and its eerie, historical presence makes me think of Chief Kitpoo, the first "real" native person I ever knew.

Kitpoo was only half Indian; he had to shave his chest. I met him one night at Camp Kandalore, where I had gone as a camper and where I was now a staff member. It was dark and I was coming back to camp after a day off. Coming across the flattened-earth playground at the centre of camp, I encountered the director, who saw who I was in the dark before I was even conscious of there being people in front of me. He said: "James, have you met Chief Kitpoo?"

"How do you do, Chief," I said, straining in the darkness to see what the Chief looked like. He was short, about five-foot-four, and smoked a clay peace-pipe with cigar stuck into the bowl like a roman candle.

Over the next several days, I learned a great deal about the Chief. He was in the process of turning over to the camp a series of Indian artefacts he thought should be housed at such a place. He claimed to be the man who played the part of Roaring Chicken on the TV program "F-Troop," and although I had never seen the program, its mythology left little to the imagination about Kitpoo's theatrical career. He was a wonderful story-teller. He had no teeth, or very few, and longish grey hair with a bald pate. He wore leggings and a wolf head-dress much of the time and sported a broad-winged eagle tattoo across his chest. He worked, so the story went, as a representative for the Canadian tobacco industry. But he had a photo album of shots of him in the Indian regalia with the likes of John F. Kennedy and the Queen. If he was a fake, he was an accomplished one, and I, for one, was convinced otherwise.

But, for all his inconsistencies and daytime shortcomings, Kitpoo was more Indian than anybody I'd ever met and around the campfire introduced us to the native notion of giving back to the land for game that is taken; of the cedar, and tobacco and other sacred herbs; and of the life and spirits in trees, and animals and people. He told stories of how things got to be the way they are today and warned of losing touch with the keepers of the four winds. Kitpoo, whoever he was–whoever he *is*–taught a generation of people at that camp that the land was alive, and this, more so than anything we learned on the archery range, at the canoe dock or in camp-craft sessions, jibed with what we saw and felt on our canoe trips through Haliburton and into Temagami.

That's what I wanted to ask the people who'd made these tent rings at the Mara/Burnside confluence. I wanted to ask them about the voices in the rocks, and in the fish, because I fear that diamond drills and commercial fishing gear have drowned out what they might have to say. Wherever the descendants of the people who made these rings are living now, and however they might be getting by (they may, in fact, still be living off the land in similar fashion), these tent rings are a powerful reminder of a way of life and of a relationship with the land that most of us know nothing about. Torn alder bushes, abundant musk-ox footprints and two human footprints on the beach only add to the mystery as we embark and head on.

I'm left wondering what the Caribou Inuit called this place. Surely they have a name that is more imaginative, and more connected to what really goes on here, than the one given this river by John Franklin in honour of one of his British patrons.

By contrast, a flood of memories comes back about hand-drawn maps in Knud Rasmussen's account of the Fifth Thule Expedition. Between 1921 and 1924, Rasmussen, a Dane, himself half Inuit, travelled 20,000 miles (32,000 kilometres) from Greenland to the Pacific, across the Canadian arctic coast, stopping along the way to find out what he could about the people and land through which he was travelling. One of the activities in which he engaged en route was to ask Inuit to draw maps of their hunting-grounds and detail the names of significant places. Rasmussen was amazed at the accuracy and detail of these maps; the distances were often incorrect, but the orientation of islands and bays was always of sufficient accuracy for Rasmussen, a stranger in the area, to travel with ease.

Sometimes these hand-drawn maps would have upwards of two dozen names on one small island. But this day, sitting atop a hill, looking north toward Bathurst Inlet, I think of the substance of the names Rasmussen's various informants put on their maps. All with one-word Inuktitut descriptions, there was the place with driftwood, the lake with many islands, the lake with many trout, the place where caribou bulls abound, the bay at the place where people gather in spring, the land behind, the place where one turns inward, the breasts, the ptarmigan-abounding island, the island shaped like a giant hare, and the place where ice is cut up by current. It's a shame that we have not adopted the native naming system for places, because, even though we are of a different culture, those names speak of a relationship with the land that we can only imagine.

Just the thought of those maps brings back memories of Theo Ikkummaq and our winding boat trip through the fog along the coast of Baffin Island. If he had an evolved mental map of the details of where we were, I could see how it would be difficult for him to navigate. That part makes sense. How he drove for hours across a gap without sighting land is still a bit of a mystery. But central questions continue to surface regarding the land and our growing relationship with it.

But the question may not be: "How do people attach meaning to space and place?" Rather, it may be: "How does the landscape attach its meaning to people?" The fundamental difference between the person who would name a natural feature after an earl and the person who would name a place after one of its salient characteristics is quite simple: one calls, one listens. One passes through, the other abides. The former thinks the land belongs to him, the latter belongs to the land.

Things are starting to make sense. My Anishnabi-speaking friend Craig Macdonald once told me that the Algonquian language is different from our subject/object-oriented speech. Algonquian verbs, he said, can be conjugated in at least nine modes and seven tenses; they are the key part of native speech. Bark-canoe-builder David Gidmark also said something that has stuck: Indians do not use an adjective to indicate that an object is coloured black; instead, they conjugate the verb that means to be black.

I begin to wonder if the alienation from the earth of people of non-native stock is exacerbated by language. Somewhere back in an old cerebral file drawer filled with useless liberal-arts facts is a theory that suggests perception of the world is conditioned by and confined within the limits of grammatical categories and structures of the mother tongue. Maybe it's true. And now I'm wondering if our relationship with the land is fading because we have not the words to describe the interaction between people and places. Maybe native people have a closer relationship with the land because they live there and depend on it for their survival–but so do we, in a disconnected sort of way. Maybe they have a language that allows them to celebrate their connection with the land in spoken and symbolic language? And that same drawer produces some notion of trouble and disconnection when the symbols on which our language is based came to represent sounds and not ideas. People of oral traditions, like North American Indians and Inuit, didn't have this problem.

Whatever the reason, be it language, familiarity with place, or something else completely different, being native in a particular place means having a special type of attachment to that place. The Inuit person or people who have sat at this same spot high over the Burnside (or whatever they called it) River valley, savouring the stillness or watching for caribou, belonged here like no European ever did. And on this day I am beginning to see distant outlines of a totally different set of understandings. I want to think that travelling slowly and taking the land on its terms, as we have done for the last six weeks, has allowed us to feel some of the same feelings and learn some of the same landscape-derived lessons as the original dwellers of this still and smokey valley.

Glenn Gould's informant in the "Idea of North" program was only partly right when he said that the North was a stage for the playing out of two great human dreams: Eldorado and Utopia. People who apply those myths give their friends' names to places they conquer. They are white dreams, dreams of people who have no enduring attachment to the landscape itself, dreams of people who have no sense of belonging, dreams of people who have no real idea of "nativity"–what it means to be native to a place, what it means to belong. There is another northern dream, and that is the dream–the mythology–of the people who consider this place their home. It is the same all over the world: there are those who believe the land belongs to them, those who do not care about the exploitation of the land; and there are those who feel they belong to the landscape, whose words and actions acknowledge the stillness and intrinsic value of a place.

If I have learned anything on this journey it is that the land has power and music of its own, and there can be, on an extended outing such as this, a meshing of the human spirit and the spirit of the land, which may well be the essence of being native to a place, a phenomenon that could be called "nativity." Some people have no sense of nativity; others' lives are informed and shaped by connections to the landscape.

The idea of nativity–belonging derived of the land–has lots of attractive offshoots. For one, it may help retire the tired old white-land-raper noble-native-steward stereotypes! There are places under native jurisdiction littered with the same skutter of disposable diapers as one might find in any city. Similarly, I know non-natives who live peacefully with the cycles of nature. There are cultural and linguistic differences, to be sure, but maybe these are a result of a fundamental difference called nativity.

It is exciting to think that there might be a set of understandings derived from sustained encounter with the land, and not from the colour of one's skin or necessarily from one's cultural heritage–a set of understandings that may well control behaviour with respect to the environment. Reconciling the differences of opinion about the future of the lower Burnside River would then become a more manageable task. All one need do is find the engineers and the park policy-makers, take them from their offices in Winnipeg and Ottawa, and help them develop some sense of nativity–some sense of belonging–in the Burnside River valley. Send them hunting with Inuit from Bathurst Inlet. Take them on a canoe trip. Walk them over these blue hills along the route of their proposed water corridor. Then, maybe things would be different.

Today I am moved by the vastness of this area, but for the first time–maybe because the linear river and its motion are out of mind and out of sight–I become conscious of a remarkable stillness, and realize how frenzied, linear and full of motion is our existence. Places, to most of us, I begin to comprehend, are always on the way to somewhere. We seem to be driven to define who we are, what we do and where we live by flows, movement, forward motion, development, progress.

Stillness is elusive. Like the perfect moment in time, disconnencted from past or future, the stillness of place may be its intrinsic value, the value that people cannot understand. Maybe stillness is one of the land secrets locked in the language of the Inuit, and maybe in the words and stories of other native people too.

This night, the images of the tent rings and of the wolves are still strong and prompt the digging-out of a dog-eared copy of Aldo Leopold's *A Sand County Almanac*. I know in there is one of the best essays ever about the vital life in the natural world. I read "Thinking Like a Mountain" in the dying light to the sound of gulls fighting over the grayling remains on the shore. Although he never used the term, Leopold knows all about nativity, and how we belong to the land, not the other way around.

21.
ARCTIC CIRCLE

THE END IS CLOSING QUICKLY. SETTLING INTO THE RHYTHM OF THE day's paddling, we all scan the hills opposite for sight of last evening's wolves. Nothing. But I am silently warmed by the thought that somewhere on those steep, greened slopes are at least three pairs of eyes, probably four, watching us leave their territory.

Quickly, however, there is no energy or time for shore-watching. The river since the mouth of the Mara is squeezed between ever-closing banks that rise 600 and 700 feet (180 to 214 metres) off the water. In the canoes we're left feeling small, insignificant and caught on a predetermined course leading–whether we like it or not–to the sea. But, instead of being fearful of the bigness of the land and of the seeming inevitability of our future with the river, riding with the water as it drops between 10 and 20 feet (3 to 6 metres) every mile is a focused and very satisfying experience.

There are no falls or major rapids marked on this stretch on the map, but with the dramatic change in elevation, we're wary, although not quite wary enough. Inside corners are usually the safe place to be, because there is always a back eddy to pull into, providing time to bail should the going get rough. But, on this occasion, in a series of switchbacks in the river, staying to the left side of the river turns one inside corner into the outside of a much-more-tumultuous bend. It is all Gail and I can do–no time for elegant ferrying–to dig deep and drive the canoe diagonally across the river to a rip current on the inside. The lateness of the manoeuvre sweeps us sideways through standing waves at the brink of this corner drop. We ignore the water that splashes into the boat as a result of our speed, thinking only of getting away from the 8-foot (2-metre) waves and swirling currents on the outside of the corner that will surely swamp us. The river drops away to our left, giving the impression of paddling down a set of steep garden stairs: for a moment I feel as if my canoe seat is a stool, and I'm perched high above the water. Adrenalin-charged strokes see us to the inside of the bend, and amid flying ribbons of spray mixed with celebratory hoots of high adventure, we pull into the inside eddy to bail.

"Phew! That was close," Gail says, twisting in her seat to have a look at the amount of water that has collected in the heavy end of the boat. Radiant life in her sun-weathered complexion shines through lingering spray that rolls off her face and onto her life-jacket. "We're getting cocky, but I love it!"

Two or three eddys later on this river roller coaster, we pull in for another bailing session and find a foam-covered hand-carved spruce canoe yoke, mute reminder of someone else's experience with this wild section of the Burnside. I think of the politician and his "polar jet" crew and wonder if this was their upset, and if it was ever reported via radio to the Yellowknife control tower and thus to the folks back home. Our good fortune on the bad corner, we realize, did have a large element of luck. The yoke is enough to renew our commitment to scouting rapids before shooting them, even if there are no marked sets in this stretch of river.

We lunch on the Arctic Circle, the earthly line above which the sun is visible for twenty-four hours, for at least one day, during the summer months. The occasion links us to the geometry of the solar system and allows us to celebrate the 23.5-degree tilt of the earth's axis, relative to the line joining the centre of the earth with the centre of the sun, that gives our planet the seasons. Ninety degrees minus the tilt of the earth gives the latitude of the Arctic

Circle. Without the tilt there would be no seasons; day and night would be twelve hours each everywhere on the planet. More importantly, there would be no Arctic Circle on which to build our northern fantasy.

For some people, the edge of the forest is the place where north begins, and rightly so, because this is a line, or at least a zone, that can be seen. For others, north begins with the line of continuous permafrost. But for us the Arctic Circle, the invisible line of latitude marking 66.6 degrees above the equator, is more significant than either of those. The Arctic Circle may be geometrically derived and have a rational explanation, but for us the mythology of the Circle – the Circle's magic that has found its way into northern songs and stories – is of great significance. Crossing the Arctic Circle places us firmly, if only in our imaginations, in the true North of this vast country. Paddling across the Arctic Circle is probably one of the most Canadian, if not romantic, acts of our lives. Why not use it as an excuse to drain the dregs of whiskey from the last of our Sigg bottles and sing a rousing chorus of "This Land Is Your Land"?

Sometime later a young golden eagle makes its way into view, flying up the valley. As if it just crossed an invisible borderline marking the territory of another bird of prey, two peregrine falcons dive out of the sun and strike the surprised eagle. They wheel, climb and swoop again, this time turning the bottom of their U-drive and striking the belly of the eagle on their way back up. The big eagle tries to dodge the striking falcons, but to no avail: it's like a sausage-sized cecropia-moth caterpillar attempting to evade a couple of angry hornets.

The speed with which the falcons drop from the sky is difficult to comprehend. They are supposed to be one of the fastest birds around, credited with reaching 100 miles (160 kilometres) per hour on occasion. From our vantage-point, the remembered statistics mean very little. The fiesty little falcons beat their wings to a point high above the eagle and then tuck them in, leaving only little missile vanes protruding. They seem to drop faster than free-falling stones. The eagle, the majestic eagle, is no match in the categories of speed and agility, but it perseveres, and as it passes overhead and further upstream, the falcons desist and disappear into the craggy green hills. Crossing the falcon's territorial boundary is a lesson that has cost the young eagle a flight feather on its right wing, but the encounter with the falcons has, presumably, been a lesson of value.

The Arctic Circle, the aerial show, the river, the hills, the rapids–all of these sights and events are laid down in sequence in my imagination, creating a special kind of bond to the corridor through which we are travelling. Knowing that eagles live here, that falcons live here, and that they have trouble getting along from time to time, is all part of an increasingly complex set of understandings I have about this land through which we're travelling. Where we are at this moment has a number on the Universal Transmercator Grid; it has a citation relative to the Arctic Circle and the ordered reticule of meridian and parallel lines of which it is a part. Where we are on the Burnside River has a time and distance from our end-point at Bathurst Inlet. But, in the fullness of this experience of journeying through the Burnside River valley, all of those place-holders seem foreign and somehow insignificant. Where are we right now? We are in the overlap of that golden eagle and those two angry falcons. We are paddling between terraced green hills. We are downstream from a tricky switchback in the river. We are on a long, sloping water corridor that is dropping to ocean tidewater at a rate of 15 feet (5 metres) per mile. We are at a high point in our lives. We are here.

22.
DAM

LOADING THE CANOES THE NEXT MORNING, A PIECE OF MILLED WOOD IN the water catches my eye. Wood of any description at this latitude is unusual, but this is no ordinary piece of driftwood. Floating in the back eddy is a blond-coloured piece of spruce one-by-two strapping about 2.5 feet (76 centimetres) long with a saw-sharpened point. Nailed to one end is an aluminum tag confirming suspicions that it's a claim stake. We keep the tag for posterity, secretly hoping it will make the claim void on a technicality. This whole river, I'm afraid, has been spoken for by somebody in the resource-extraction industry.

By this time, in spite of the majesty of land and water, the accumulating tension of constant whitewater decision-making and the ongoing worry about getting to the coast on schedule have taken their toll. There is unspoken disagreement about where and when to camp, some wanting to move on, others wanting to stop and savour the landscape. We are moving now into the area of a proposed national park, whose recreational and interpretive potential Gail and I have been contracted to assess for the Canadian Parks Service. The stay-or-go bind experienced by the whole group is especially vivid in Gail's mind and mine: even though we are many days behind our original schedule, we wish to do all the exploring we can in the Bathurst Inlet area, but we also have no desire to crash down the lower river and thereby miss the highlands outside the river corridor. The to-camp-or-not-to-camp dilemma spreads us out on the swift-flowing river, sails us right past at least a dozen excellent campsites, and puts us, for lack of a better place, on a tiny rock-strewn and very uncomfortable terrace high above the river. The only redeeming feature of the site is that it is just downstream from the location of a proposed power dam on the river. I'm dying to get up into the hills to have a look at the land that would be flooded.

The next morning, my birthday, I arise early to an overcast sky, shake the kinks out of my back and pack up for a celebratory stomp in the highlands. Fourteen-hundred-foot (427-metre) hills flanking the river would shadow our tents at this hour if the sky had been clear. This time alone may slow the group if I'm not back by breakfast time, but this day I'm filled with a sense of freedom and adventure derived from the conjunction of a special day in a very special place. The others may hike too, I rationalize between laboured breaths.

I continue up the hill, attracting a gyrfalcon from a nearby eyrie to dive-bomb the stranger. Like the Doppler effect of a passing train whose whistle-call is intensified and then stretched by movement, the bird's scream sharpens and fades with its swoops at my head. I duck and run sideways on the hill until the bird again settles, and wish Gail was here to share the moment. Footing is made easier by caribou trails that criss-cross the hillside. I wonder if they too are ambushed by the bird, or if, to the falcon, the passing ungulates are just part of the summer landscape.

Deep breaths of cool morning air charge muscles that labour to lift me ever higher in the river valley. In my neck, straining against the straps of a heavy camera pack, and in my temples and flushed earlobes I can feel my heart delivering oxygen and flushing away the metabolic products of exertion. By now my body is used to hard physical exercise. Just living a canoe-journey life requires an inordinate amount of bending and lifting. A walk like this becomes a celebration of fitness and of the simple joy found in self-propelled exploration of a new place.

At the top of the climb, I look northeast, down the line where the 10-mile (16-kilometre) penstock might run, to hill after hill, first green, then tan, fading to blue upon blue, upon misty blue. In the distance I can only imagine Bathurst Inlet past a horizon of melded rock and sky. The logical place to sit on this peak is a prominent rock festooned with streaks of white bird droppings intermixed with blotches of vermillion lichen, but that is the falcon's place. Instead, I plunk down cross-legged, and lean on the rock. What a place this is.

This, like every piece of land on the planet, is the object of competing human interests. If power is required in these parts to extract the minerals out of this Precambrian rock, then the 275-foot (84-metre) contour, which now exists only in the minds of map-makers and hydrological engineers, will mark the edge of a massive reservoir held back by a Burnside River power dam.

In a thick report entitled *Power Site Survey Northwest Territories* commissioned by the Canadian federal Department of Indian Affairs and Northern Development, Underwood McLellan (1977) Limited–the UMA Group–assessed the hydroelectric-power potential for five river basins in the NWT: the Burnside, Hood, Camsell, Back and Hayes rivers. UMA concluded that "ultimate development of the five river basins, together with four external diversions, could provide a firm generating capacity of 1516 MW using a total of 16 sites. In excess of 75 percent of this firm capacity would be on the Back River where the largest plant, at Site 76, has a firm capacity capability of 666 MW. The second largest plant, with 300 MW of firm capacity, is located at Site 3 on the Burnside River."

When demand is sufficient, the power dam could be built. It would be the cost-effective thing to do. UMA points that out in the early pages of the report: "Within the study area there are no settlements which have any significant demand for electrical energy. Transmission distances from the potential major plants on the Burnside and Back Rivers to the larger population centres such as Winnipeg, Saskatoon and Edmonton are in order of 1500 kilometres. Future demands for substantial amounts of energy in or near the study area will be related to natural resource based developments such as mines and pipelines.

"The Burnside River drains over 19,000 sq. km of the northern Mackenzie District. The headwaters are in the Contwoyto Lake drainage basin, elevation 450 m. The river flows a total of 350 km north northeast into Bathurst Inlet. The upper reaches of the river have a fairly regular gradient of about 0.9 m/km with some minor rapids and falls. A major fall of 35 m in 1.5 km occurs at the Burnside Falls which is only 5 km from tidewater. The basin lies entirely above the tree line and within the zone of continuous permafrost."

That's it. The Burnside River from a resource-exploitation perspective. Hard to believe that it's the same place.

The report goes on to detail plans at Site 3 for a 24-foot (7-metre) tunnel, over 10 miles (16 kilometres) long, to take water through the hills to a powerhouse in the river estuary. I stare at the map showing the score of this pipe against the natural meanders of the river, and then look again at the soft curves and gentle shapes in the valley before me and feel an upwelling of anger at the audacity of a fellow human to suggest such a scheme.

But what bothers me about this bald-faced assessment of the Burnside River is the fact that there is not so much as a hint that this land, this river valley, could have value derived of anything other than its 300 MW "firm capacity" for hydroelectric-power generation.

The problem, however, does not lie with the engineers who drafted the report, or for that matter, with the bureaucrats who commissioned it. The problem lies with a society that has lost touch with the land, a society that defines itself by competition in every sphere of life. Money–the fiscal axis, the bloody bottom line–is the only tool we seem to have with which to make decisions and resolve conflict. Nobody ever seems to stop to ask about the consumptive life-style that drives the competition. Nobody ever asks, "What would the Burnside River think about a reservoir to the 275-foot contour?"

We, as Canadians, are just as bad as everyone else. Our greed for wilderness has taken us to the ends of the earth, where we can conveniently forget about our consumers' life-style, which includes buying plastic canoes and other assorted paraphernalia whose production sullies the air and water of southern Canada. It is entirely conceivable that one day Gail and I will wear wedding rings that are made from Lupin mine gold! We would then be part of the demand that makes feasible the building of this dam that seems such a repugnant idea. We have to expose the contradictions in our lives.

During this journey we have done our utmost to "no-trace" every campsite. That, in itself, has been an honourable goal. We have felt good about cooking with gas stoves, trying not to leave fire scars on the land, using as little wood as we can for fires, taking care to make sure that our toilet paper is burned or set into the active layer of the tundra soil. If only we worked as hard at home to do the same.

The beauty of this unmanaged landscape is that we can see and appreciate the effects of our living on the land. Here, there are no mysteries when it comes to waste disposal. There is no action, like flushing a toilet or putting a bag of garbage out at the curb, that is unconnected to the land. Everything we do, from stepping onto a beach and leaving footprints, to walking into a herd of caribou or eliminating, has effect that we can fathom. Part of learning to belong in this landscape involves coming to terms with our own effects on its natural cycles.

When I was a kid paddling the Speed River through Guelph, Ontario, my trips were always marred by the presence in the river of shopping carts, park benches, old tires and penis-like pipes that spewed brown water and foam. Maybe that brown water had elements in it that came from our house. Maybe it's time we left the wilderness to be wilderness and tried to reconnect with the landscape closer to home. It's not no-trace camping we need– although that has been an important start in the process of environmental enlightenment–it's no-trace living!

The Burnside must not become a northern Speed. Stopping the demand for gold and gas and uranium is a long-term, complicated socio-economic problem. Parks are shallow solutions to deep problems. There is no doubt that parks are paradoxical: putting boundaries around small pieces of territory interrupts the natural ecological cycle of life, and making parks attracts people to regions that suffer from the traffic, but at least the notion of a park provides a context for compromise, a forum for talking about various ways of valuing landscape, and, in the short term, at least, stopping or slowing uncontested and irreversible development of an area.

This particular park idea, for which Gail and I are supposed to be gathering on-the-ground information, stems from the demarcation of a series of Canadian areas of natural significance, including six arctic areas: Wager Bay, parts of Ellesmere Island and Axel Heiberg Island, Banks Island, northern Yukon, and the pingos of Tuktoyaktuk. Its proposed boundaries make a big footprint–130 miles (208 kilometres) long and 50 miles (80 kilometres) wide–with the place I'm sitting right at the outside edge of the instep.

Until now, I have been thinking in terms of a park's recreational potential for people who might come here to hike or canoe, but, as a place-holder, the park may be the only legislative tool we have to keep this land undeveloped. Even at that, the park is an imperfect solution. But it's a start, until we find a way to rationalize preserving the land for its own sake.

No matter what schemes might be conceived to leave this land the way it is now, they all seem to involve rationalization in human terms, whether it's national heritage, resource potential, or a legacy for our children's children. This seems to be the limit of our language and perception. Nobody, except maybe native people, seems to have the ability to conceive of land for land's sake, or leaving undeveloped a section of green tundra hillside, or a stretch of arctic water for the goodness of the earth.

I wander back down toward camp, filled with the beauty of this remote arctic river valley, and acutely aware that I may be walking the line of the proposed 10-mile (16-kilometre) tunnel linking the 275-foot (84-metre) contour reservoir with a powerhouse at Bathurst Inlet. An arctic hare hops across my path and sits beside a rock, almost invisible against the grey and green lichens. I'm sure it thinks I can't see it.

On the last terrace before dropping to our river level, the

unmistakable vapours of wood smoke and double-smoked bacon waft over the rise. At the campsite, Norm is up and cooking. Closer to the fire, I can smell coffee too. Already it's August 7. There won't be many more mornings like this before our time runs out.

23.
CANYON PORTAGE

PADDLING THE FINAL 10 MILES (16 KILOMETRES) OF THE BURNSIDE
River leading up to Burnside Falls and canyon is an experience that
weaves terror and exhilaration. Quick drops and big waves are
separated by sinewy stretches of curving fast water that in turn dive
around corners and drop out of sight. Every nuance of style and
technique, every intuition of true partnership we have learned, is
stretched and tested in these last hours on the river. But all that is
cut to an abrupt halt when the entire course of the river is forced left
by a rock face and sneezed through a narrow chasm of red and white
quartzite. It is here the final physical challenge begins: a 3-mile
(5-kilometre) portage to the Burnside estuary. We disembark and
walk the edge of the gorge, but stop when the enormity of the task
before us sinks in. Again, and reminiscent of the Back River, we will
portage as far as our eyes can see. It is a daunting prospect. But, first,
a birthday celebration!

After being asked to "disappear" for a while, I descend the
riverbank and see in the distance a red and white gingham tablecloth
and brightly coloured balloons festooned over the water-rounded
boulder beach. The ensemble is completed with party serviettes,
favours, paper hats, and six adults wrapped in the unlikely festivity

of this tundra occasion. The meal of freeze-dried steaks, dried hash-brown potatoes, Surprise-brand peas and cheesecake–the same bagged meal we have had now at least five times in the menu rotation–tastes better than ever, mostly because the occasion is warmed and spiced by the simple pleasures of camaraderie, surprises and good fun.

As if the table dressings are not enough, presents and an iced chocolate cake with candles are produced. How all of these items survived nearly seven weeks on the trail astounds us all. Over coffee, presents are produced that round out the finest birthday celebration a person could imagine. Lorraine has made a pair of home-sewn cowboy boots complete with stars and sequins, for campsite wear. Norm has wrapped a package of Century Sam cigars and a much-needed lure after countless snags and line breaks have depleted personal stocks. Gail produces a carefully wrapped hand-crocheted nose warmer and a pair of Groucho Marx glasses, complete with plastic nose and moustache attached. Jake sheepishly hands over a container of powdered shoe deodorizer and a spanking new and *clean* "Summer North of 60" T-shirt, which, after living in the same paltry but functional few clothes for the summer, is a welcome gift indeed! And Cath–Cath has sewn a set of outrageous costumes for the ladies, which add magnificiently to the general bawdy saloon atmosphere of the post-party card game! It is a scene that totally bamboozles six canoeists who hie up when the party is in full swing.

A professor and five strapping male students from Dartmouth College in Hanover, New Hampshire, have paddled the Burnside and have had a fine time indeed. Like us, they are a little surprised to see another group on the river, but they have hiked and travelled slowly and enjoyed the land as we have. We have more in common than it at first appears, and before long, the leader of this crew has put fears of being strangers to rest when he trots out the names of half a dozen Canadian canoeists of our acquaintance with whom he has either travelled or corresponded about his travels in the Northwest Territories. The meeting with this crew is quite different from another encounter with American university students on a northern river.

I was to be lying on the shore of a steeply dropping rapid, photographing mergansers swimming through the white water. Reminiscent of the famous scene inside the Nazi channel block-house on D-Day, I scanned once up the valley of the river looking for ducks and saw nothing, and then, an instant later, looked again and saw a flotilla of nearly a dozen canoes and twice that number of people bobbing down the river! The sense of being invaded was palpable. No wonder the ducks were swimming through the rapid! I stood up and tucked in my shirt.

Several minutes later, I was still standing in the same spot. The canoes had landed upstream and long lines of people were making their way down the river to scout the rapid. One of the leaders of the group was well out in front of the rest and was caught by surprise to see us sprinkled along the shore of the river. "What are you fucking dingos doing on *our* river?" was his first utterance.

"Nice to see you, too," I said, still a little shocked by the whole set of circumstances. "Where have you come from?"

As it transpired, this group had been out for weeks longer than we had and had chosen a route that crossed many watersheds and touched a great number of lakes and rivers. It was as if they had drawn a line from one place to another and had gone cross-country, using only the waterways that touched the line. It sounded like a canoe route planned by the UMA engineers who conceived the 10-mile penstock idea!

Among the group were undergraduate and graduate students from a variety of disciplines and a variety of universities. There were history majors, anthropologists, sociologists and a variety of liberal-arts majors; most of them, it seemed, were getting university credit for their participation on the canoe trip. What a great idea!

On that occasion we leap-frogged down the river with this crew, running into them at various places en route, and getting to chat with some of the members. The leader turned out to be somewhat less Ramboesque than his first impression had led us to believe, but he did have a wonderful story about stalking a sleeping musk-ox, which eventually awoke and charged him, leaving him, the stalker, no other option than to give the unsuspecting animal a John Wayne smack right on its snoot. "That gave me time to get my camera and get out of there!" he said, with a grin. "Whoowh, it was a close one!"

There were twenty-three of them altogether, paddling in eleven canoes and sleeping in eighteen tents. They were eating a rotation of four types of pasta and sauce for their main meals and every dessert was one of two or three flavours of dried pudding. The participants, many of whom were on their first canoe trip, had split lips and burned noses; their feet were blistered; they were trail-weary, having moved constantly with a daily average distance that was nearly twice ours; and on day fifty-odd, they were tired, very tired, of the food. For many of them the trip was not a happy experience, at least at that moment.

The first reaction when canoeist meets canoeist is to make an automatic assumption that one's own way is right and superior to all other ways, be it with respect to cooking, packing, paddling, menu-planning, wanigan-making, portaging, trip-scheduling and just about every other aspect of the tripping process. On that occasion we lived up to the stereotype. The monotonous food, the large group size, the top-down leadership style–all of which were different from ours–I see now, after the fact, as matters of taste. But straight-line travel and prodigious daily mileage can totally cripple the land's ability to teach and to nurture the journeyers. Canoeing for the sake of covering miles, or journeying for the sake of getting from A to B is strictly a functional enterprise. Such travel may have some lasting spin-offs, but I see now that to allow an account of the journey and of the land and its teaching to form in one's imagination, the process cannot be rushed. There must at least be openness to and acceptance of the possibility that a journey can be etched in the imagination–a journey in six/eight time. One must acknowledge the spiritual, the mythical dimension of a journey, which has a genesis separate from that of the strictly physical journey involved in getting from one place to another. That is so much more significant than simply a matter of taste.

But the Dartmouth crew was different. They had gone to the place where canoeist Alex Hall described a 1975 sighting of a grizzly taking down a musk-ox, and found the musk-ox skull! They are carrying it with them, and Norm impulsively takes the skull, holds it up to his own head and does his best to imitate a rutting bull musk-ox. The Dartmouth lads are impressed with the impromptu acting, but say that they didn't think a real musk-ox would wear a Mickey Mouse party hat. They seem to be catching on to our trail-worn sense of humour. They're a good crew, but it is nevertheless unsettling to think, for the first time on our journey, that we are not alone in this place. How spoiled we have been, and how comforting it has been to realize that we have momentarily lost touch with worries about what other people might think of our behaviour. The absence of a society mirror for our activity, it becomes apparent, has been a significant factor in allowing us to live a simple, unaffected life out here on the tundra. But, suddenly, the Joneses are back, and back with them is the undeniable, irrepressible need to worry and to compare. How refreshing it has been to be alone. How disappointed we are to run into people before the end of the trip, even if, intellectually, we understand that they have equal right to be here.

The next day brings baggy eyes from lack of sleep and the onerous prospect of carrying our gear off the face of the visible earth. After the sharp left-hand turn, the river courses north through a quartzite canyon, into a smallish pool ringed with sandstone bluffs, then over 40-foot (12-metre) Burnside Falls, and down the remaining 60-foot (18-metre) drop in elevation to a final island split in the river before reaching the alluvial sandflat leading to tidewater. To our dismay, to walk the edge of the river gorge would mean doubling the portage distance. The most direct route from one end of the carry to the other cuts the corner formed by the river and involves hiking up and over a 350-foot (107-metre) hill! Gail and I each decide to carry one of our two loads to the other end of the portage before walking back along the river.

The substance of this carry is much the same as it was at any other place on the trip, except at this point we have a lot less in the food packs. The tenor of the portage is dramatically different from any other, because, from the top of the killer hill, we can see Bathurst Inlet Lodge and the end of our journey. Seven and a half miles (12 kilometres) distant is a little collection of red and white buildings sprinkled on a verdant green slope at the edge of Bathurst

Inlet. We can make out the structure with field glasses, but see no people. But also visible from this superb vantage-point is the shadowed spine of the Bathurst cuesta, a geological formation that cuts out of the Burnside Hills, forming a chain of dramatic peaked islands in the inlet itself. And between those islands and the shore is tidal water of varying depth that does for the colour blue what tundra does to green–expands it into every shade possible.

We take time to reflect on the origin of this little community nestled onto the shore of this remote northern body of water. John Franklin was here; Knud Rasmussen was here; history has kept those events prominent; but also living at this place, perhaps as long as 4000 years before, were Caribou Inuit who first made this oasis their home. From this distance, the buildings that dot the landscape are nothing more than a symbol of many generations of human habitation.

The buildings themselves were originally constructed in the early decades of the century by the Hudson's Bay Company to facilitate trade with the local people. Some of those people came to live at the post site. But now, since the business was abandoned by the HBC and the buildings were purchased by an ex-RCMP corporal and some partners, Bathurst Inlet is a remote summer naturalist's lodge catering to keen birders, photographers, botanists and artists from the south. We watch a small float-plane take off silently from the water in front of the lodge and move toward where we are sitting. Now, we are really not alone. No time to dilly-dally. We've got a big job to do!

The view and the not-so-simple act of reaching this headland has energized the pair of us. Gail's back is still tender and she's got herself trussed up tight into her brace, but, like us all, she can see the end and is determined to finish the portage. She strides off downhill, leaving me to shoulder the canoe and catch up.

By now the wind has come up. It twists the boat on my shoulders and makes me miss steps in trying to compensate for the rotation. The gusts make it impossible to gain any kind of walking rhythm, kindling a fire of frustration. I'd dump the pack, but on this carpet of green we'd very likely never find it again. So, I carry on.

The next obstacle is a series of 6-foot (3-metre)-wide 4-foot

(122-centimetre)-deep ditches, which I realize, only after stopping, are tundra polygons, similar to the ones we saw on the shores of Contwoyto Lake from Dwayne's airplane, only this time, instead of appreciating the pleasing geometric symmetry of the phenomenon, I am left cursing the difficulty in gaining enough momentum in the rounded bottoms of these ditches to be able to port me and my load back to ground level! Taking short steps down the leading incline of one ditch the canoe slams into the opposite bank, jumps the yoke off my shoulders and lands the full 85 pounds (38 kilograms) squarely on my head. It is a good place to sit down for a rest.

Next appears an esker-like ridge of sand and gravel that must be scaled on an angle. By the time the top of that is reached, Gail is a steadily moving dot in the distance and I am thoroughly fed up with the whole business. Following Norm's example, I load the pack into the canoe, jump in myself and ride it like a wild green toboggan down the other side. The canoe slides so well over the heath that I carry on, with Norm as my hero. I extract the bow lining rope from under the front deck, throw it over my shoulder and commence dragging the empty canoe. It's a doggedly satisfying alternative to carrying in the wind, but one I fear will ultimately wear out the bottom of the canoe. At this point, who cares? We could walk to Bathurst Inlet Lodge if we had to!

Damn! I've been caught by two of the Americans engaging in this barbarian portaging technique. They top a nearby rise, apparently having been sitting with their packs for some time, and, after asking me about the Jimmy Hoffa portaging technique, join in on the merry route to tidewater. The conversation makes distance and pain fade to subconscious levels. All the while, though, as we walk and share experience of our journeys, I am miffed and embarrassed at being caught dragging a canoe across a portage. Surely, if there is anything, anything at all, in which Canadians should set a stellar example for Americans it should be on the ins and outs of canoe travel. And I blew it! These guys must get the right impression of who we are and how we do things up here in the Great White North. What a time to be burdened with national pride!

We arrive at the end of the portage, some four hours after

starting with this load, to find Jake and a couple of the others watching a dozen 15- to 20-pound (7- to 9-kilogram) lake trout resting in a shallow eddy beside the Burnside's final drop. Oddly, no one even mentioned fishing. The sight of these magnificent fish idling in the slow-moving current was enough to satisfy curiosity. Perhaps they were spawning, perhaps not. In any case there was a sense among all of us that we were the invaders. These fish seemed better left alone.

Gail, by this time, had teamed up with Lorraine or someone else for the walk back along the canyon, which left me alone to wander at will back to our campsite for the second load. I had purposely left my camera bag for the second trip, mostly because I didn't want to carry it across the portage four times instead of just once, because I was sure it would accompany me on this hike back up the river. Instead, I had pocketed my sketchpad and paints.

Predictably, I am met almost immediately by a peregrine falcon that rises on the currents roiling out of the gorge and stoops angrily at my head. The perfect curve of its little patterned wings, the hook of its beak, the fanning of its tail feathers as it brakes and turns away, time after time–these were all aspects of this bird that I would not have seen through the lens of a camera. I would have been so intent on focusing, or just getting the moving bird into the frame of the photo, that all that would have been missed. If you do happen to get good snaps, they can be savoured over and over again, and much can be learned, but I'm pretty sure now that a camera, unless you can somehow manage to leave it behind from time to time, is a net liability to seeing, really *seeing*, what goes on in the world about.

I stand high above a right-angled corner in the river near a lichen- and scat-encrusted raptor-roosting stone and gaze down at the perfect rectangle of Burnside Falls. One hundred feet (30 metres) wide, maybe 50 feet (15 metres) high, and etched in a million parallel white, grey and blue lines, the falls gather energy in taut reflections of cliffs in the upper pool and release it onto the roiling whitewater dancefloor below.

Beyond the falls, in compressed, purposeful zigs and zags, the river reaches upward toward the Contwoyto Plateau. It was Canadian author Rudy Wiebe who observed that, when you approach a river from the ocean, instead of perpetuating the inland mythology of rivers running from mountains to sea, it is more enlightening to imagine rivers as the gnarled fresh fingers of the sea reaching for the mountains. Wiebe went on to say that if endless tentacles of the sea lie everywhere on the land, it is "both philosophically proper and imaginatively pleasing that the first whites to systematically explore the Canadian Arctic tundra and its coast were sailors."

Today, Wiebe's construction, while linking my thoughts back to Hearne and Franklin, serves no other purpose than to highlight the feeling, nurtured by this long journey, that everything is connected to everything else–the river to the sea, the plants to the rivers, the animals to the plants, the people to the animals, the gorge to the wind, the birds to the gorge, the rocks to the beach, and everything, ultimately, to the sun, which marks our place in the universe. How easy it is, here, to celebrate that fact, and how quickly I have forgotten the constraints to seeing that are the walls and microwaves of our urban existence.

If we have lost anything that only a journey such as this can find, it is connection, that link to the land and the interconnectedness of all living and non-living things. It makes me think of another kindred spirit, Brian Fawcett, who wrote: "Disneyland is a kind of laundered, cartoonized replication of the world. It allows people to experience history and geography without physical risk or threat to their value structures. Everything is translated into a very simplified version of basic Western consumer capitalist values. Instead of sharks you get shark fishsticks."

But this experience does more than bring into focus relationships in the natural world and the essential aspects of human nature. I had never before thought of time, linear time, clock time, as anything other than a fact of our lives, something about which we can do nothing and with which we must learn to live. I'm getting the sense, now, that even time can be examined, like any other technology. We can pick it up, examine it, and put it down again; or, we can do the same and recognize that there may be other ways to think about the chronology of events.

One of the reasons why stillness is so foreign to us could be because we are always conscious of time. We think linearly. An event passed is an event put into history, and time provides a means by which we can conceptualize movement away from that event and into the future. We're always, it seems, on the way to somewhere, and maybe time is partly to blame.

The Inuit travelled extensively in search of food, and also for other reasons–I think again of the "journey in search of itself"–but their concept of time, at least as represented in language, is radically different from ours. Anthropologists who have looked at this aspect of Inuit culture tell us that there is no Inuit concept for time as indicated by such expressions as "to save time," "to kill time" or "to gain time." I remember Edmund Carpenter's comment about Aivilik Eskimos and their concept of "the timeless present." Carpenter observed that the Aivilik regard the past as merely an attribute of the present, as something immanent. Mythical and historical past events become, as essence, part of everyday life.

By putting ourselves at the unexamined mercy of linear time, and in the face of an information explosion, we are tempted to leave past events and focus instead on now and what is to come. We have no ability, or so it would seem, besides thousands of dusty history books, to incorporate the essence of the past into the dealings of today. This, surely, must have had something to do with our alienation from the landscape.

The natural tendency on the canoe journey, however, seems to be more akin to the "essence" thinking of past events. Everything that has happened to us over these last few weeks, without a steady flow of information from television and radio, has been shaped into a journey in our heads, a journey in the imagination. Like the sketch maps given to Knud Rasmussen by willing Inuit throughout the North, there are spatial and temporal distortions in the imaginary journey, but the essence remains, probably for all time. It remains, with fullness of taste, smell, sound and sensation, to inform and enliven everything else that we will do in our lives.

The journey has taken us to the edge of our thinking and allowed us to come to a state of mind in which we can hear the music of the land and the music of the journey itself. The journey has connected us to this place in the barren lands and given us the sense of belonging that we people probably have only for our immediate home environment. But, more importantly, and this may be one of the mechanisms by which the journey becomes such a significant factor in the life and times of the journeyer, this journey has drawn, in our imaginations, a mental map rich in tangible places and connections to the landscape that is more like that of Rasmussen's Inuit informants than any chart produced by the National Topographic Map Service.

At another corner upriver, there is time to stop again. This time, in the stillness, I can feel the river pulsing through the rocks below. How good it feels to be without fear–of this place, of not getting to the coast on time, of being eaten by a grizzly bear. How deeply satisfying it feels to just *be* here, alone, but with friends who have shared this experience, attached to the land, and detached, if only for a moment, from the business of that other life. A lone bull musk-ox ambles into view and grazes its way along the opposite bank of the river.

24.
SALT WATER

WE SLEEP AGAIN AT THE BIRTHDAY-PARTY CAMPSITE, AND BEGIN
the second and final portage trip of the expedition in the morning.
By the time we six are assembled at the foot of Burnside Gorge, it is
3:00 P.M., and there is a decidedly queer feeling in the air. By this
time, the Americans have moved on toward Bathurst Inlet; our time
is running short, but no one seems in any kind of rush to go, or, for
that matter, to stay. There is tension among us that, I begin to
realize, has been building for days. But not one of us seems able, or
willing, to articulate to the rest what the problem is. The problem is,
I fear, that the trip is coming to an end. But the question remains:
should we stay put for the rest of the day and go to the lodge in the
morning, or should we head out now and finish today?

Although no one seems satisfied with the decision, like a herd
of leaderless creatures of habit, we get into our boats and, one by
one, move into the current below the final whitewater gasp of the
Burnside, turn, each of us, and look upstream into the maw of the
gorge, and then dawdle our way downstream. A musk-ox appears on
the right-hand bank. We look, but not a soul makes an effort to land
for a closer look.

These last 8 miles (13 kilometres) of the river, from Burnside

Falls to Bathurst Inlet Lodge, are different and some of the prettiest we have seen to date. The predominant impression is one of sand–compressed sand bluffs with layer upon layer of delicately shaded greys, tans and buffs; shifting free-patterned beaches of gold and white; and tear-drop islands in the stream braiding the variegated blue river channel into separate routes for a hundred canoes. This is the part of the river the Inuit call *ayepapartorvik* meaning "where a pole is used." For a while we instinctively fall into a competition to see who will be first to get stuck and be forced to push or drag their canoe to deeper water. No one does.

At length, still perhaps 4 miles (6 kilometres) from the inlet, everyone stops paddling, then starts again, and stops, then starts for a few more strokes, and finally we stop and rest. We raft up in mid-stream, no one saying anything, everyone, presumably, conscious that we have reached some kind of milestone in our journey. We sit, avoiding eye contact. The tension is excruciating. I want to yell!

Lorraine suggests a meeting. Someone else calls for a paddle-or-not-to-paddle vote–four votes either way would decide. We do that. The tally is three yes-let's-go and two no-let's-camp-here votes. Norm abstained–he "didn't care" one way or the other. We're trapped by our allegiance to democracy. Eventually Jake says "three votes win," and on we go. It is the damndest and most frustrating situation imaginable, and reflects the mix of feelings created by the prospect of ending our arctic odyssey. The lodge is our destination, but the cups are out as Bathurst Inlet opens before us, and we sample water until we can taste salt. Mouthfuls of seawater mark the official end-point of our journey–430 miles (700 kilometres), two heights of land (not three, as we'd originally planned), six and a half weeks and a lifetime of experience. Whatever vapours caused the previous moment of group indecision, we are reunited by union with the sea. There is private satisfaction in accomplishment, but overshadowing any individual triumph is the lifetime group bond we seal with a saltwater toast.

For all the beauty, clarity and cold goodness in fresh water and in the streams and rivers that have buoyed our canoes, there is a powerful sense of completion, of return, in reaching the ocean.

There is a sense that we have travelled with the clouds that have fallen to earth high on the Contwoyto Plateau and split on the Burnside Divide, that we were with them as their potential energy stores were expended in bends and rapids and wild falls along the way. At the ocean, the river is spent. Our journey is done.

We are terrestrial animals and drinkers of fresh water, but in recognition of the primordial sea from which we came, our blood, still roughly the salinity of the ocean, circulates and sustains us. Without the sea, without salt water, we would all surely perish. Strange that we have lost any way of saying thank you to the ocean, or to any significant part of the natural world. The rounded head of a curious seal pops up before us, then disappears. Activity on the beach in front of Bathurst Inlet Lodge has caught our attention.

25.
DRUM DANCE

TRISH WARNER, OWNER AND HOSTESS, STEPS FORWARD OUT OF THE group of guests and local Inuit, greets us warmly and invites us all in for coffee. Kids swarm over our beached canoes as we walk forward in dying light, up a path that is marked with whitewashed stones. On the front of the main, one-storey lodge building, still maintained in the classic HBC white with red trim, are the words "Bathurst Inlet Lodge" spelled out in strategically hung caribou antlers. At the sight of electric light, I turn just before going inside and savour the sun, five times larger than life, magnified by its low angle in the atmosphere, dipping down behind the hills on the Burnside Canyon portage. After two days of grunt and toil, never again will those particular hills be anonymous.

And the sun, the setting arctic sun, how tuned we have become to its daily circle. How foreign it seems to be stepping inside, but how good the coffee smells. So much for the hard work and romance of campfire cooking; let's get at those Oreo cookies!

In the functionally appointed large living-room of the lodge, we meet Glen Warner, Trish's husband and the person who saw potential in the HBC post when, in the 1960s, as an RCMP officer, he came here by dog-team to visit the Inuit families who lived beside the post. He's a strapping specimen of a host, every inch the northern mountie, younger-looking than I had expected, but every bit as congenial. Some of the dozen guests staying at the lodge this week have gone to bed after busy days on the land, he explains, but, like the consummate host, he introduces us to the guests who greeted us on the beach.

There is a couple from New York City who, until their visit, "hadn't been farther north than the Hudson River." There are a Medieval Literature professor from the University of Western Ontario, a middle-aged lady and her husband who are "keen birders," and an octogenarian lawyer from Kingston, Ontario, whose name is Henry Cartwright–"Henry was legal council in the Gouzenko trials;" and Nancy Stride ("Eighty-year-old Nancy who's here with us for the ninth time," Glenn quips) is here with her grandson. Several other guests smile as they're introduced, and we do our best to remember their names. My impression is that the Warners have done splendidly in making these people feel at home. They flop easily into an arrangement of comfortable sofas, invite us, too, to sit and pump us with questions about the trip: How long have you been out? What did you eat? Did you catch any fish? How many upsets did you have in rapids? Were bears a problem? Did you see the big caribou herd? How long did you say you've been out? What do you do when you're not galavanting around the North in canoes? Did you all get along? How did you manage to keep clean all that time?

"We didn't," says Gail, with a smile, looking longingly toward the lodge showers.

"It's not every day that a bunch of people come paddling up to our door," says Glen, pouring another round of hot coffee. "Make yourselves at home."

"Does that include showers?" Gail asks as sweetly as possible.

"Certainly, my dear."

The room is a combination lounge, living room and bar. On one wall is a skin kayak sporting a Bathurst Inlet Lodge sticker. Underneath it is a selection of spears, projectile points, tools and other artefacts. On the other walls are everything ranging from Travel Arctic posters to home-made prints, photographs of guests and a shelf of "Genuine Eskimo Carvings." It is kind of an all-purpose room, reminiscent of many an Ontario Legion Hall–stately when it has to be, but one gets the sense it's just dying for a rollicking good party.

The big news this night in the lodge is an imminent visit of Governor General Ed Schreyer and his wife, Lily, and a mixed band of dignitaries, including the American ambassador to Canada, former NWT commissioner Stuart "The Big Muskox" Hodgson; Metric Commission chairman Sandy McArthur; and Southam News columnist Charles Lynch.

We're curious about other news, since we've been out of touch. The American hostages are still in Tehran. One was released in July because of ill-health. Jimmy Carter is in hot water because his little brother Billy has been to Libya to visit Muammar al-Qaddafi. It looks like Ronald Reagan will win the Republican nomination. A one-legged runner called Fox caused quite a stir when he ran through Toronto on his way across Canada. Prime Minister Trudeau is still adamant that the constitution should be brought home from Britain. A scientist has determined that 140 lakes in the Nickel Belt area of Ontario are dead from acid rain and apparently another 50,000 will go this way in the next twenty years if nothing is done about air pollution. The first Global Conference on the Future was held in Toronto in late July. Peter Sellers died. Mount St. Helens in Washington state erupted. Pay-telephone calls doubled in price from 10 to 20 cents. The Moscow Olympics were boycotted by many countries, including Canada, but while Canada did not send an Olympic team to Moscow because of the invasion of Afghanistan, we in fact doubled wheat exports to the USSR. Two hundred thousand workers in Poland are on strike. The Winnipeg *Tribune* and the *Ottawa Journal* went under. The Jays are about twenty-five games out of first place and the Expos are tied for first in the American League.

But the substance of talk is high-paced babble about what the lodge patrons have seen on their travels, the lone musk-ox up the Burnside estuary, orchids, wildflowers, birds of every description. They're as excited as we are, it seems, about this land and have done it with a minimum of hard work; $1550–everything for every need, all they had to do was get to Yellowknife and the Warners take it from there: flights, food, guides, the works, for one week.

I catch a glimpse of Gail chatting to Henry Cartwright, the lawyer from Kingston. In comparison to Henry's pallid complexion, Gail's ruddy cheeks and sun-browned forehead radiate warmth and a sense of gentle satisfaction, but she's hot. As is the case for all of us, being outside for this length of time has turned up her personal thermostat; our bodies routinely churn out enough heat to keep us warm in even near-freezing temperatures. Being indoors for the first time in weeks, especially in a place with added heat, is stifling, to say the least. All our faces are quite red. My ears are burning. Dealing with all of the new information about what's happening in the rest of the world is bamboozling, but it is escape from closeness and heat that comes as much-needed relief when we say good night and head out into the cool night air to pitch our tents.

On the way out to the grassy place Glen has suggested we pitch our tents, we're just dying to know what has been said about possible spaces on the lodge charter for getting us and our canoes back to Yellowknife. Gail tells us that we're in luck. The load of dignitaries is coming in on a Northwest Territorial Airways Executive DC-3 on Monday, and because there are only a dozen patrons going out, a smaller number than usual, there will be room on the big plane for us and our canoes, two hundred dollars a person. We'll be on our way home the day after tomorrow. Things couldn't be better.

Sleep doesn't come easily. I am totally awash with mixed feelings, impressions and thoughts–of home, of the trail, of interesting people, of how to best spend tomorrow, of our journey, of work . . . of the people who live year round at this lodge and who use the electrical generator only in the summer when the lodge is operating.

Through the bug-smeared no-see-um netting on the door of the tent, I can see several turquoise structures in which some of the local Inuit families live. If Buckminster Fuller were here, he would call them geodesic igloos. Apparently Warner has funded the building of these to house the families of people who work for the lodge. Electric floodlights nailed onto loosely standing sections of grey two-by-four illuminate caribou hides, antlers, caribou heads and various other bits thrown up onto the roofs of plywood ante-chambers that break the hexagonal symmetry of the little structures. The new is well mixed with the old throughout this little encampment.

The following day, when guests are packed up into boats and driven away by their Inuit guides for a final day of arctic exploring, we pick through the last of our plasticized packages of food to decide what gourmet concoctions we can tease from the dregs of the wanigan. The food has lasted, but just. By now we have a couple of packs full of folded packs, sure sign of journey's end. I pass a container of old jerky, keeping in mind a piece of green jerky I ate at this juncture on another trip, a simple snack that left me in a sorry mess, marvelling, between panic trips outside the tent, at my digestive tract's ability to simultaneously expel its contents from every available opening.

A couple of the kids who greeted us on the beach stand by with dried meat of their own. One can't be a day over three and the other might be five years old. Both of them have strips of dried caribou, which they nonchalantly bite and then slash with blades that look more like Sikh short swords than any sort of kitchenware. To them the knives are routine. They cut and chew away, pointing and laughing at the remains of the party kit in the top of the wanigan, more independent than any comparable southern children.

When things at the campsite are set for departure, we head down to the canoes for a sightseeing paddle out to Quadjuk Island where there is an archaeological site Glen says is worth visiting. The canoes feel tippy and hyper-responsive to paddle strokes without the weight of gear in them. But, by now, our positions in the seats are well established; people in the bow know what their stern paddlers are doing without having to look, and we make quick time to the site.

The tent rings look similar to those we have seen farther up the river. They lie in a semicircle on a gravelly outwash at the south end of Quadjuk Island, and give the impression that this was a fine campsite in its day. There is a cast bronze plaque bolted to one of the rocks at the site that makes the feel of the place quite different from that of any site we've come across on our own. Some of the artefacts on the lodge wall have come from this site. Archaeologists say it may be thousands of years old. I wish–I wish–we had the power to know what the spirits of these people are saying this August day. There is so much we have felt and so much we have learned on our travels, but, at a site like this, the possibility of knowing–really knowing–the significance of this place seems remote. The plaque doesn't bring it any closer. Maybe that's a role the lodge's Inuit guides play. I wonder if they still know the stories? I wonder if anyone's interested?

We find shrimp skeletons on the beach as we're getting back into our canoes. Another seal surfaces offshore. A peregrine falcon catches the updrafts off the face of the cuesta. The earth has turned the sun through its southern zenith and is dropping toward another tranquil evening. The wind, from the southeast, brings with it the distant moan of a couple of motor boats. Always, always, I'm now thinking of home.

That evening, we're invited to the lodge for the final evening festivities that happen every week. Glen is dressed in his caribou-skin leggings and parka that he has pulled from the freezer for demonstration purposes. He gives an animated talk about the history and uses of the various artefacts on the wall, and hands out Bathurst Inlet pins and "Order of Arctic Adventurers (Arctic Circle Chapter)" certificates for all of the guests. He even presents the visiting canoeists with enamelled lodge pins. But, as a special treat, and in honour of the impending visit of the governor general, William Kwaha, "the best damn drum dancer in the whole Bathurst Inlet country," has come six hours by boat from his home at Brown Sound, and will do a traditional Inuit drum dance for everyone, as a warm-up for his Royal Command Performance.

Kwaha is a crooked little man, about five feet tall, of slight build. He's shy, but eventually is coaxed to enter the circle of eager bystanders. With the dustbin-lid-sized drum, he's hunched over and looks even smaller, but there's a twinkle in his eye that is infectious. He takes the striker, a thick, rolling pin-like piece of wood, and hits the drum. A dead sound dribbles away from the flaccid skin. But Kwaha stands motionless after hitting the drum. Not knowing what to expect, people clap. He looks up, laughs, and hits the drum again. The head is too loose to begin. He spends the next five minutes rolling the edges of the sealskin head around the striker and tightening the drum surface onto the 2-inch (5-centimetre)-wide wooden hoop. At length he is satisfied that the drum is tuned and the dance begins.

He shuffles sideways around the circle, striking first one side of the drum and then the other with a lilting rhythmic motion. All the while he sings a two- or three-note song with words that often repeat–Ayii–Ayii–Ayii at one pitch and then again at a lower pitch. His body movements and voice move and modulate synchronously, and, in time, it becomes apparent that the song itself has a larger pattern as well. He is building in volume, in complexity of step and beat, and, without looking up, seems in complete communication with his audience.

Ayi–ayi–ayi–ayi, hae–ai, yaeek, ayi–ayi–ayi. The heartbeat drumming is mesmerizing. The movement, the sounds, the rhythms draw us into the dancer's concentration. He lifts his drumstick hand, as if holding a spear, drives it through the air and resumes beating.

This is the dance of the land. Fishing and hunting held first place in the thoughts and lives of the Inuit and as such were the subject of many songs in the big igloo. Songs recounted the joy of hunting success, the details of a great conquest or the disappointment in failing to get game. But there were other songs too, travelogues that described a long journey, or songs to describe the beauty of an arctic night or to welcome the return of the sun in spring. Songs and the drum dance are somewhere near the heart of the Inuit mythology, which in turn celebrates their relationship with the land and all its creatures.

As Kwaha circles and circles again, each time with more fervour than the time before, I wonder what he's singing about. Perhaps his dogs at Brown Sound. Or about hunts before the arrival of the Hudson's Bay Company. Maybe he drums and dances of a journey he has taken somewhere, perhaps to visit friends to the west or to the east or to the north. Or is he singing about what it feels like to dance for a gaggle of southern strangers?

Songs are part of the journey, of the hunt, of travails on the land, that are left in the mind of the journeyer, of the hunter, of the traveller, when the physical travel is done! Songs are a celebration of the journey of the imagination, a way of sharing the essence of what has happened on the trail. Songs capture the spiritual and mythological dimensions of the Inuit experience. Kwaha's drum dance may well be a perfect model for what I've been struggling to understand on this canoe trip. Like us–like anybody–the Inuit have physical journeys that create journeys in their imaginations, but *they* have a way of getting at the mythical part of *their* travels; they have developed a cultural tradition to access the essence of who they are! The slides and journal entries that most of us take home from these canoe trips seem so far removed from the ideas of the drum dance.

Kwaha works himself to fever-pitch with the drum and stops with a flourish. The house goes wild, as Glen leads the dancer aside for a cold drink. There is little doubt that for most people Kwaha's dance had transcended the boundaries of the lodge experience and connected people, if only momentarily, to the raw power of the Inuit relationship with this remote northern land. The room fairly bubbles with people's excitement and enthusiasm for the dance, and for one another, with animation that makes it difficult to believe that these are the same people we met here the night before.

Glen is explaining drum dancing to Mary, the Medieval Lit prof; eighty-year-old Nancy is examining the drum, talking a mile a minute to Kwaha, who looks and smiles and understands not a word; the lady from New York has brought out a sombrero and is imitating the drum dance off in the corner while talking to a small group of onlookers; Trish is showing a book of lodge snapshots and telling about previous performances Kwaha has made for lodge patrons; another guest, artist Al Hochbaum is chatting quietly with Henry, his Inuit guide; Jake and Lorraine are telling a guest about their encounter with the grizzly bear.

This is it! This is live "contrapuntal radio" that Glenn Gould used so effectively in the "Idea of North." The net message I am getting this night is about enthusiasm for the North and all of its mysteries–bears, Inuit, drums, songs, dancing, exploring, painting and remembering a vast and tantalizing land–but the message comes, not in one lump of information, but as the mixture of many different conversations. The point is that simply paying attention to the facts of the situation may be tantamount to missing the actual experience of being in this place.

And now I begin to see that the musical metaphor can help prescribe a way of looking at journeys too. The process of journeying is superficial and fundamental. What elevates it to the imagination is the fact that every time the journey melody is reiterated by the voice of a new day and a new place, you hear new harmonies and become cognizant of new meaning and new understanding. The longer the journey, the more you listen, the richer the music, the richer the reward.

Maybe what Kwaha did with his dance, in bringing everyone to life, was, with elegant simplicity, to highlight the fact that music has an important role to play in any significant relationship with the land, if, for no other reason, than it is music that touches the part of our consciousness that is sensitive to matters of the spirit. Every person in this room has had some experience on the tundra, each creating some blend of facts, sensory impressions and emotions. Perhaps it took William Kwaha's drum dance to reframe, focus, and coalesce those experiences into some kind of manageable meaning for each of these assembled souls, or maybe there is just some sort of synergistic magic in the air this night.

Lorraine gets out Stella for the last time on our journey. Kwaha is back at centre-stage with the drum, dancing to the guitar music! People are clapping, singing and beginning to stomp their feet to the music. A couple of the guests join Kwaha in the centre of the circle, then a couple more. Suddenly Jake yells, "Snowball," and in less than a moment, pandemonium is in a full-faced downhill slide. The Inuit guides and their families are up now. Eighty-year-old Nancy is jumping around like a little sic-sic on dexadrine. Kwaha is now doing the rounds of all ladies, taking his turn to wheel them around the dance floor, why even Medieval Mary is pried away from her spot near the bar and is swaying to the music!

During a lull in the dancing a few folks begin to sing "I've Been Working on the Railroad," a tune that everyone seems to know. As the chorus comes around on the guitar, and with precision timing and finesse, old Henry Cartwright, who's been sitting in the corner throughout the evening, stands up and bellows at the top of his lungs, "DINAH, BLOW YOUR HORN!" and sits down.

Bonnie, the whimsical lady from New York City, throws her sombrero in the middle of the floor and begins to circle around it, picking up people as she goes. In no time, we have created the most multicultural Mexican Hat Dance ever performed north of the Arctic Circle. Glen and Trish Warner are in the thick of the action, as are most of the Inuit, all the guests and all of our gang, except Norm, who is off in the corner, doing an Arcto-Mexican version of the Highland Fling! Plaid shirts, brightly coloured slacks, boots, shoes, and slippers–all galloping around the room in a frenzy. Kwaha is more energized now than ever, and on one pass past Lorraine with the guitar yells "Kabloona good!" and carries on.

It is a remarkable blending of bodies and souls. Little Nancy, who's got more energy than people half her age, says she overheard Glen say that this may have been the best Sunday-evening party they have ever had. Maybe he says that every Sunday night, but there is no denying that something memorable and possibly quite magical has happened at Bathurst Inlet Lodge this night.

By now everyone has gone to bed and the sky is starting again to get light, but I'm too tired to go to sleep and too energized to stay awake. I sit by a bookcase and pull out Knud Rasmussen's narrative *Across Arctic America*. In it is the transcript of an Inuit song that resonates deeply in my soul:

THE KAYAK SONG

Ayii–Ayii
I think over again my small adventures
When with the wind I drifted in my kayak
And thought I was in danger.
My fears,
Those small ones that seemed so big,
For all the vital things
I had to get and to reach.
And yet there is only one great thing,
The only thing,
To live to see the great day that dawns
And the light that fills the world.

26.
HOME

THE DC-3 ARRIVES FASHIONABLY LATE AT THE DUSTY BATHURST Inlet airstrip and, as promised, out pours a whole load of dignitaries in new casual hats. They are welcomed by Glen and Trish and quickly trundled off to the lodge in a pair of blue BUGS–old, U.S. Air Force blue Bombardier half-tracks brought down from the old Dew Line Station at Cambridge Bay. We're left with the pilots, attempting to find the best way to fit eighteen people, three canoes and quite a pile of luggage into the plane.

Everything is stowed with a minimum of trouble, the door is closed, the piston engines cough to life and, in a flurry of sand and fine gravel, we're airborne and headed southwest for Yellowknife. We fly directly over Burnside Canyon and then up the river to about the junction of the Mara River before striking out cross-country for Contwoyto Lake.

The six of us are scattered throughout the plane, but I watch as everyone cranes to see out the windows to pick up familiar landmarks. This journey has bonded us to this land. To these people and thousands more who fly over the pole each year, the North is very likely just millions of miles of trackless wasteland. Cath points out the window at a huge herd of caribou she's spotted. I can just imagine the amount of hair such a group of animals will put on the shores of every little lake they'll cross.

Gail has been following our route on the map. Fifty miles (80 kilometres) north of the margin of Contwoyto Lake, she puts down the map and walks forward into the cockpit. We watch as the blue sleeve of a freshly pressed flight suit reaches around and pulls down a jump seat for her. Next she dons a headset with attached microphone. Although we can only see her back, it is apparent that she's laughing and having a great time talking to somebody–perhaps the pilots–on the intercom.

But no, she comes back to her seat and says with a broad grin, "Steve and Peter send their best! I remembered that all planes check in at the Contwoyto Lake Weather Station, so I thought I'd just go up and say hi and goodbye to the guys. It was great fun! Just like Peter said when we offered him more brandy out of the Sigg bottle when we were all sitting together around the ping-pong table–he said, 'Dump 'er in, Gail!' It was good to talk to them."

Beyond Contwoyto Lake, we pick up Yamba Lake and then Desteffany Lake. It's hard to believe at 20,000 feet (6000 metres) or however far from the ground we're flying, that we have paddled in some of those lakes. I found my first set of caribou antlers ever on the shores of Desteffany Lake on a day when I would have killed to see a live caribou–the *first* live caribou of my life. But that was not to be, not until Point Lake, off in the distance on the right-hand side of the aircraft. These little recollections, these little attachments to particular places on the land, on the map, and etched on the imaginary map in my head have new significance, because they're starting to come together into something larger. Or at least I'm beginning to see that they are–and probably have been for some time–part of something larger, a growing sense of attachment and belonging to the tundra, but also to north as a phenomenon central to who I think I am.

Wally Maclean, or one of Glenn Gould "Idea of North" informants, said that north is the moral equivalent of war in the power it seems to have for the development of character. North for me has been a place where I have become acquainted with the possibility that there is more to life than facts and figures, that there is more in the ground than minerals, that there is more in the flowing water of a river than whitewater frolic, that there is value in uncertainty and hard work, that the land is a living land–that connections to the natural world are central, whether we like it or not, to our survival.

The journey itself has been a great teacher. Much of what we have learned about ourselves and about the way we live could well have been learned by travelling in almost any part of the world, in any cultural and natural setting, as long as it was substantially different from home's. Recognizing and learning to see that these are worlds apart that thrive without our knowledge has been a significant boon of this journey.

This great undeveloped land through which we have journeyed, however, has served a purpose in our lives that only a wild place could serve. Devoid of the technological supports and markers that buoy and guide our workaday lives, the North represents the edge, the margins of who we are and what we know. It has allowed me to see, for example, that the categories science would have us impose on the natural world are not necessarily the *only* lens through which to perceive the world. There is a plane of understanding that supersedes the rational mind. The world, and we humans as a part of it, are spiritual beings. Education, said the cynic, kills by degrees, but what it has killed in the culture that has surrounded my life is the possibility that there could ever be value in something as difficult to hear as music from the land.

We have come to rely too much on the use of transport like this DC-3, and on the map instead of the land that it represents, aided and abetted by spiritually constipated culture and probably by the grammatical constructs of our language–not to mention time–that have alienated us from the land and from who we are, or, more precisely, who we could be. We live a life of profound contradictions. On an edge-place like the Arctic we can begin to get a glimpse of just what those contradictions are. Sensible living can come after seeing the contradictions, but *definitely* not before. For that reason, among many, north is central to our continued awareness of who we are.

These days on the tundra trail have given me recurring images of nativity, belonging derived of the land. It's a sense of kinship with the place of our existence that comes right from the spiritual centre of this earth that is our home. I have learned things, and thought things and felt things on this journey that have spoken to me in ways I have never been spoken to before.

Life is connected to the earth and to the stars and, while those connections are made in places other than wilderness, they are most often made under conditions of privation and solitude–they are made by people exploring the rough and uncertain edges of their understanding.

Paddling a canoe in the Arctic has been a co-operative venture, not by choice, but by necessity. We could have conducted our affairs differently but it is abundantly clear that if anyone or anything were to have persisted in a competitive mode and "won," then someone or something would necessarily have had to "lose." Sometimes those losses do not justify the win. And when compromise and co-operation *can* be implemented and *can* work, narrowly competitive assessments of mineral rights, hydro potential, land use, river quality, or even how a group of people spend their summer holidays, must be examined and rethought.

It is difficult to conceive, as I look around the plane at the twelve lodge guests with whom we shared these last two days, that any one of these people will not take a keen interest in matters concerning development of Bathurst Inlet. A journey through the same land, such as the one we have just completed by canoe, simply deepens and intensifies the commitment to the place, the knowledge of what goes on there and the great feeling of nativity that rides on spiritual as well as physical dimensions of the landscape.

WE LAND, STOW OUR GEAR IN THE NORTHWEST TERRITORIAL cargo hanger, taxi into town and pick up the van. Back out at the airport, the canoes are tied on top and everything is tucked away for the drive home. Jake and Lorraine will fly home this trip, leaving Norm, Cathy, Gail and me to drive the van home. We make sure there is room in the back of the van for two people to rest while the other two are driving. We head to the long lake campground across the street from the airport, set up our tents and then head back into town for dinner at the famous Wildcat Café. Max Ward's Bristol is still there, and still looking like a fiery crash is imminent.

Sitting in the old log Wildcat Café in Old Town, a guy sticks his head in the door and yells: "Hey, who owns the green Old Town canoe out here?"

We turn around, say nothing and watch him scan the tables. There must be something obvious about how we look, or, more to the point, how we smell, that brings him directly to our table, at which juncture he asks again, "Do you own the green Old Town canoe out there?"

"That's us."

This is Kevin. He's from Ontario and has been up in Yellow-knife for several years now, working at the Giant Mine. He's been canoeing a couple of times, but always with a borrowed boat, and now he sees one that he'd like to buy.

"Canoes are hard to get up here. There's not much variety. And if you get one shipped up from Edmonton or somewhere the shipping costs'll kill you. How much do you want for it?"

"Just a minute," Gail teased. "Nobody said it's for sale."

"Oh come on, everything's for sale. Name your price."

"Not that canoe," I said, not wishing to bore him with the details of how you can't just sell a canoe in a café after it's taken you safely from one end of the NWT to the other.

"Would you be interested in the Woodstream or the green fibreglass that are also out there?" I offered.

"Nope. I want an Old Town."

"Sorry."

We return to the campsite after gorging ourselves on fresh milk, salad, sandwiches and cold beer, in that order. It's Saturday night at the O.K. Corral. The place is hopping: cars ripping around the campsite roads, music blaring, and the people's voices cutting through the night air. At one point, soon after crawling into our sleeping-bags, the roar of a passing car brings back a taste of forgotten fear–fear of people and the crazy things we'll do. There is nothing stopping a drunk from leaving the road and driving right over us.

For all of the uncertainty, for all of the surprises, for all of the caprice of northern weather and white water, we learned on the trail to expect events within predictably unpredictable ranges. Now, however, we are at the mercy of human unpredictability, and that is more frightening than anything we have encountered this summer.

A car pulls in at the next campsite and illuminates our tent. The motor keeps running, and it becomes clear from the sounds that this is a taxi-cab dropping off someone next door. We're wide-eyed and fully awake by the time the lights veer off and the sound of the motor disappears into the distance.

"Hey, fuck, will you loogat that," comes the beery voice of our new neighbour. "JEE-ZUS, will you look at them lights! Come on, yous gotta look at this! FUUUUUCK!"

"If you can't beat 'em, join 'em," says Gail wearily.

We dress and step out into the darkness. It's cold, but the man was right. A loon calls from the black waters of Long Lake. Above, stretching from horizon to horizon, red, green and white sheets of Northern Lights seethe and shimmered in the night sky. These are unborn Inuit children dancing with their umbilical chords. They are certainly robust little souls.

A pattern begins to form and all of the colours swirl together like phosphorescent bath water emptying into some huge bathtub drain.

"Hey! Hey!" beers a familiar voice in the dark. "Whistle and they'll dance."

He tries to whistle and ends up in a coughing spasm. The lights are like the most delicate sheer fabric drawn over speckled black marble. Somewhere out there are Voyager 1 and 2, with Toronto Airport and Glenn Gould playing Bach. And right overhead are the eight stars of Canis Major.

"It feels like home when you can see into the darkness," Gail says, squeezing my arm.

We settle back into our sleeping-bags, watching the shadows of the drying lines in our tent dance to the Northern Lights. The tranquillity of the moment is jarred by "Put Another Log on the Fire," sung at the top of his lungs. Buffalo Bob is frying a steak.

"That guy needs a canoe trip," I said, putting a coat over my head to block the din.

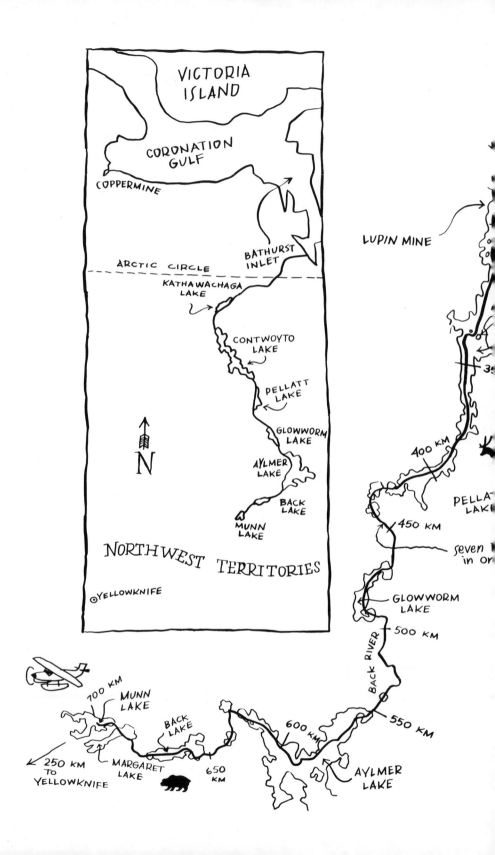